DOLLY PARTON

PORTER WAGONER

JOHNNY CASH

JAN HOWARD

RAY PILLOW

CARL AND PEARL BUTLER

LORETTA LYNN

ARCHIE CAMPBELL

DEL REEVES

JIM ED BROWN

STU PHILLIPS

WILMA LEE AND STONEY COOPER

ROY DRUSKY

SKEETER DAVIS

JUSTIN TUBB

BARBARA LEA

MARTY ROBBINS

KITTY WELLS

DAVID HOUSTON

ERNIE ASHWORTH

JIMMY NEWMAN

BILL ANDERSON

EDDY ARNOLD

NASHVILLE'S

GRAND OLE OPRY

TEXT BY
JACK HURST

————

INTRODUCTION BY
ROY ACUFF

HARRY N. ABRAMS, INC., PUBLISHERS, NEW YORK

TO THE MEMORY
OF THE LATE
JOHN W. HEMPHILL, JR.
THIS BOOK IS RESPECTFULLY
AND AFFECTIONATELY
DEDICATED

Nai Y. Chang, Vice-President, Design and Production
John L. Hochmann, Executive Editor
Margaret L. Kaplan, Managing Editor and project editor
Barbara Lyons, Director, Photo Department, Rights and
    Reproductions, and project photo editor
Patricia Gilchrest, copy editor
Arnold Skolnick, book design
Richard Nusser, photo research

Library of Congress Cataloging in Publication Data

Hurst, Jack.
    Grand Ole Opry.

    Discography: p.
    Includes index.
    1. Grand Ole Opry (Radio program)
ML68.H87   791.44'7   75-14486
ISBN 0-8109-0268-0

Library of Congress Catalogue Card Number: 75-14486
Copyright © 1975 by Harry N. Abrams, Incorporated, New York

INTRODUCTION

There is something about our kind of music that is different from anybody else's, I've always thought. I know that none of our boys can play a violin as perfectly as people who play symphony music, and I know I could not attempt to sing a classical song. Symphony music is beautiful music, played correctly by note. Our boys play by ear, and we slide into and slur some of the notes.

But what we do is pretty to us. We put a lot of feeling into it, and we reach the hearts of our audiences.

The people who watch us understand that we're not really professionals at it. They understand that we're not trained. But they also understand that what we do is part of a sort of inheritance. In a way, nobody really writes our music, you know. If we write a song, we're only writing what we've felt and heard, the way we've been raised and the way our people have lived. Those things are not created, they're inherited. And we sing them with a feeling of sincerity, because they are part of ourselves.

The boys and girls of the Grand Ole Opry had to come to Nashville with a hard determination to play this music. Nashville, with all of its colleges and universities and high society, is a blue-blooded town, and for a long time the elite people in this city would have liked to see the Opry destroyed and done away with. They thought it was belittling them.

They were wrong, but they had to be shown they were wrong, and I think we have finally convinced the greater part of the Nashville elite people that they were mistaken in thinking that the Opry should have been kicked out and put somewhere else, like back into the mountains. I believe the majority of the Nashville people, even the high society people, admire us now for the determination we've shown here.

If the Opry hadn't been in Nashville, Tennessee, this city would never have become Music City U.S.A. The rest of the music industry would never have come here, and Nashville would have been just like any other state capital city—pretty dead.

Through the Grand Ole Opry and country music Nashville has prospered, but even today the big tourist businesses that surround the Opry here would die if the Opry should stop operating. All the other things we've got here aren't big enough to keep the tourists coming. During our good-weather months we are visited by upwards of 20,000 people in a weekend, but they don't come here to see the Hermitage, or the Parthenon, or the Country Music Hall of Fame. They don't come here to ride around the Capitol or drive by and look at Roy Acuff's house. They come here to see the Grand Ole Opry, and while they're here they go out to look at all these other things.

I give the Grand Ole Opry all the credit for what success I have been privileged to have in country music. If it hadn't been for the Opry, I think I might have fallen by the wayside, because I don't think I would have ever really become known. I don't think I would have had what it took to become a star just on recordings, and without the Opry I wouldn't have known what to do. I would have just had to move from one station to another, working the little territories of a hundred miles or so radius that the smaller stations reached.

But when I came here, I realized this was different. It was like a network show. Because of our 50,000-watt clear channel, we were covering everything from the Rocky Mountains to Maine and from Canada into the islands off the Florida coast. We almost blanketed the country, especially late at night, and that gave me the opportunity to work every state in the Union. I have even received mail from ships at sea.

The Grand Ole Opry that I came to was nothing but down-to-earth country music. When George D. Hay first started the Opry there was some singing, but most of the numbers they featured were instrumental. I was possibly the first one that came here with what they call a voice. When I sang "The Great Speckled Bird" on my audition night, it started a career for Roy Acuff.

I came to the Opry from Knoxville on the 19th of February, 1938, and on the 20th I played Dawson Springs, Kentucky, with the Delmore Brothers, who were a well-known act back then. I worked every day, including Sunday, for many years. In those days, only sickness or death allowed us to be off the Opry, no matter where we were during the week. We were traveling in Fords on two-lane highways, so we couldn't get too far away, but I'd go over in the Carolinas or down in Georgia or somewhere, and I'd play my Friday night show and then come back in here for the Opry. My wife would meet me down there with my clean clothes, and I'd change at the Opry and perform and kiss her goodbye and head back to Asheville or Atlanta or somewhere for a matinee on Sunday.

They used to call me a tear-jerker, and it is true that I would tear-jerk an audience. It is true that many times I would cry when I sang songs like "Sweeter than the Flowers" or "Don't Make Me Go to Bed and I'll Be Good."

I sang "Don't Make Me Go to Bed" a lot after my boy was born. It was easier then for me to see how a little child could beg its mother or father not to make it go to bed just because it had been mischievous. The story in that song comes down to where the little child is on its deathbed, and finally it dies, and the last thing it says is, "Don't make me go to bed and I'll be good."

"Sweeter than the Flowers" is about a funeral. The boy who wrote it could see his mother lying there, and how they were all lined up in front of her—"brother and I close to Dad," one line goes. Things like that are very touching. The people who wrote those songs actually saw those things, and for you to sing them you've got to see them too. When you sing them onstage, tears may get into your eyes and into your voice, but that doesn't hurt. You needn't be ashamed of it. Whoever wrote the song would love the way you're performing it, because you're sharing his sorrows. I've sung those songs with tears in my eyes many a time, pleading for the people to understand how they made me feel. That wasn't just showmanship. That was feeling.

Our music has got showmanship to it, but there is more feeling than showmanship, and that's one of the things that make it different from a lot of other entertainment, I think. Hollywood—I was out there and worked in some pictures, and I came to find out it was phony. It's kind of disappointing to go out there and see how they make pictures. I'd say that 75 percent of Hollywood is phony and maybe 25 percent is pure, whereas I'd say that our business here with the Grand Ole Opry is maybe 90 percent pure.

You might find a little part of us that would be on the phony side, but not much. I don't really see anything in my act that would be misleading to anybody. Of course, we have Oswald playing a character, but the character that he plays is in the character of the people where he was raised. You can go into his part of the world, and my part of the world, and you'll find a lot of Oswalds walking around the streets, especially on Saturday.

I've shared the stage with performers who want to be country but overdo it, over-emphasize it. I accepted the Beverly Hillbillies show on television, for instance, because I enjoyed it and I knew a lot of those people who were on it, but we here in this part of the country would look at it and laugh. There's hardly anyone in our part of the world now who is as far backwoods as that is.

The Grand Ole Opry's strength has been that it has so little of the phony. I think the downfall of the National Barndance in Chicago was when they moved it from Chicago to the West Coast and put a band in front of it, so that you didn't just have Lulu Belle and Scotty performing on the stage anymore—you had horns and things like that in front of them. Cowboy stars and different things were brought in, and all the changes just took the show completely out of country music.

I got here at about the right time to be of assistance to the Opry in achieving prominence. My group was strictly country—no electrical instruments, no horns, nothing except our own mountain way of presenting music.

That period was the start of the Opry's growth from just a little program. During that time the country people learned where to tune in to find the type of music they enjoyed most. When I came here WLS was much more powerful, much more of a name than the Grand Ole Opry, but right after that, when they changed their format and put in the band, the thing started to change. You can't put horns and a band in front of a group playing "Good Old Mountain Dew." It just doesn't work. That's what gave the Grand Ole Opry the lead in country music.

Other country shows died because they tried to go with trends, fads. That was what happened to the Big D Jamboree in Dallas and the Louisiana Hayride in Shreveport. They went with rock and roll, thinking they were hitting on the right course, but the fad drifted away, and they drifted off with it.

Down-to-earth country music has always been the backbone of the Grand Ole Opry. I had a lot of conversations with George D. Hay, and I found out a lot about how he started the Opry.

My information from Judge Hay is that the Possum Hunters, who were led by Dr. Humphrey Bate, were the first band and were here before the Grand Ole Opry started. They were on the station, and then Judge Hay invited Uncle Jimmy Thompson to come in and be part of the show. Uncle Jimmy was an oldtime fiddler who was accompanied by his niece on the piano. As I got the story from the Judge, Uncle Jimmy and his niece were the first featured act on the program.

At that time the Possum Hunters included Burt Hutcherson, who is still with the Opry, and Staley Walton, who also is, although at this moment he is a very sick person, and Dr. Bate's daughter Alcyone. A few of the people who came in right after the program started are still here too—Sam and Kirk McGee and Herman Crook. All these are the originals that are still living, and they are getting pretty well up into their years.

Naturally you change a little bit with your times, and the Opry has progressed from the old days. The Ryman Auditorium played its part in this progress, although we outgrew it ten years ago. A lot of things grew up around the Ryman—drinking parlors, and beer joints, and massage parlors—and it got to where it was not nice at all down there. It didn't represent the Grand Ole Opry or country music. It just represented the fact that some people are going to get around where there's a crowd and sell their wares.

We are now in a beautiful spot at Opryland, and we have enough land out here to protect it. Now we can say to the governors and senators and presidents who come into our state, "Come and see us. We are located now where you can be proud of us, and we can be proud that you came." I'm satisfied that no celebrity from New York or Hollywood has ever stood on a stage any finer than what we have now, and we're proud of what we've accomplished.

But we oughtn't to change too much, and especially the music. When I go to Ireland, Scotland, Norway, or any of the other countries, I go out in the evening to hear their authentic music, to see their types of dances and shows. When I'm there I don't go out to hear some American sing, and when they come here they want to see what we have. They come to the Grand Ole Opry to see what is going on in the hills of Tennessee. They don't come to see something that is just like what they've got.

As times change, we must perform some of the other music that's around. The younger people feel they want to hear some of this music that's sort of on the fence between country and pop and doesn't know which way to drop. That's good, as long as it's presentable. But we don't want the Opry to get to playing music that you don't feel your whole family can enjoy. When you leave the Grand Ole Opry you should be able to say to yourself that you got some good out of it, that it was maybe like going to a good church service.

Nobody can define country music, but the people who listen to it know what it is. Country music to me is the kind made by Grandpa Jones, and by Stringbean, who's dead now. That's the kind of music the Grand Ole Opry was built on. I'm thankful to have had a chance to be a part of it.

ROY ACUFF

CONTENTS

A city fellow and a country boy got to asking riddles, and the city fellow wanted to bet a dollar on every one. But the country boy said he should have odds, since city people are smarter and better educated. The city fellow finally agreed to pay a dollar for every riddle he couldn't answer, while letting the country boy pay only fifty cents. The country boy advanced his first riddle.

"What is it that has three wings, four heads, and five tails?" he asked.

After considering fruitlessly for a while, the city fellow handed the country boy a dollar. "Okay, what's the answer?" he asked.

"I don't know," the country boy replied, returning fifty cents.

—1920s-vintage wit from
the Ozarks, the region
and era which inspired
the Grand Ole Opry

1

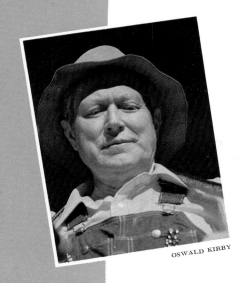

OSWALD KIRBY

GRANDPA JONES AND RAMONA JONES

OPENING NIGHT AT THE NEW OPRY HOUSE

BILLY GRAMMER

The new Opry House

◀ Please lift page

Nashville's Music Row.
FROM THE TOP: The offices
of Window Music; Mercury
Studios; Combine Music;
Columbia and Capitol
Records; MGM Records;
a studio built by pop
recording star Ray Stevens

n the chartless geography of the Middle-American soul, Nashville is the capital of the world. Its principal sphere of influence is America's last, largest frontier, the great national heartland so quickly passed over, and so largely ignored, in history's three-hundred-year trek from money-minded Manhattan to harebrained Hollywood. For five full decades now, Nashville has been in the process of becoming the entertainment center of everything between those geographic poles. A fabled town of drawling minstrels, of curios and autographs and heart songs, Nashville is a great American melting pot, the principal distillery in which the national experience of the common man becomes his music.

Nashville's dominance, perhaps rooted in nostalgic yearning for the simplicity of the past, has grown ever more powerful with each new pressure of urbanization, mechanization, alienation.

The motion picture, outflanked by vastly increased popular mobility and sophistication, relinquished its place as repository of the American Dream; its spiritually weaker successor—television—came to be regarded as an absorbing plaything, but not so much a barometer of common opinion as an ofttimes resented spokesman for the nation's influential but out-of-touch edges: New York and California.

Meanwhile, little Nashville grew.

A once-aristocratic mid-South capital where odd, impassioned people like Roy Acuff and Hank Williams kept coming to be discovered, it became forever marked by the howl and whine of their high, lonesome music. More and more of them kept arriving, becoming popular, and building recording studios; then envious others, some of them so-called pop singers who had always made their recordings in New York and Los Angeles, began to come down too. Suddenly, carefully mellowed versions of Nashville's long-scorned "red-neck" music began to be heard in cities, big cities. Whereas in 1952 (when Hank Williams was still writing and singing his tragic songs) there were only a handful of influential "hillbilly" radio stations, there were 115 full-time "country" stations by 1963, 225 of them by 1965, and 1,170—including one in Manhattan—by 1974.

The music's appeal lay in its authenticity, authenticity in everything from its preservation of old mountain folk ballads to its portrayal of today's life as it is. As more and more average Americans wearied of the complexities of a city-controlled life, they sought solace in the nostalgia of a "country" music, and what had once been a scorned, regional, lower-class art form became praised and patronized by presidents.

Finally, in the spring of 1974, one president—in great public disfavor, attempting to ride out a scandal that would ultimately force his resignation—visited the source of this Nashville revolution, apparently seeking to draw some strength from its awesome national power. Richard M. Nixon, the thirty-seventh president of the United States, attended a performance of a wild old radio show that has run continuously (except for a couple of unavoidable power failures and some Roosevelt fireside chats) every weekend in Nashville since 1925, its very name—Grand Ole Opry—standing as a monumental illustration

Downtown Nashville. A pawn shop, a couple of
adult moviehouses, a guitar company, a record
shop, and the famous Tootsie's Orchid Lounge
contribute to the gamy atmosphere of Lower Broadway,
the Opry's neighborhood for three decades

FRIEDMAN'S

S. FRIEDMAN

OANS

KEY'S
SHOP

Sterling

MELLOW

BEER

GET YOURSELF A
BEER!

TOOTSIE'S
ORCHID
LOUNG

A

Bud

AL'S

edman
USIC &
N

OAN

FILMS

hose w how"

SHO

NITURE
STO

ABOVE AND LEFT: The crowded sidewalks and traffic-congested streets in front of the historic Ryman contrast dramatically with the tree-lined walkways of the new Opry House at Opryland U.S.A. BELOW: Opryland U.S.A. sits in a lovely grove of trees on the banks of the Cumberland River

of the country boy's ability to laugh at himself just enough to succeed.

The presidential visit meant a great deal to the Opry and its corporate parent, Nashville's National Life & Accident Insurance Company. Its historical significance, however, may someday seem little more than a footnote to the principal event of that chilly March evening: the first performance of the Grand Ole Opry in a lavish, permanent new home.

Having outgrown the ramshackle, historic Ryman Auditorium in downtown Nashville where it had played for three decades, the Opry moved into a luxurious, cushioned, air-conditioned Opry House in a sprawling suburban family entertainment park. In its first six months as part of "Opryland U.S.A.," it would surpass the record annual attendance figure of its last full year at the Ryman.

The audience at the presidential performance differed considerably from a typical Opry crowd. There were only a few of the usual talkative children, the harried mothers in print dresses, the sun-reddened fathers wearing sport shirts and white socks. Rather, most of the people filling the 4,400 seats of the $15 million building that night were influential leaders of politics and business who had come to congratulate the old show on its new affluence. The performance they saw was no more typical than they were, but both served to highlight the Opry's earthy grandeur.

The last of the audience filed in to the sound of sprightly old country instrumentals played by the Fruit Jar Drinkers, a string band made up of seventy- and eighty-year-old men who had first stood on an Opry stage nearly forty-nine years before. The numbers they played were introduced by mellow-voiced Grant Turner, an Opry announcer for thirty years.

Then the formal proceedings began.

Opry cast member Billy Grammer, a guitarist and singer, gave the invocation.

Irving Waugh, president of National Life's 50,000-watt Nashville Radio Station WSM, announced winners of the first George D. Hay awards for "vast contributions to the Opry and the world of country music"; recipients included the chairman of the board of the longtime Opry advertiser Martha White Mills, a deceased executive of National Life, and musicians Roy Acuff, Chet Atkins, and Bill Monroe.

Waugh pointed out that in 1976 the United States would observe its bicentennial.

"By then," Waugh said, "for more than one-fourth of the nation's years there will have been a Grand Ole Opry."

Then William C. Weaver, Jr., chairman of the board of National Life, rose to recount a little of the Opry's homely epic.

"It was November 28, 1925, when an eighty-three-year-old fiddler named Uncle Jimmy Thompson sat down in front of a microphone in the WSM studios and started playing," Weaver noted.

"Now, Uncle Jimmy claimed to be able to fiddle the bugs off a sweet tater vine . . . but no one who was there that night, or listening in, could have foreseen where that beginning was going to lead. I'm sure there were a lot of people in Nashville who thought that country

TOP: Announcer Grant Turner reads live radio commercials. CENTER: Guitarist-singer Billy Grammer, shown here with his wife Ruth, began the opening ceremonies with a benediction. BOTTOM: William C. Weaver, chairman of the board of the National Life and Accident Insurance Co., briefly recounts the Opry's half-century saga

LEFT: An island in a sea of attentive darkness,
the opening night show hurries along.
ABOVE: On a board floor shining with newness,
the clustered Opry musicians aim their music
at the spotlights

music would eventually go away. Instead, as other musical forms came and went, country music just kept on getting bigger and bigger.

"Every now and then George D. Hay, 'The Solemn Old Judge,' would say to the Opry musicians, 'Keep it close to the ground, boys.' And if I had to explain the enduring success of country music and the Opry, I would say it's because it has stayed close to the soil, close to the simple truths of life."

Weaver, a tall man, drew himself up to his full height as he reminisced about the Opry's early wanderings.

"As country music grew," he continued, "the Grand Ole Opry grew—or maybe it was the other way around.

"Anyway, the Opry moved several times within the WSM studios to larger and larger quarters on the fifth floor of the old National Life home office building. Finally, in 1934, we built Studio C, which seated five hundred and which we thought was the living end.

In this early Opry montage, the friendly face of George D. Hay, Opry's earliest guiding force, is surrounded by pictures of some of his performers

But even that wasn't big enough, and the Opry moved on to the old Hillsboro Theater, then to the Dixie Tabernacle on Fatherland Street in East Nashville, then to the War Memorial Auditorium, and finally to the Ryman Auditorium, where it settled down for its longest run so far. Now, this new Opry House is the sixth, and, unless I am terribly presumptuous, final location.

"Last year, the Opry drew a record total of 464,000 persons from all over the world to see a live performance, and countless millions listened in on their radios. Nashville long ago gave its name to a sound and became the world's number one recording center—and the National Life & Accident Insurance Company became known as an affiliate of the Grand Ole Opry."

The laughter of the audience at that final sentence was carried not only over WSM Radio in Nashville, but also over a live, two-hundred-station network reaching to the Rocky Mountains and a delayed broadcast over 1,135 stations on the Armed Forces Network.

Weaver reintroduced Grant Turner, who in turn began to present the late, mysterious, parson-like figure who is credited with creating an American institution.

The stage curtain behind the speakers' rostrum slowly rose, revealing at center stage a gigantic motion picture screen suspended from the ceiling. A projector crackled, a light beamed onto the screen, and suddenly the 1941 image of George D. Hay—the man who had long ago named himself "The Solemn Old Judge" and his show "The Grand Ole Opry"—squinted hospitably at the 1974 audience from under his black hat, behind his thick spectacles.

"First," the Judge said in a low-pitched, laconic monotone, "we're gonna hear from Roy Acuff and his Smoky Mountain Boys. Smoke it up, Roy."

The camera then switched to a young and serious-looking Acuff, who immediately began the immortal wail that in its time had kept entire military barracks awake at night and literally blasted small radio stations completely off the air.

> From the great Atlantic Ocean to the wide Pacific shore,
> From the queen of flowing mountains to the south bells
>   by the shore,
> She's mighty tall and handsome and known quite well by all:
> She's the combination on the Wabash Cannonball.

On that night's special, far-flung radio network it may not have sounded like much more than a recording, but to the people in the new Opry House it seemed as though the past had been stunningly recaptured. They began to cheer wildly, and then in a great rush they all rose together as the screen started drawing up into the ceiling, because there behind the screen stood seventy-year-old Acuff, singing along with the recorded voice of his younger self, never missing a note as his present Smoky Mountain Boys took up where the film left off.

The standing ovation was impassioned. It continued as the

Stony-faced Bill Monroe, one of American music's cherished originals, receives one of the first George D. Hay awards on opening night

"King of Country Music" walked gravely out toward the front of the stage. Nearly sixty member acts of the Grand Ole Opry filed out behind him. They all were singing.

"This is nonrehearsed," Acuff shouted, grinning now. "Believe me, this is the first time we've been on this stage together."

He made a short speech, welcoming the crowd and proclaiming his pride at being part of the occasion. Then the Grand Ole Opry swung into a respectable approximation of its Saturday night ritual, although under the pressure of getting everybody on for this landmark performance, the show's stylized format had to be forgotten.

This time, there would be none of the usual segments of fifteen or thirty minutes, sponsored by such products as Martha White Flour, Coca-Cola, or Stephens Work Clothes, each with a "host" performer who sang two or three songs and introduced two or three "guests," who each sang one or two. Tonight the performers merely came out and sang, one by one, in roughly alphabetical order.

Ralph Sloan and the Tennessee Travelers, four men in work shirts and white slacks and four girls in crinolined skirts, started it off with the kick, swirl, and stomp of traditional square dancing.

Then Bill Anderson, a tall South Carolinian who had graduated from the University of Georgia with a degree in journalism, sang a verse and a chorus of his slightly incongruous theme song, "Po' Folks." Ernie Ashworth, a blond Alabamian in a gold sequined suit trimmed in red lip designs, sang his biggest hit, "Talk Back, Tremblin' Lips." Jim Ed Brown, a soft-voiced Arkansan, crooned "The Three Bells," a tune which had lifted him and his sisters to stardom as The Browns in the late 1950s.

Like a normal Opry show, however, it was not all music.

Comedian Jerry Clower, a huge Mississippian, told a true story about a pulpwood hauler named Marcell Ledbetter who demolished a roadside beer joint with a chain saw one hot afternoon because the proprietor refused to sell him a cold drink and called him a red-neck.

One after another came a seemingly endless succession of entertainers, their very variety a celebrated feature of the Opry. Behind them on the stage was another: a spectacle of nearly absolute chaos. Some background musicians were playing and singing along to the songs being performed, but others—and apparently their relatives and friends—wandered around kibitzing with each other in full view of the audience as the show hurried along in front of them.

Backstage, meanwhile, sat legions of others.

"I've been waitin' so long to go on, my dress has gone out of style," Minnie Pearl would cackle when she finally got to the microphone at 9:30 P.M.

The presidential party arrived after the show started.

Someone suddenly stopped everything for a moment by shouting "Ladies and gentlemen, the President of the United States!" and everybody rose. But although the Opry cast members were obviously much impressed, the arrival did not inhibit them. Clower told his Marcell Ledbetter story after the Nixons came in, and Jeannie Seely, a pretty blonde songstress who came onstage with her partner,

OPPOSITE PAGE:
The opening night crowd watches in awestruck silence as a young Roy Acuff and his old-time Smoky Mountain Boys serenade them from the silver screen of a 1940 motion picture

LEFT: Appearing, in silhouette, like participants in some primeval rite, Ralph Sloan and his high-kicking Tennessee Travelers rattle the boards of the new Opry stage

ABOVE: Smoky Mountain Boys Bashful Brother Oswald, right, Charlie Collins, in glasses, and Howdy Forrester, far left, surround their boss, Roy Acuff, as he brandishes his fiddle and greets the crowd. BELOW: In their trademark Stetsons, Ernest Tubb and the Texas Troubadors do Tubb's classic "Walkin' the Floor over You," a hit since 1941

OVERLEAF:
The Opry's grand old men, the Crook Brothers, center, and the Fruit Jar Drinkers, right, make some of the Opry's most traditional music in accompaniment to the flying feet of Ben Smathers and his Stoney Mountain Cloggers. INSETS, FROM LEFT: Bill Anderson sings about something he is most decidedly not—"Po' Folks"; Jim Ed Brown croons "The Three Bells"; Jeannie Seely's opening night attire is stunning, especially by traditional Opry standards; Ernie Ashworth, appropriately attired, sings his biggest hit, "Talk Back, Tremblin' Lips"

Jack Greene, appeared in a bare-midriff pantsuit that elicited wolf-whistles as she soulfully sang "Don't Touch Me."

The Opry's earthy informality was not subdued even when the President came down from the balcony after about half an hour; "Hail to the Chief" was played, but on traditional bluegrass mandolins and banjos.

Acuff came out again to welcome the President—a usually formal man who appeared to have been taken by the Opry's straightforward spontaneity. He walked out to Acuff at center stage and produced a yoyo, which is an Acuff trademark, from his coat pocket. He let it dangle at the end of its string.

"I haven't learned to work this thing yet," he said.

At Acuff's urging, he went over to a piano and played "Happy Birthday" and "My Wild Irish Rose" for Mrs. Nixon, who was celebrating her sixty-second birthday.

The expected wild applause went up and died down, and then Acuff and Nixon assisted National Life chairman Weaver in the unveiling of a plaque dedicating the new Opry House. Afterward, on his way back to a chair onstage, Nixon stopped in front of the center-stage microphone and wryly observed, "It must be time for the commercial."

Acuff then introduced the President for his formal remarks, and even in these the Chief Executive felt impelled to begin with an appropriately informal reference.

"Somebody was telling me that there is only one thing stronger than country moonshine, and that is country music," he began. "I saw a couple of fellows outside that were combining the two, and believe me it was plenty strong."

He went on to praise the character of the Opry's music.

"First, country music is American," he said.

"It started here, it is ours. . . . It is as native as anything American we can find. It comes from the heart of America, because this *is* the heart of America, out here in Middle America. Country music talks about family. It talks about religion, the faith in God that is so important to our country and particularly to our family life. And we all know country music radiates a love of this nation — patriotism. Country music, therefore, has those combinations that are essential to America's character, at a time when America needs character."

He finished his impromptu speech moments later, and the audience applauded warmly, but then suddenly there was old Acuff again, clowning around, heeding Judge Hay's venerable admonition to keep it close to the ground. He began instructing Nixon in the art of the yoyo, meanwhile suggesting, "You don't need to be in a hurry to get back up there [to Washington]—we need you down here for a while."

"I'll stay here and learn the yoyo," Nixon offered, "and you go to Washington and be president."

Acuff bent over with laughter.

"This is such a wonderful program," he exclaimed in his choppy East Tennessee drawl. "We'll never see another one like it in our state. Never have before."

The presidential part of the program ended shortly thereafter.

LEFT: As many cast members as are able crowd onto the stage to sing "God Bless America" as former President Nixon accompanies them on the piano. BELOW: Alabama Governor George Wallace chats with Ernest Tubb while Wallace's wife Cornelia chats with Teddy Wilburn of the Opry's longtime troupe, the Wilburn Brothers

Coached by Roy Acuff, the former president attempts—without notable success—to master the subtleties of the humble American yoyo

Acuff led the crowd in singing a rousing old country song called "Stay All Night, Stay a Little Longer," and then the President returned to the piano to play "God Bless America." Then he and his wife bowed, waved, and left for Nashville's Metropolitan Airport.

After this exodus the show went on as it had been accustomed to doing for nearly half a century. Jan Howard, a red-haired singer who has been a prominent performer for a decade, took the stage immediately after the departure of the Nixons. She came out to the center microphone and ruefully shook her head.

"I've had some tough acts to follow in my career, but this is unreal," she said simply.

"I wouldn't wish a spot like this on a drycleaner."

Although considerably behind schedule, the Opry finished the first of its two Saturday night performances, then opened its doors to the crowd lined up outside awaiting the second one. These people outside were not politicians or business leaders; they were the show's regular patrons, the factory workers from Detroit and Gary, the insurance agents, farmers, and shoe salesmen bringing their wives and families from Kansas City, Bald Knob, and Bessemer.

GEORGE MORGAN

TAMMY WYNETTE

THE YOUNG GIANTS

For half a century, the music of the Grand Ole Opry has eloquently chronicled the decline of rural America. And it will probably continue to recount the ongoing, simultaneous process that John Egerton, a Nashville writer, has characterized as "the Americanization of Dixie and the Southernization of America."

Country songs started out as Elizabethan ballads and Protestant fire-and-brimstone hymns that were sung on the hearths and porches of farmhouses, mountain cabins, and tarpaper sharecropper shacks. As rural America came more and more into contact—and, often, into conflict—with onrushing urban bigness, the traditional songs began to be changed and modernized to satisfy current needs and moods. Newer songs were written, molded both by the old music and the new times; modern songs of remorse or self-pity or even occasionally of happiness took the place of similar Elizabethan ballads, and songs of this world increasingly supplanted ones yearning for the next. Songs of separation and wanderlust reflected migrational upheavals, Western ballads romanticized the noble cowboy, train and automobile songs enumerated the blessings and perils of progress. As city life closed in, honky-tonk songs began to reflect the hopelessness of redneck ghettos.

Each Friday and Saturday night, in a picturesque and unsystematic way, the Grand Ole Opry revisits all these successive eras.

The venerable members of the Crook Brothers and the Fruit Jar Drinkers, relics of early days when the Opry consisted of string bands, are likely to play something like "Old Joe Clark" and "Arkansas Traveler." Acuff may do his "Wreck on the Highway," and Bill Monroe "Blue Moon of Kentucky." There is apt to be a honky-tonk love song by Ernest Tubb and a train song by Hank Snow, and perhaps the classic woman-left-behind song, "The Dear John Letter," by Jean Shepard.

But interspersed among these historic, archetypal songs are other, newer ones reflecting the neon sophistication and hungover cynicism of times as recent as last night.

In "City Lights," Bill Anderson dramatizes the emptiness a country boy can feel in town. Loretta Lynn warns a husband "Don't Come Home A-Drinkin' (With Lovin' on Your Mind)." Del Reeves whimsically profiles a truck driver's infatuation with a half-naked girl on a billboard, and Marty Robbins romanticizes a racing-car driver. Barbara Mandrell agonizes about cheating on a faithful husband, while Tammy Wynette spells out "D-I-V-O-R-C-E" so her four-year-old Joe won't understand.

They are new songs, songs relevant to today's Middle America, and yet they somehow remain extensions of the old songs. "Detroit City" is the dismal destination of a luckless "Arkansas Traveler," and the heroine of "D-I-V-O-R-C-E" could well be the daughter of "Dear John."

The new giants come from practically everywhere, but they grew up in a world built by the old giants. There is hardly one of these new ones who does not begin an interview autobiography by noting, as a matter of course, the one great common denominator:

"Of course, as a kid I listened to the Grand Ole Opry . . ."

The voice and instrumental style of Bill Monroe, an Opry performer for more than thirty-five years, have influenced generations of younger country music stars

Roy Acuff, the Opry's first great singing star, fired the imaginations of countless young country boys, showing them that one could make a living on the homely kind of music common people knew

Hank Snow, a Nova Scotian whose first job was that of cabin boy, became an Opry star with Ernest Tubb's assistance and remained to help many other younger stars develop

Ernest Tubb, who was among the first to introduce the steel guitar to Opry audiences, not only influenced many young performers stylistically but also helped many of them—including Hank Williams—become stars

Jean Shepard, a member of the show since 1955, is the matriarch of the Opry's women singers

Dressed in thoroughly contemporary style,
Marty Robbins signs autographs in the doorway
after the last Opry show at the Ryman
Auditorium

Marty Robbins, whose numerous and mostly self-written hits include some of country music's best-known cowboy songs, was born in Glendale, Arizona. During part of his youth his family raised goats and lived in a tent in the desert, and he and a brother earned some of their first money catching and breaking wild horses. Somewhat of a thrill seeker ever since, he has spent considerable time racing automobiles against professional drivers. His Opry encores are so taken for granted that it has become almost a tradition for him to close the show; when he does, the sign-off always runs several minutes past the midnight deadline.

Porter Wagoner is country music's king of the small screen. A homespun singer of old-style fiddle and steel guitar songs who is being increasingly seen as a latter-day Hank Williams, Wagoner acquired his famous, nationally syndicated television show in 1960 when officials of its principal sponsor, the Chattanooga Medicine Company, learned that he could bring to their commercial announcements the same kind of deep sincerity with which he performed his country hymns and sentimental recitations. A tireless road trouper whose repertoire is among the most traditional within the circle of younger stars, Wagoner was born on a Missouri hillside farm and got midway through grammar school before he had to go to work full time to help support his family.

Porter Wagoner and the cast of his TV show about 1970

Loretta Lynn, born to the large and talented family of an eastern Kentucky coal miner, changed the role of women in country music with her rise to stardom in the early 1960s. Instead of quietly and righteously bemoaning their lot, as women had done in the earlier country songs, in Loretta's lyrics they fought back and talked about marriage and its foibles in a straightforward manner they had never used before. Loretta's frankness won her country music superstardom in an era when even the thought of such stature for a woman had hardly been contemplated. (See also Chapter 12)

Jack Greene and Jeannie Seely are one of the most closely identified male-female teams in country music. Miss Seely, a native of Townville, Pennsylvania, had worked as a secretary in Los Angeles before she came to Nashville and was discovered by prominent Nashville songwriter Hank Cochran, whom she later married. Greene, of Maryville, Tennessee, was a drummer for Ernest Tubb before striking out on his own. Their show combines traditional country emotional power with a contemporary look and a wide variety of music.

Dolly Parton and her longtime friend and partner
Porter Wagoner chat with the Opry audience between songs

Dolly Parton, a native of Sevierville, Tennessee, became a star as the featured lady singer on Porter Wagoner's television and road show. Miss Parton, the closest the Opry cast has ever come to a pinup girl, was raised in a fundamentalist-church family in the Smoky Mountains; both her singing and her original songs bear the firm imprint of fundamentalism's spontaneity and unrestrained feeling. The many songs she has written are stamped with old-time simplicity, but her voice has shown itself capable of enough variety to be called "popular" as well as "country." She left the Wagoner Show in 1974 and formed her own band. (See also Chapter 12)

George Jones remains a distinctive and highly popular traditionalist amid country music's increasingly sophisticated song stylists. A native of Saratoga, Texas, who grew up in Beaumont, Jones got into the music business through the help of a record executive who later said his hardest job lay in convincing Jones to stick to his own natural style rather than imitate the styles of other, smoother country singers. Jones's highly rural sound has made him one of the most imitated "white soul" singers.

Franklin Delano (Del) Reeves is perhaps the Opry's most popular exponent of truck driving and honky-tonk music. A native of Sparta, North Carolina, Reeves is as hip and zany as his friend Porter Wagoner is homespun. (Reeves once compared his and Wagoner's similar profiles and said, "If me and Porter didn't have billfolds, we wouldn't have no figure a-tall.") With his band, the Good-Time Charlies, Reeves has another in the group of Wagoner-inspired country television syndications. He also performs in another medium of country music popularity; so far he has acted in more than half a dozen low-budget country music motion pictures.

Jim Ed entertains at an Opry birthday celebration in 1968

Jim Ed Brown is one of the foremost exponents of the soft, intimate singing style popularized by Eddy Arnold and by the late Red Foley and Jim Reeves. A native of Sparkman, Arkansas, Brown and his family listened to the Opry on a battery-operated radio, and he and one of his sisters often ordered Opry-advertised songbooks so they could sing along with the performers. In the mid-fifties he and his sisters Maxine and Bonnie formed The Browns, a soft-singing trio that became popular amid the din of early rock and roll. For several years now, Brown has had his own syndicated television show and traveling troupe.

53

Bill Anderson became a part-time disc jockey
and songwriter before he graduated from college

Bill Anderson is a Southern city boy, born in Columbia, South Carolina, and raised in apartment houses in the nonpastoral environs of Atlanta. A journalism graduate of the University of Georgia, he entered the country music business via the oft-used avenue of songwriting. Because there were so few collegians in country music when he started his career in the late 1950s, Anderson kept his college education a secret until he became established. Perhaps in compensation for his lack of rural background, Anderson has been one of the more conservative country songwriters, emphasizing traditional American viewpoints and values.

Texas-born, diminutive Barbara Mandrell is the proprietress of a highly popular touring show. She is one of the youngest of the Opry's major stars, and her music reflects that. Usually set to an urgent, pounding beat, it often deals with situations which women country music fans would not even have discussed privately a few years ago; a first-person ballad about a housewife's infidelity is a recent example. In her own way Miss Mandrell is helping — as Loretta Lynn did a decade earlier—to enlarge the "woman's place" in country music, to allow reality to enter where only stereotypes of home, motherhood, and other, "bad," women used to exist.

Dottie West, the singer of nationally broadcast commercial jingles for Coca-Cola, has become one of the best-known voices of American radio and television. One of ten children born to a McMinnville, Tennessee, farm family, she worked her way through a small Tennessee college and then spent five years at an electronics plant in Cleveland, Ohio, before getting her first recording contract. She has won awards both for singing and for songwriting, including some for the Coke jingles. The degree of warmth in her singing style is rare in that it manages to be at once passionate and motherly.

David Houston, a godson of 1920s recording star Gene Austin and a descendant of both Sam Houston and Robert E. Lee, is nevertheless on the opposite side of the spectrum from the Opry's traditionalists. Houston is a crooner, a highly individualistic stylist whose rangy voice moves easily from a mellow baritone to a high, soft, lilting quaver. A college graduate born in Shreveport, Louisiana, he became an overnight national star with one huge hit, "Almost Persuaded," which was released as the "other side" of one of his first recordings.

Tammy Wynette was country music's first and most eloquent full-time spokeswoman for the middle-class American housewife. With hit after hit, the Alabama-born former hairdresser has sculpted and profiled the lonely married female animal. To great songs, some of which she wrote or co-wrote, Miss Wynette brings a classic style, raw emotion combined with simple dignity. A rock producer just beginning to familiarize himself with Nashville once marveled at Miss Wynette's ability to sweep into a powerful, up-tempo chorus and then recede with a moaning whimper into the next verse. "Her voice," he said, "is like a steel guitar."

Jerry Clower, a mountain-size native of Liberty, Mississippi, one of the South's master storytellers. A former football playe for Mississippi State University, he majored in agriculture an served as a county agricultural agent for two years before be coming a fertilizer salesman. To bolster his sales pitch, Clowe would tell true stories of his own rural youth, getting his pro pective customers to identify with him and laugh at him at th same time. He was one of the most successful fertilizer salesme of his time when somebody recorded one of his routines and became a hit. He joined the Opry in 1973.

Bobby and Sonny Osborne, natives of eastern Kentucky but raised in Dayton, Ohio, played bluegrass music for several years on electrified instruments. Their sound, "electrograss," was controversial in bluegrass circles for its departure from the instrumental tradition, and they abandoned it in late 1974 after seven years. It did, however, make them known far beyond the usual boundaries of bluegrass, and one of their recordings—"Rocky Top"—has become a country music standard. Bobby says they returned to acoustical instruments to satisfy smaller audiences after large, expensive package shows began to be abandoned in the recession of the mid-1970s. The Osbornes' style, electric or acoustic, combines Bobby's mandolin and chilling tenor voice with Sonny's frenetic banjo.

Onstage at the new Opry House, the Osbornes display the electrified musicianship that has made them a revolutionary force in bluegrass

WILBURN BROTHERS

SAM AND KIRK MCGEE

COUNTRY MUSIC TAKES TO THE AIRWAVES

Beecher R. (Bashful Brother Oswald) Kirby has been a member of Roy Acuff's Smoky Mountain Boys for nearly forty years. ABOVE: A young Oswald poses with a banjo. After first playing for pay in Chicago, he went to work in a Knoxville bakery before seeking employment with Roy Acuff, then a Knoxville radio musician. BELOW: Backstage at the Opry, Oswald gets together with Ed Dopera, manufacturer of the "dobro," or slide guitar. The name of the instrument is derived from that of the Dopera family

eecher Kirby, an impish old gentleman with iron-gray hair, has played dobro guitar behind the great Acuff for going on forty years. His standard uniform is a pair of bib overalls, oversize clodhoppers, a shapeless hat, and an irrepressible grin. They call him "Bashful Brother Oswald" onstage but, as Acuff observes, the name has gotten woefully out-of-date; Oswald has long since grown considerably more brazen than bashful. On Opry nights he clogs joyously with the square-dance troupes, bawls loudly into a checkered handkerchief during love ballads, and doffs his homely hat expectantly toward every brandished camera within sight.

Oh, he plays his howling, plaintive instrument during the breaks of such classics as Acuff's inscrutable "Great Speckled Bird," and shouts his high tenor into the choruses of "Build Me a Cabin in the Corner of Glory Land." But even Oswald will acknowledge that he is much more of a clown than a musician, a throwback to bygone days when the Opry's makeup was almost equally slapstick comedy and impassioned music. It was a time, Oswald sometimes reflects, when members of the Opry cast were more intent on entertaining their audiences than on selling them records.

Like his famous boss, Oswald is a period piece, a colorful relic of another time. In many ways he is typical of others his age and older, the ones the Opry has fewer and fewer of as time goes by. They are men (almost exclusively) who remember the look of Southern crossroads communities untouched by electricity and concrete pavement; they remember the feel of a time in which some of the most important things for a man to know were how to plow mountainsides, make whisky, and entertain oneself with music.

Beecher Kirby, for instance, a member of Roy Acuff's Smoky Mountain Boys, was a real Smoky Mountain boy long before he ever met Acuff.

"My daddy was a barber in Sevierville, Tennessee," Oswald says of his beginnings.

"The rest of us lived out on the farm. At least, I thought it was a farm until I got out and seen some farms. It was about sixty acres, I guess. There was ten of us in the family, and my oldest brother worked with my daddy in the barbershop. Daddy'd stay in Sevierville all week and would come home Sunday morning. A car would let him out at the end of the gravel road, and us children would come down to meet him there with the mules and take him back up the dirt road —or the mud road, which it was sometimes—to where we lived. It was ten miles to Sevierville from there if you cut through the fields, but it was probably twice that far by what roads there was.

"I'm the only one that took up music to try to make a living at it, but they all played a little bit. There was more people at our house all the time than any other house in the whole country around there because we all played. People would gather in there on Saturday and Sunday nights. We sang old hymns and anything else anybody knew. I don't know how we learned to play; nobody taught us. I guess people up in there are just born with something in them or something. I don't know how in the world they learned the songs,

Much of Oswald's contribution has been as a player of the dobro, a howling instrument with a circular steel pan in the center of the body where a normal guitar has only soft wood and a hole

Oswald still clogs joyously with the Opry's square dance troupes. Here he romps with Ben Smathers's Stoney Mountain Cloggers

either; there was no radio up there, nor nothing. Anyway, on Monday mornings we'd take my daddy back down to the gravel road, and the car would pick him up."

That was in the early 1920s, four or five years before Kirby left home for the first time to try to get a job in a Flint, Michigan, automobile factory, and nearly fifteen years before he met an ambitious young musician named Acuff while working in a Knoxville, Tennessee, bakery.

Even in the days before Oswald and others first began to leave the mountains, however, a few intense men who called themselves "folklorists" were already coming into the mountains. These educated outlanders were eager to learn something that such men as Beecher Kirby were little concerned with: where their music had come from.

Eventually, much of it was discovered to have come from the same places the people themselves had, two hundred years before. Between 1916 and 1918, an Englishman named Cecil J. Sharp collected forty-five English and Scottish ballads that had survived for

Country music was born in starkly humble circumstances on southeastern mountaintops and westerns plains. This house in Crisp, Texas, birthplace of Opry patriarch Ernest Tubb, epitomizes the simplicity of country music's beginnings

more than two centuries in the Appalachian region; he found them in three counties in Tennessee, two in West Virginia, eleven in Virginia, eleven in Kentucky, and seven in North Carolina.

Sharp was only the first of the folklorists, and they found what they were looking for in various parts of America. The Appalachians are only one of these areas, but because the region remained virtually isolated for some two centuries, it is one of the richest.

The difficulty of mountain travel and the consequent lack of schools made formal education almost impossible, but the mountaineers clung tenaciously to what culture they did have. They carefully passed on the ballads and religious songs of their fathers, sometimes putting new words and variations to old, handed-down tunes from Elizabethan or even pre-Elizabethan sources.

Such old music doubtless made up some of the repertoire of such families as the Kirbys in Oswald's youth. Other songs were probably brought into the mountains by peddlers, circuit-riding preachers, and other travelers, and by former mountaineers returning home from towns and cities.

Dr. Sharp and the first folklorists were soon followed by other, less selfless men.

Until the early twenties, city theaters and vaudeville circuits had ignored the music of mountaineers and other working-class, rural Americans of the South and the West. These people had been described as "hillbilly" since the turn of the century, and by 1925 that homely term began to be applied to their music. Even for that to happen, the music had to be noticed, and the fledgling recording industry, which had been increasing its sales volumes steadily since its start in the Gay Nineties, was even less interested in hillbillies than vaudeville had been.

"The music then was all Broadway stuff," recalls Art Satherly, one of a handful of recording-company scouts who began to seek new singers and instrumentalists after World War I.

"If a song hadn't been written by the coffee-and-cake boys in New York, then it wasn't supposed to be a song. They didn't figure anybody else was smart enough to know anything about music people would buy."

Until Satherly and his fellow so-called field recording men came on the scene, the executives of the recording companies paid no attention to music found outside the cities—or even outside upper middle-class neighborhoods. There was no economic motivation to do so. The popular singers, men like Al Jolson and Gene Austin, were selling unprecedented numbers of records with songs like "Rockabye Your Baby," "My Blue Heaven," and "Melancholy Baby." Recorded music was all of one kind.

Then, haltingly at first, came a revolution.

Satherly, a British-born ex-cavalryman who got into the business after serving as Thomas Edison's secretary in 1916, strayed off the popular path together with a few other recording men. They first ventured into black blues—or "race music," as they called it then—going into black urban areas in the South and West and recording

Gene Autry with Art Satherly, who first recorded Autry and dozens of other early country, or "hillbilly," performers

the music they found there. Having recorded it, they set out to prove there was a market for it.

"We found we could get ads for nearly nothing in a black newspaper called the *Chicago Defender,* as well as other places where no recordings had ever been advertised," Satherly recalled recently.

"And it happened like a bomb. Those black people heard their own dialect being sung for the first time on recordings. For the first time, in other words, they could hear themselves."

After race music became popular, the field recording men began to turn their attentions to white, "hillbilly" music, to see if the race music phenomenon could repeat itself in another area. About the time they did so, something happened to make the recording companies more anxious to hear the recording men's opinions.

Radio, hitherto a novelty, suddenly began to make its presence powerfully felt. By the mid-twenties, record sales had begun to decline as radio stations went into business. The radio stations, seeking all the listeners they could get, began to put all sorts of local musicians on the air. Radio thus began to supply the kind of home entertainment that had only been obtainable through the phonograph up to then, and much of its programming was "live"; it was also satisfying some musical demands the record companies had ignored.

The troubled industry soon started to rectify its earlier mistake. Faced with shrinking markets, it sought to build new ones.

Talent scouts invaded the South and West and recorded music by such homely "artists" as Georgia moonshiner Fiddlin' John Carson, a Georgia fiddler named Gid Tanner, a Tennessee banjo player named Dave Macon, a Tennessee guitarist named Sam McGee, a blind Georgia guitarist named Riley Puckett, and hosts of string bands with such names as the Dixie Mountaineers, the Virginia Reelers, the Virginia Breakdowners.

Noting the appeal of rural music, an established popular singer from Texas named Vernon Dalhart persuaded the Victor Company to let him record two hillbilly songs, "The Wreck of the Old 97" and "The Prisoner's Song." The latter became one of the biggest hits of that or any other time, going on to sell six million copies.

Suddenly this thing they were calling "hillbilly" music, a homely sound that had been around the mountains and the rural valleys and plains for generations, was found to be commercial.

Nor was this development the strangest of the era. The entire decade was a raucous and zany one, and its music only added to the national dizziness. The twenties were born in the depths of a postwar depression and died in the beginnings of a prewar one, but in the decade between those pinched times Americans briefly created a glittering yet strangely sad era.

Nationally, the twenties are stereotyped as a frenetic age of jazz and flappers, of contraband booze in the pockets of raccoon coats. It was, of course, an age of many other things, too, and most of them eventually filtered even into the growing cities of the historically insular South. There they blended with other, more local events, some of them recognized as important at the time, others only seen as important later.

ABOVE: Riley Puckett, left, and Gid Tanner, two of the earliest "recording stars." BELOW: Sam McGee played on some of Uncle Dave Macon's early recordings

ABOVE: This exact-size replica of the Greek Parthenon is located in Centennial Park. It was built in Nashville's Roaring Twenties, a multifaceted era that saw the Grand Ole Opry grow up practically alongside Vanderbilt University's vaunted Fugitives, a literary group that included such famous figures as Robert Penn Warren, John Crowe Ransom, and Allen Tate. LEFT: From a hill above the Cumberland River, Nashville's State Capitol overlooks the rest of the city

In Atlanta, for instance, Radio Station WSB went on the air in 1922 and put hillbilly musicians in front of microphones for the first time. In Memphis in 1923, an amiable but introverted ex-reporter named George Dewey Hay gained his first but not last fame as an announcer on Radio Station WMC. In 1925, high school teacher John T. Scopes was convicted of teaching Godless evolution in innocent Dayton, Tennessee, spelunker Floyd Collins died in a dark cavern in Kentucky, and a worldly, tubercular former railroad brakeman named James Charles (Jimmie) Rodgers, who had moved northward from Mississippi for his health, lost a radio singing job and became a city detective in Asheville, North Carolina.

In Nashville, meanwhile, a small insurance company was trying to decide whether to get itself a radio license.

At that time Nashville would have seemed the unlikeliest of all southern locales for an outbreak of hillbilly fever. An aristocratic capital which had put two presidents—Jackson and Polk—in the White House, it had haughtily been calling itself "The Athens of the South" for seventy-five years. In 1920, to underscore the city's right to that title, the city fathers commissioned the construction of a full-scale replica of the Greek Parthenon in one of the municipal parks. That same year the Nashville Symphony presented its first concert, employing a total of sixty-two musicians.

During the years immediately following, a group of agrarian-minded undergraduate writers at Vanderbilt University strongly advocated a rejection of the urban values of the twenties in favor of the earlier ones of an agricultural society. These "Fugitives," as they named themselves, included such later literary lions as John Crowe Ransom, Donald Davidson, Allen Tate, Robert Penn Warren, Merrill Moore, and Cleanth Brooks, Jr.

"These writers ... had a certain freshness, appearing at a time when (1) H. L. Mencken and others were stressing, quite unfairly, the 'intellectual sterility of the South' and (2) F. Scott Fitzgerald and others had convinced millions of Americans that college youths primarily aspired to roadsters, raccoon coats, and that sort of thing," observes Jesse C. Burt, a Nashville historian.

A number of Nashvillians of the time, however, appear to have cared more for Fitzgerald—or at least his style—than they did for the austere principles of the Fugitives. During this period, "a certain lady bootlegger with a Hupmobile Straight Eight once hit 120 miles per hour on Franklin Pike," Burt notes, adding that the Kit Kat Night Club in the Hermitage Hotel was advertising "Manhattan-style diversion" that even included a comic master of ceremonies.

Radio, which was to change everything in the nation almost immediately and everything in Nashville eventually, came on the scene unobtrusively in 1921. That year a fifteen-year-old prep-school student named John H. (Jack) DeWitt, Jr., acquired a ham radio license and began conversing with other like-minded radio pioneers around the country. A year later he built Nashville's first radio station, WDAA, for Ward-Belmont College; the Southern Baptist institution soon gave up the exotic toy, however, because it was thought to use too much electricity.

Edwin Craig, the young insurance executive who convinced National Life officials that they should buy a radio license, at one of the early microphones of the station whose affairs he would oversee for forty years

DeWitt then built another station in his father's home, and it soon brought sophisticated local bandleaders and their orchestras trooping into the DeWitt living room for the broadcasts, which were held whenever anybody showed up to be on them. This station also closed down after a while; Luke H. Montgomery, who helped DeWitt build both the Ward-Belmont station and this one, has said that DeWitt's mother wearied of "all those strangers traipsing through her house." Meanwhile, the First Baptist Church became interested in radio as a prospective medium for broadcasting religious services, and DeWitt—Nashville's resident expert—built the church a station with the call letters WCBQ.

By this time he had also done another important thing: he had constructed a battery-operated receiver for Edwin Craig, a young insurance executive who had become enthralled with ham radio.

"Mr. Craig became a long-distance radio enthusiast—or DX fan, as the hams call it," DeWitt recalls. "DX fans were people who would sit up all night listening to people around the country talk on the radio. It got Mr. Craig terribly excited."

A vice-president of the then fledgling National Life & Accident Insurance Company, Craig began toying with the idea of formally linking his ever more consuming hobby with his job.

Craig was the son of one of the seven men who in 1901 bought a small, five-year-old insurance firm named the National Sick and Accident Association. Within a year, they had changed its name to National Life and it had begun to grow. Assets of $33,200 at the end of 1902 had multiplied to $694,155 nine years later, and to $7 million by 1920. By the end of the twenties, the decade that would see Edwin Craig involve the company in radio, the company's assets grew to $26 million.

Several stations had operated for short periods in Nashville during the interval since DeWitt built WDAA in 1922, but only two were on the air in the autumn of 1925. These were WCBQ in the Baptist Church and WDAD, a small station owned by the proprietor of a hardware concern called Dad's. Even though both were very small, their signals covered considerable territory because there was no interference.

Craig worked hard to persuade the National Life founders that radio could be an "advantageous force" in promoting the sale of insurance policies in the twenty-one states in which the company then had agents. When they finally agreed, he began setting up the only station in the South—except for Atlanta's WSB—that had a power of 1,000 watts. He also set about obtaining call letters that would fit National Life's motto, "We Shield Millions." This was no easier than persuading the founders must have been.

"The letters WSM were then the call letters of a Navy ship, a lifeboat of the *Leviathan,* I think," DeWitt recalls.

"Mr. Craig got the Department of Commerce, which licensed radio stations then, to withdraw those call letters from the *Leviathan* lifeboat so somebody else—National Life—could get them. Herbert Hoover, the Secretary of Commerce, signed the license."

The new station opened on October 5, 1925, with DeWitt,

C. A. Craig, Edwin's father, in 1940. At this time he was president of National Life. Persuaded by his son that radio could sell insurance, he had helped dedicate WSM in 1925

This **WSM** transmitter, then called "the world's largest radio tower," helped beam the new **WSM** signal across the southern and midwestern United States

who was by then a student at Vanderbilt, at the controls as a part-time member of a five-person staff. It was, in the parlance of such functions, a gala affair.

The studio and control room, located on the fifth floor of National Life's home office building in downtown Nashville, were too small to allow the public actually to attend the broadcast, but loud-speakers were set up in the windows of the building to transmit the proceedings to hundreds of people who gathered in the street to listen to the first program.

Edwin Craig put the station on the air for the first time with the simple announcement, "This is WSM, 'We Shield Millions.' The National Life & Accident Insurance Company." Soon afterward his father, C. A. Craig, dedicated the station to community service.

Assembled to watch and participate in the ceremonies were the most important people who could be gotten there. They included

OPPOSITE PAGE
ABOVE: Judged by today's standards, WSM's first studio looks
oddly elegant. BELOW: The old National Life & Accident
Insurance Company home office building in Nashville in 1924
the year before Radio Station WSM was founded within its walls

Tennessee's Governor, Austin Peay, Nashville's Mayor, Hilary Howse, several of the city's finest musical bands, and three of the best-known · radio voices in America at that time—Lambdin Kay of Atlanta's WSB, Leo Fitzpatrick of WDAF in Kansas City, and, most important, George D. Hay of WLS in Chicago. The twenty-nine-year-old Hay had just been named the most popular announcer in the United States as the result of a poll of radio owners conducted by *Radio Digest* magazine. He had received more than 120,000 votes.

A tall, soft-spoken Indianan, George Hay had fallen in love with the South when he was sent to Camp Gordon, Georgia, for training during World War I, and as soon as he could do so after the war, he returned to it. He got himself a reporting job on the Memphis *Commercial Appeal,* and almost immediately, during an era in which Memphis was nationally publicized as having the highest violent crime rate in America, he was given the police beat.

"I covered 137 murders in one year," he said later. "It was the human interest in it that I loved."

Eventually he got a by-lined column, which he called "Howdy Judge" because of the nickname ("Judge" for "George," apparently) that he had acquired in childhood. In 1923, when the *Commercial Appeal* founded Radio Station WMC, Hay was named "radio editor."

"Then it wasn't so much what you put on the air as how far you could hear it," he once recalled. He did a nightly one-hour broadcast talking about the things he had seen on his beat during the day. He also started calling himself "The Solemn Old Judge," but he seems to have done it ironically. "None of this stentorian baloney."

He moved reluctantly from Memphis to Chicago when WLS was founded there in 1924. That year he broadcast what may have been the first talkathon appeal for funds in the history of radio, raising $215,000 for the Red Cross to help victims of a Midwest storm.

When he came to the WSM opening in 1925, he was offered a job. "We were looking for something which would give us national identification," Edwin Craig recalled much later. Since Hay had been voted America's most outstanding announcer, he would be a distinctive feature. Another might be a hillbilly music show something like the WLS barndance which Hay had helped develop in Chicago a year earlier.

"Hay had become acquainted with string bands when he worked in Memphis, and he thought there was a great future for folk music," Craig remembered. "He met with us, and we decided to feature a Saturday night folk music program."

A discussion of folk music between Craig and Hay was a meeting of like minds. The thirty-four-year-old insurance executive had played a mandolin in a string band at school, and he liked the music played by rural people. He knew its heritage, once remarking that the folk music in the central South had derived from North Carolina camp meetings and that the camp meetings preserved songs brought to America from Scotland.

Hay was perhaps even more of an enthusiast than Craig. He believed, as Art Satherly had believed, that rural people deserved the chance to hear their own music on the radio, rather than having to accept programs dictated exclusively by urban tastes. Unlike Satherly, however, Hay was not attracted by the commercial possibilities of the idea. A generally amiable loner, a man whose conversation and prose were sprinkled with both the romanticism and the guff of the hustling and yet sentimental twenties, George Hay was a dreamer, a crusader for the common man.

"Our show is presented for the rural and industrial workers throughout the states," he was to write many years later. "Above all, we try to keep it 'homey.' Home folks do the work of the world, they win the wars and raise the families. Many of our geniuses come from simple folk who adhere to the fundamental principles of honesty included in the Ten Commandments. [The show] expresses those qualities which come from these good people."

At the keyboard of the typewriter that remained his companion long after he left newspapering for radio, a jovial George D. Hay—self-described "discoverer," rather than "founder," of the Grand Ole Opry—looks at his watch to check the nearness of a deadline

Hay's dream of such a show had been born in 1919 not too far from Memphis. That year, at the age of twenty-four, he was sent by the *Commercial Appeal* to cover a war hero's funeral near the small Arkansas resort town of Mammoth Spring—"one of the most typical small towns in America," as he described it.

The soldier whose funeral he covered had been a farm boy, and Hay was driven the thirty miles up into the mountains to the young man's home community by mule team.

"It was a beautiful day," Hay later wrote. "The neighbors came from miles around in respect to the memory of this United States Marine who gave his life to preserve their way of life. The young man's father welcomed them as he stood on the crude platform in the country churchyard, but closed his brief remarks in this manner: 'Let all those who were against the government during the war pass on down the road.' We didn't see anyone leave.

"After the services, the automobiles and mule-drawn wagons which had brought the mourners to the services headed slowly back down the rutted road, and Hay went back to Mammoth Spring to file his story. After doing so, he decided to spend the next day in the little Arkansas town, which he described as "a beautiful place for rest and quiet." He spent the first part of his holiday just looking around.

"In the afternoon, we sauntered around the town at the edge of which—hard by the Missouri line—there lived a truck farmer in an old railroad car. He had seven or eight children, and his wife seemed to be very tired with the tremendous job of caring for them. We chatted for a few minutes, and the man went into his place of abode and brought forth a fiddle and a bow. He invited me to attend a 'hoedown' the neighbors were going to put on that night until 'the crack o' dawn' in a log cabin about a mile up a muddy road."

Hay readily assented, never having seen anything like that before. He and the truck farmer journeyed to a two-room cabin where wagons already filled a bare yard and mules were tethered to trees. When he and his host went inside, Hay's companion brought out his fiddle and joined two other musicians, a guitar player and a banjo player. About twenty other persons, their work-worn faces lighted by two coal-oil lanterns, sat around the walls of the room waiting.

Then the three-man band struck into some lively old tunes that Hay remembered the rest of his life. They were tunes like "Old Dan Tucker," "Casey Jones," "Whoop 'Em up Cindy," "Turkey in the Straw," and "Pop Goes the Weasel."

"They danced, they danced, they danced all night long," Hay told another reporter many years later. "They laughed and yelled and had a wonderful time, and I tucked it away in my mind as the happiest scene I ever saw. Years later, when I got into radio full time, the whole scene came back to me—the music, the laughter, the little Arkansas cabin."

That scene stored away in his mind became to Hay the epitome of the South he had fallen in love with. When WLS in Chicago, which had just started a radio barndance show, offered him a job in 1924, he intentionally set his price at $75 a week, thinking it would be too high. He was mistaken. WLS wanted a man with a style, something that would give the barndance show that quality called "human interest," and the WLS management knew from Hay's work on WMC in Memphis that he was such a man. WLS would have paid him $100 a week if he had asked for it, Hay found out later.

Now, in 1925, WSM wanted him for the same reason WLS had wanted him. This time he was being offered the opportunity to set up his own show instead of running one already formed, and he was being invited to return to the South. He accepted, and he seems to have done so for love rather than money. Jack DeWitt, who remembers seeing some of Hay's paychecks in later years, estimates that he came to Nashville for $250 to $300 a month.

CROOK BROTHERS

FRUIT JAR DRINKERS

THE OPRY IS BORN

National Life's radio station seems to have been of considerable interest to a few musicians in the outlying environs of Nashville even before it went on the air. During that summer of 1925, a National Life purchasing agent named William R. Craig (apparently no relation to the founding Craigs) contacted a rural physician friend who had a string band. The doctor, Humphrey Bate, lived some forty miles northeast of Nashville, and Craig asked him if he would bring his band down occasionally when the new station opened. Dr. Bate said that he would be happy to, and his daughter recalls that he was so anxious to do it that he would not accept a similar invitation from WDAD until he had cleared it with Craig.

"But Mr. Craig said it was all right, and we went down to WDAD and played before WSM went on the air," his daughter, Mrs. Alcyone Bate Beasley, recalls.

Dr. Bate's band, in which his daughter played piano, performed mostly "pretty, old-time country songs and the fiddle breakdowns," Mrs. Beasley says. Fifty years of age that year, Humphrey Bate was a robust man, completely bald, whose three passions in life were medicine, music, and fishing. He had graduated from the now defunct University of Nashville School of Medicine and been a surgeon in the Spanish-American War. His family was a historically prominent one; one of his ancestors was both a governor and senator. But in his teens Bate had played a harmonica on a steamboat plying the Cumberland River and money had been thrown at his feet. Show business was about as deep in his blood as his pride of ancestry. He and his family—a wife sixteen years younger than himself, his daughter, and two younger sons—lived in a six-room house on an acre and a half in the crossroads community of Castalian Springs. He drove his own automobile on his trips to Nashville or wherever his music or medical rounds took him, and he accepted pay for his medical services in whatever currency was available, including vegetables, chickens, molasses, and hams.

Less than three weeks after WSM went on the air, Dr. Bate and his group presented an hour-long program on it, Mrs. Beasley recalls. "I remember that night after it was over, we drove back home in the old Ford car and Daddy, who always called me 'Booger,' said, 'Booger, we might've started something down there tonight, you just don't know.'

"We played there for about four or five weeks before Mr. Hay came. We would drive into Nashville and perform on WDAD in the afternoon, then we would walk up the hill [between where the two stations' studios were located] and play on WSM later in the evening. I remember we would give Jack Keefe, who was the WSM announcer then, a list of the numbers we were going to play during the hour we would be on the air. And within just two weeks or so, bands from everywhere began to come up to be put on the air. One of the first of them was Mr. Ed Poplin's band from Lewisburg, Tennessee."

Dr. Bate, who died of a heart attack in 1936, may well have

Dr. HUMPHREY BATE
And His
"POSSUM-HUNTERS"
From Radio Station WSM

thought he "started something" on WSM after that first October evening when he brought his string band up the hill, but who started what, and when, in the early country music at WSM has been a controversy ever since George Hay wrote a one-dollar history of the Grand Ole Opry a quarter-century after he arrived in Nashville. It was even later than that—apparently too late—when historians and scholarly-minded fans began to be interested enough in the subject to try to trace the Opry's origins.

"If everybody who claimed to have been on the first show actually had been, there wouldn't have been room enough left in the studio to do anything," observes Minnie Pearl, who has tried to research the origins herself.

One of the few things generally agreed upon is that George D. Hay did not arrive in Nashville to assume his duties until a few weeks after the station went on the air, apparently five or six weeks afterward. When he arrived, he brought along his trademarks: his self-coined nickname, "The Solemn Old Judge," and an old Mississippi River steamboat whistle which he had blown at what seemed to him appropriate intervals during his first announcing stint on WMC in Memphis and more recently on the WLS barndance show in Chicago. He became the first director of the station, and according to the ac-

George D. Hay, holding steamboat whistle and agenda, with fabled Uncle Jimmy Thompson, the first featured performer on the WSM barndance

count he later wrote he first went on the air with a program of hillbilly music on November 28, 1925. This show featured Uncle Jimmy Thompson, the venerable fiddler whom legend has made even more famous than he was at the time.

Hay's account of this and many other events is a pamphlet titled "A Story of the Grand Ole Opry." A rambling saga which jumps back and forth across time spans of a decade or more, and sometimes digresses, it is nevertheless probably the most important single document about the birth of country music in Nashville. Whatever its disputed worth as history, it is a Bible of the genre and a powerful piece of homely Americana. Its earthiness, so typical of its author, gives it a neighborly charm.

"Your reporter, who was the first director of WSM, had considerable experience in the field of folk music when the station opened in October 1925," Hay says in opening his account of the creation.

"Realizing the wealth of folk music material and performers in the Tennessee Hills, he welcomed the appearance of Uncle Jimmy Thompson and his blue ribbon fiddle, who went on the air at eight o'clock Saturday night, November 28, 1925. Uncle Jimmy told us that he had a thousand tunes. Past eighty years of age, he was given a comfortable chair in front of an old carbon microphone. While his niece,

Grave-faced Kitty Cora (Mrs. Grundy) Cline, one of the early performers on the barndance, with her zither

Mrs. Eva Thompson Jones, played his piano accompaniment, your reporter presented Uncle Jimmy and announced that he would be glad to answer requests for oldtime tunes. Immediately telegrams began to pour into WSM.

"An hour later, at nine o'clock, we asked Uncle Jimmy if he hadn't done enough fiddling, to which he replied, 'Why shucks, a man don't get warmed up in an hour. I just won an eight-day fiddling contest down in Dallas, Texas, and here's my blue ribbon to prove it.'

"Uncle Jimmy Thompson, Mrs. Jones, and the Solemn Old Judge carried on for several weeks for an hour each Saturday night. Telegrams poured into the station."

About this time, the account goes on, automobile magnate Henry Ford presented an award for the best old-time fiddling in the United States to a Maine resident named Mellie Dunham. Plainly seeking publicity for itself, the new Nashville radio station invited Dunham to come down and "fiddle a duel" with Uncle Jimmy. Dunham's advisors, "realizing he had nothing to win," refused to allow him to accept the challenge, Hay says, adding that Uncle Jimmy then observed (on the air, doubtless) that Dunham "is affeared of me."

"The fact that Mr. Dunham was advised to refuse our invitation probably gave Uncle Jimmy more publicity than he would have received if the Hon. Mellie had come to Nashville," Hay gleefully notes. "It added up to the fact that WSM had a good-natured riot on its hands. After three or four weeks of this fiddle solo business, we were besieged with fiddlers, banjo pickers, guitar players, and a lady who played an old zither."

Not much further along in this history, the first parts of which were written in 1945, Hay notes that to the best of his recollection the first old-time band to play on the WSM barndance was the one led by Humphrey Bate. When Bate died in 1936, Hay wrote in the National Life bulletin *The Shield* that the country doctor had been "among the very first on the program. . . . As a matter of fact, he played on the station before the barndance started. . . ."

The latter seems a curious admission, for it would seem that if Humphrey Bate played hillbilly music on WSM before the barndance in 1925, he deserves some credit for bringing the barndance into existence. Mrs. Beasley, who was thirteen at the time, says that the show was being called a "barndance" before Hay arrived in Nashville to stay, and that it was announced by the late Jack Keefe, who became a Nashville lawyer.

Several of the few old-time musicians left on the show today agree with Mrs. Beasley—and with Hay's 1936 column in *The Shield* —that Bate preceded Hay and Uncle Jimmy. Such people include Burt Hutcherson and Staley Walton, both of whom played in Bate's band in 1925. If what these people remember is indeed true, then the only question seems to be whether what Bate did constituted the beginning of the show that became famous.

Hay does not appear to have thought so, although he gives no clear clue as to why. Perhaps, since he was not there for the first month or so, he assumed that the show he put on the air November 28 was the first of its kind the station had carried. Or perhaps Bate's performances occurred on some night other than Saturday, and Hay figured they did not count. Perhaps the Dunham "feud" stunt put Uncle Jimmy Thompson foremost in Hay's mind. Or perhaps, in the score of years that intervened between the events and his recording of them, he simply forgot; he was beset increasingly with emotional problems during his later years at WSM.

"I never felt badly about it toward Mr. Hay, because he wasn't well," Mrs. Beasley says, "but the fact remains that nothing was ever said about Uncle Jimmy Thompson being the first one on the show until long after my Daddy died in 1936.

"How that came to be the story has been the puzzle of my life."

Whatever the truth, and whatever the reasons for the latter-day mystery about it, the shrouding of the show's beginnings adds to the richness of the legend. The ambiguity of its heritage makes it all the more the offspring not of one man but of an era, and of the hard yet colorful life of rural people.

Almost immediately after it went on the air, the country people whose music it had captured began to show up in little groups in the hall of the National Life home office building on Saturday nights. Gathering outside the studio from which the show was broadcast, they would press their noses against the glass of two large windows that commanded views of the proceedings inside, and week by week their numbers grew. So did the number of radio listeners.

An item from *The Nashville Tennessean* dated December 27, 1925, notes: "Old tunes like old lovers are the best, at least judging from the applause which the new Saturday night features at Station WSM receive from listeners from all parts of the country. Jazz has not completely turned the tables on such tunes as 'Turkey in the Straw' and 'Pop Goes the Weasel.' America may not be swinging its partners at a barndance, but it seems to have the habit of clamping on earphones and patting its feet as gaily as it ever did when the oldtime fiddlers get going."

Those words sound suspiciously like George Hay, and some people who knew him believe his continuing interest in reporting may well have led him to call in occasional items to the newspapers. He was putting together a distinctive show, building it according to his conception of what it should be. On the first broadcasts on which he introduced Bate and his group, he referred to them as "Dr. Humphrey Bate and His Augmented String Orchestra"; very soon, however, he changed the name to fit his image of his production. They became the Possum Hunters. Other string bands that came for auditions got similar names if they did not have them already: Ed Poplin and the Old Timers, Paul Warmack and the Gully Jumpers, The Binkley Brothers and The Clod Hoppers, George Wilkerson and the Fruit Jar Drinkers —this last being a term widely used in the twenties to describe imbibers of moonshine whisky.

Others among the earliest groups were the Crook Brothers and Sam and Kirk McGee. Burt Hutcherson, who now plays with the Crook Brothers, says that for the first two years the musicians played

OVERLEAF:
LEFT ABOVE: A few years after the barndance started, the performers began to take on more rural trappings and to see themselves as entertainers of country people. Here the Possum Hunters look much less formal than they did in their first WSM pictures. Left to right are Dr. Bate, Staley Walton, Oscar Stone, James Hart, Walter Liggett, and Oscar Albright. LEFT BELOW: Another early barndance group was Ed Poplin's band. Standing, left to right, are guitarist Jack Woods, his daughter Louise, and Poplin, fiddle. Seated are Woods's daughter Frances and Ed Poplin, Jr. RIGHT ABOVE: According to legend, Judge Hay often made up names for the bands that came in to audition. The Gully Jumpers may well have been named by him. Here we see banjoist Roy Hardison, fiddler Charlie Arrington, guitarist Burt Hutcherson (originally a Possum Hunter), guitarist Paul Warmack, and an unidentified pianist. RIGHT BELOW: The Gully Jumpers a little later, after country clothes really came into vogue. Left to right are Burt Hutcherson, Roy Hardison, Charlie Arrington, and Paul Warmack

83

for nothing, except for one two-week Loew's Theater engagement that Hay got for them. After two years, they began to be paid five dollars a week, he says.

"It was purely a labor of love," Hay says in his history. "Whoever showed up went on the air sometime, and usually several times, during the Saturday night show. By that we do not mean it was a free-for-all. We passed upon all of them in a crude sort of an audition."

One performer who went on without such an audition, according to Mrs. Beasley, was DeFord Bailey, a black harmonica player who was one of the performers on programs at WDAD. Dr. Bate asked him one afternoon at WDAD if he would like to go up to WSM, she says, and Bailey said he would. Bate took him with them up the hill to the WSM studio, where the barndance was already in progress.

"As they started in, Mr. Hay said, 'Doc, where you goin' with this boy?' " Mrs. Beasley recalls.

"Daddy said, 'Let this boy in here, Judge—let him play a tune.' And the Judge said, 'Why Doc, I can't let this boy go on the air without hearin' him.' And Daddy says, 'I'll stake my reputation on the ability of this boy, Judge.' So he went on the air and played, and Mr. Hay, he was just thrilled to death. He pitched his old steamboat whistle up in the air."

Hay already was exhorting them to "keep it down to earth, boys," meanwhile laying down stringent rules about the music. He notes in his history that Ed Poplin's band specialized "in folk music, although once in a while, before we could or did stop it, Uncle Ed would slip in an old popular song, such as 'When You Wore a Tulip and I Wore a Red, Red Rose.' "

Mrs. Beasley and the old-time musicians do not question that George Hay shaped the show and made it the homely ideal against which its later years forever will be measured. What secures his place as its spiritual father is that he named it—and instantly transformed it from just another hillbilly radio show to a distinctive phenomenon that has become the archetype of its kind.

He did it, he says, "out of the blue" one Saturday evening in 1927 as his barndance show followed a New York network production onto the air.

"It so happened that on Saturday nights from seven until eight o'clock, WSM carried the Music Appreciation Hour under the direction of the eminent conductor and composer, Dr. Walter Damrosch," Hay recalls.

"Dr. Damrosch always signed off his concert a minute or so before eight o'clock, just before we hit the air with our mountain minstrels and vocal trapeze performers. We must confess that the change in pace and quality was immense, but that is part of America, fine lace and homespun cloth, our show being entirely covered by the latter. . . . The members of our radio audience who loved Dr. Damrosch and his Symphony Orchestra thought we should be shot at sunrise and did not hesitate to tell us so. . . .

"The monitor in our Studio B was turned on, so that we would have a rough idea of the time which was fast approaching. At about five minutes before eight, your reporter called for silence in the studio.

OPPOSITE PAGE:
ABOVE: The Binkley Brothers and the Dixie Clodhoppers were another early group on the show. Left to right, they are Amos and Gayle Binkley, Elmer Simpson, a mandolinist who occasionally played with the Binkleys, and left-handed guitarist Tom Andrews. Notice the cigar-box fiddle propped up at left. BELOW: Grandpappy George Wilkerson, second from left, is shown here with his Fruit Jar Drinkers, who all appear ready to engage in a little of the art they were named for

Kirk, left, and Sam McGee serenade a WSM microphone surrounded with evidence of their virtuosity

Watched by an awestruck admirer at far left, the Crook Brothers group gets together for an early publicity picture on the steps of a country store. Sitting on the top step are harmonica player Herman Crook and his cousin Lewis, the banjo player

The Opry cast about 1930. Front row, from left: Buster Bate, Claude Lampley, H. J. Ragsdale, Tom Leffew, George Wilkerson, Charlie Arrington, Tom Andrews, Gayle and Amos Binkley. Second row: Oscar Stone, Oscar Albright, Dr. Humphrey Bate, Walter Liggett, Dorris Macon, Uncle Dave Macon, Paul Warmack, Roy

Hardison, and Burt Hutcherson. Third row: announcer David Stone, Herman
Crook, Kirk McGee, Arthur Smith, Sam McGee, Robert Lunn, Bill Etter, Staley
Walton, and George D. Hay. Fourth row: Blythe Poteet, Alton and Rabon
Delmore, Lewis Crook, Dee Simmons, Nap Bastian, and DeFord Bailey

Out of the loudspeaker came the very correct but accented voice of Dr. Damrosch, and his words were something like this:

"'While most artists realize that there is no place in the classics for realism, nevertheless I am going to break one of my rules and present a composition from a young composer from 'Ioway,' who sent us his latest number, which depicts the onrush of a locomotive. . . .'

"After which announcement the good doctor directed his symphony orchestra through the number, which carried many 'shooses' depicting an engine trying to come to a full stop. Then he closed his programme with his usual sign-off. Our control operator gave us the signal which indicated that we were on the air. . . . We paid our respects to Dr. Damrosch and said on the air something like this:

"'Friends, the programme which just came to us was devoted to the classics. Dr. Damrosch told us that it was generally agreed that there is no place in the classics for realism. However, from here on out for the next three hours we will present nothing but realism. It will be down to earth for the earthy. In respectful contrast to Dr. Damrosch's presentation of the number which depicts the onrush of the locomotive, we will call on one of our performers, DeFord Bailey, with his harmonica, to give us the country version of his 'Pan American Blues.'"

Bailey, to whom Hay refers in his account as a "wizard with the harmonica," played the number, which was also a train tune. When Bailey had finished, Hay went back to the microphone and delivered one of the most stunning ad libs in the history of American radio.

"For the past hour, we have been listening to music taken largely from Grand Opera," he told his audience. "But from now on, we will present the Grand Ole Opry."

DeFord Bailey and his harmonica,
on which he was known as a "wizard"

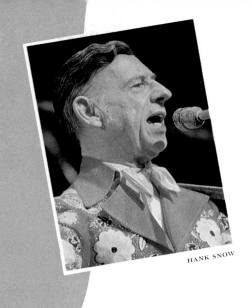

HANK SNOW

BILLY WALKER

THE FIRST STAR—UNCLE DAVE MACON

THE CARLISLES

A little fiddler by the name of Sidney Harkreader, introduced as the fiddling fiddler of Mount Juliet, [who was] teamed up with a banjo player by the name of Uncle Dave Macon of Readyville, Tennessee, introduced as the struttingest strutter that ever strutted a strut with a banjo or guitar, set the hundreds to stomping their feet with 'Turkey in the Straw,' 'Sugar Walks down the Street,' 'Ain't Goin' to Rain No More,' and 'Go away Mule.'

"Six thousand people roared their approval."

According to some yellowed, anonymous research notes in the files of the Country Music Hall of Fame Library, the above concert occurred at the Ryman Auditorium on November 6, 1925, some three weeks before the date George Hay cites for the establishment of the WSM barndance.

The crowd estimate seems a bit inflated (the Ryman's crammed-full capacity during later years when the Opry occupied it was always set at 3,500), but the notice does illustrate that David Harrison Macon was a popular entertainer in central Tennessee for some time before WSM became a functioning station.

Macon was a squat bull of a man with a mouthful of gold teeth and a little goatee which he sometimes pulled violently during a show, while bleating like a billygoat.

He had begun performing professionally at the age of forty-eight, after being discovered by a Loew's Theater talent scout at a rural party hosted by one of Macon's neighbors. Before that, he had earned a living driving mule teams for his Macon Midway Mule and Wagon Transportation Company, which hauled goods between the towns of Woodbury and Murfreesboro, just south of Nashville.

Born in the nearby rural community of Smart Station, he moved to Nashville when he was very young and attended Hume-Fogg High School there. His parents operated the Broadway Show Hotel, a favorite stopping place for traveling performers who came through Nashville. He became fascinated with their way of life and was particularly taken by the banjo playing of a performer named Joel Davidson.

By the time he began to appear on the WSM barndance in late 1925 or early 1926, Uncle Dave had been making public appearances since 1918 and had been to New York twice to make recordings. He was, in fact, already a composite of all the things the barndance would someday come to typify—singing, picking, and comedy—and he may well have been the most colorful Opry star of all time.

Nipping whisky which he carried with him in a little black suitcase, he was by turns religious and boisterous, a tiny bit vain, very thrifty and practical, and almost always funny—whether he meant to be or not.

"All day long, from morning 'til night, it was a show," remembers Kirk McGee, who worked with him on the early Opry.

"To my opinion, he was the greatest. He was an entertainer that could perform anyplace. Even if it was a church, he could make a fine talk."

Sid Harkreader fiddles before the Opry microphone in the Barndance (early Opry) era

Uncle Dave Macon

On his first New York recording trip Uncle Dave entered a Manhattan barbershop, asked for the full treatment and got it, including a bill for $7.50. He paid the outrageous sum without flinching, even telling the proprietor that he would have expected such service to cost $10, but later noted in his expense book: "Robbed in barbershop: $7.50."

Roy Acuff recalls that on one trip to New York Uncle Dave was "walking around, maybe looking up at the skyscrapers or something," and one of the locals asked whether it was not true that there were "a lot of ignorant people down in those hills where you come from, Uncle Dave?"

"Yes, sir," Uncle Dave acknowledged, "but they don't come in droves like they do up here."

Honey Wilds of Jamup and Honey, a long-time blackface comedy team, recalls that Uncle Dave was a little eccentric in some respects.

For instance, although his size was about forty, he purchased his long underwear—"complete with the trap door in back," Wilds says —in size fifty, "because he didn't like it tight on him." And at his home in Readyville he had a large safe; he opened it one day when Wilds was there, and its entire contents consisted of two pints of Jack Daniel's whisky, two pairs of suspenders, and three pairs of new shoes.

An extremely funny man himself, he was a frequent target of the jokes of others. The Jamup and Honey troupe once locked him out of his room in a "little wasp-nest hotel in Arkansas" when he went down the hall to the bathroom in his long underwear.

Another time, they tricked him into sharing the contents of his little black suitcase, something Wilds says he was normally loath to do. That time, Wilds says, they had been riding all night and were going into Oklahoma on a Sunday morning when they passed a sign warning motorists that there would be road construction for the next several miles. Uncle Dave's eyes were not so good, apparently.

"I was driving and he was sitting in the back seat," Wilds recalls. "He raised up back there and said, 'Brother Honey, what's that sign say, what's that sign say?' I said, 'That sign says "No Whisky Allowed in the State of Oklahoma on Account of the Indians. Anybody Caught with Whisky, Automatic Ninety Days on the Public Road."' Uncle Dave sat back there a minute, and then I heard him opening his little suitcase. 'We better drink this up, boys,' he said."

Macon's early recordings are said to have been one of the most important sources of authentic folk songs—such songs as "Rock About My Saro Jane," "Jordan Is a Hard Road to Travel," "Way Down the Old Plank Road," "Buddy Won't You Roll Down the Line," "Sail Away Ladies," and "Bully of the Town."

His style was boisterous; he would kick and shout while performing a number. He was a consummate showman, but although some folk-music scholars seem to disagree, musicians who played with him do not consider him a particularly gifted banjo player. He carried three of these instruments with him on performances, each tuned in a different key because he played only one set of chords. If he wished to

OPPOSITE PAGE:
ABOVE: One of the first organized Opry road troupes was this one, which toured a circuit of RKO theaters in 1931. Seated from left are Sam McGee and Uncle Dave Macon. Standing are Kirk McGee, Dr. Humphrey Bate, Dorris Macon, Humphrey Bate Jr., Alcyone Bate, and Lou Hesson. BELOW: Some of the Opry's early performers gather around the porch of a rural general store to watch Uncle Dave Macon do his famous kick. Seated are Uncle Dave and his son Dorris. Arrayed behind them, from left, are Amos Binkley, Tom Andrews, Walter Liggett, Paul Warmack, Burt Hutcherson, an unidentified man, Charlie Arrington, and Dr. Humphrey Bate

change key, he might simply say to his son Dorris, who usually accompanied him on guitar: "Dorris, hand your pappy that D banjo."

Aaron Shelton, a WSM engineer who began part-time work at the station in 1928, says he and the rest of the technical personnel used to dread Uncle Dave's Saturday night performances.

"He was so hard to control from a volume standpoint," Shelton explains. "You had to watch your levels much more closely back then, because they might overmodulate and possibly damage some of the equipment. Uncle Dave and Dorris would always sit in chairs and play, and we would set the microphone up about three feet out in front and sort of between them. There was one song in particular, Uncle Dave's famous 'Way out on the Mountain,' in which at some point he would always jump up and holler 'Whur?'—and the following phrase was, of course, 'way out on the mountain.' But you could never tell at exactly what point he was going to jump up and give you this wild 'whur?' I've heard engineers get pretty wrought up during it sometimes, and not call him nice names."

Shelton remembers that during his first two or three years at WSM, the show was referred to as the Grand Ole Opry with increasing frequency as listeners' cards and letters made it plain they had accepted Judge Hay's off-the-cuff name for the program. He also recalls that the attitude of technical people like himself toward this new institution was "mixed," although they agreed that the proceedings were certainly "entertaining."

Jack DeWitt, who left to work for Bell Laboratories in New York for three years before returning as chief engineer in 1932, readily acknowledges that he did not like the music; the musicians themselves, however, he found colorful and interesting. "Real hickories, we used to call them," he recalls.

It was a spectacle even in its earliest days.

Shelton recalls that some of the performers would "bring along certain refreshments to help them along with their performances toward the shag end of the evening, so they sang with a lot of abandon."

Meanwhile, the show was growing and changing. The performers were being paid now, and there were more and more of them.

Around 1930 Sam and Kirk McGee, who had been on the show since its first weeks and had appeared frequently with Uncle Dave Macon, brought in a fiddler named Arthur Smith from Humphreys County, Tennessee, who worked on the so-called "Dixie Line" of one of the railroads; the three of them began to call themselves the Dixieliners.

About that same time, Asher Sizemore and his six-year-old son, Little Jimmy—singers of "heart songs who closed their programme with a prayer," Judge Hay notes—joined the show. So did Robert Lunn, the "talking blues boy," a performer whose best-known song had so many verses that he used different parts of it on the Opry for years.

In 1931 a group named the Vagabonds—Herald Goodman, Dean Upson, and Curt Poulton—came to the Opry after prior stints on WLS in Chicago and KMOX in St. Louis. They are credited by some with being the first really professional group to join the show.

OPPOSITE PAGE:
ABOVE: Sam and Kirk McGee flank Arthur Smith, a young fiddler whose regular job was working on the Dixie Line of one of the railroads. They called themselves the Dixieliners. BELOW: These early Opry performers, Asher and Little Jimmy Sizemore, always closed their performances with a prayer

"People like that came down as acts of their own and were on other programs on WSM before somebody got the idea that they would be appealing on the Opry," Shelton says.

"In those years Sarie and Sally [Mrs. Edna Wilson and Mrs. Margaret Waters, a comedy team] and the Delmore Brothers [singers] and several others ended up on the show that way."

Another performer who came to the show that way was Lasses White ("dean of minstrelsy at that time," Hay says), who joined WSM to present a radio version of Lasses White's Minstrels. White, who did not remain long, brought a partner, Lee Davis (Honey) Wilds, who later founded the team of Jamup and Honey.

Others who joined the show in the early or middle thirties included Zeke Clements and His Bronco Busters, the team of Fiddlin' Curly Fox and Texas Ruby Owens, and Jack Shook and His Missouri Mountaineers.

The crowds that came gathered first outside the two windows of little (twenty-five by thirty-five feet) Studio A, then outside the larger, glass-paneled Studio B, and finally inside specially constructed Studio C, which seated five hundred fans.

They seemed to be largely farm people from close around Nashville, Shelton recalls. They came in cars and flatbed trucks to see their picturesque new musical heroes, particularly Uncle Dave Macon.

"They were not the kind of people who responded very much," Shelton says.

"They sat on their hands, sort of in awe. They would not applaud; wild applause was a later development of the show-business techniques that grew up around the show as it became more famous, drawing people who were used to that kind of thing. No, the first audiences had the reserve of the real Anglo-Saxon type of people from the hills." But although they were reserved, they seemed to come in greater and greater numbers each week.

"They were hungry for the rhythm of the soil and the heart songs, plus the rural flavor and humor which spiced it," says George Hay. "Finally the crowds stormed the wrought-iron doors of our Home Office Building to such an extent that our own officials could not get into their own offices when they felt it necessary to do so on Saturday nights. People in crowds are apt to lose their heads, and finally the payoff came one Saturday night when our two top officials were refused admittance to their own office building. They were forced to seek out the night engineer and be admitted through the back door. Our audience was very politely invited to leave the building.

"For some time we did not know whether or not the Grand Ole Opry would be taken off the air. We broadcast for some time without any audience, but something was lacking. So we went into a huddle, and it was decided to rent the Hillsboro Theater, a neighborhood house not too far from the center of Nashville. It was a great relief to the audience and the performers."

At the Hillsboro, Hay notes, the show for the first time acquired dressing rooms and a staff of ushers.

Because the theater was small, the show played to two audi-

ABOVE: Dashing fiddler Curly Fox teamed with Texas Ruby Owens. LEFT: Sarie and Sally, a comedy team, were one of the most popular early Opry acts

OPPOSITE PAGE, FROM THE TOP: Jamup, or Bunny Biggs, and Lee Davis (Honey) Wilds do their routine before the WSM microphone; Lasses White, left, and Honey Wilds shoot dice next to a boxcar in a publicity picture that probably came from Hollywood rather than Nashville; Curt Poulton was a member of an early Opry trio called the Vagabonds, one of the first professional groups to come to the Opry from another show; Husky Zeke Clements sings to a large street crowd in Nashville

OVERLEAF:
ABOVE LEFT: Rabon, left, and Alton Delmore, seen here flanking Uncle Dave Macon, started the Opry tradition of duet-singing brothers. Later and better-known ones include the Louvins and the Wilburns.
BELOW LEFT: Bunny Biggs, left, and Honey Wilds, here without the usual black-face disguise, do a daily segment of their Jamup and Honey radio show. ABOVE RIGHT: Left-handed guitarist Robert Lunn, left, whose "talking blues" had a seemingly endless number of verses, with fiddler George Wilkerson, mandolinist Glen Stagner, and minstrel Lasses White with ukelele. BELOW RIGHT: Jack Shook and the Missouri Mountaineers. From the left, Shook, Dee Simmons, Bobby Castleman, Arthur Smith, and Nap Bastian

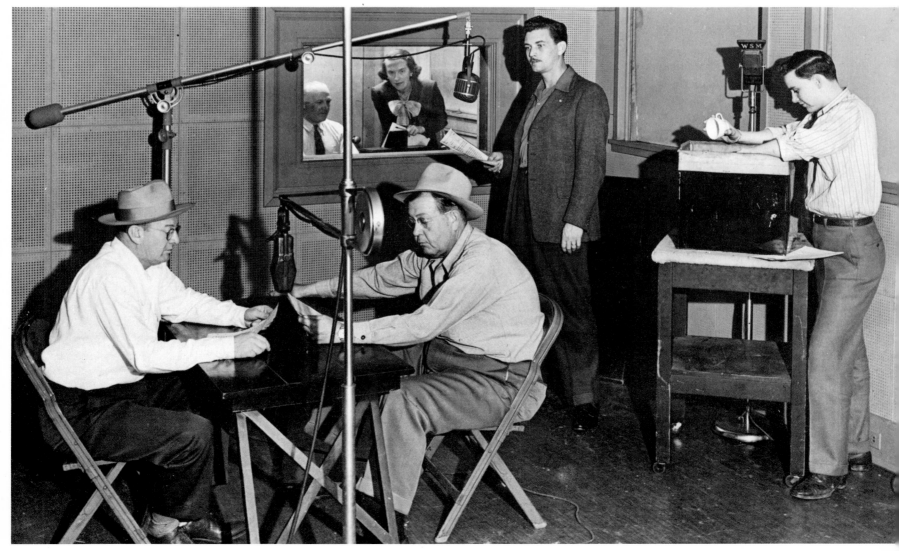

ences between eight o'clock and midnight. The tickets were still free, but they were only allowed to be distributed, and in limited numbers, by the 3,000 agents of National Life.

Alcyone Beasley recalls that soon after the move to the theater, Hay for the first time began to ask the performers to try to wear costumes that would identify them as performers on a rural show.

Other, subtler changes had been occurring steadily since the show's inception.

In 1927, WSM increased its power to 5,000 watts and affiliated itself with the newly organized National Broadcasting Company. In 1932, it acquired a clear-channel frequency and was permitted to increase its power from 5,000 to 50,000 watts. (A clear channel means that no other station in the country can operate on that frequency.)

Around 1930, Judge Hay was replaced as the station's director by Harry Stone, a more business-oriented announcer who was about Hay's own age. A native of Jacksonville, Florida, Stone's family had drifted into Nashville after his father went bankrupt on a Coca-Cola franchise in North Carolina. Harry and his younger brother David got "what education we received" in the Tennessee capital, David recalls today. Harry began his radio career in Jack DeWitt's father's living room while working in a Nashville retail store. Later, when a drug firm took over WCBQ from the First Baptist Church and redesignated it WBAW, Stone became a full-time announcer. Around 1927, he was hired by WSM. His brother David joined the station as an announcer the following year, remaining until 1940.

Hay seems to have been replaced because he was emotionally unsuited to regimented schedules and detail work. There are indications that he already had begun to suffer the nervous breakdowns that would plague him increasingly later on.

"Judge Hay's health was not the best at that time, and he was in and out of work a lot," David Stone says. "Sometimes he would leave for a few days to see a relative in Indiana. I served as the Opry's announcer much of the time when he was out during those years."

Harry Stone, who began directing WSM's activities about 1930, was one of the most powerful influences in the Opry's history

Hay was much more of a creative artist and show business personality than he was an executive, according to many of the performers and businessmen who worked with him.

"He just wasn't a practical kind of man," DeWitt recalls. "He was up in the clouds all the time."

Stone was just the opposite in that respect, but like Hay and Edwin Craig—and unlike almost everybody else connected with the show then—Stone really liked the Opry.

"He also saw a commercial value in it," DeWitt adds. "Harry Stone was the man who commercialized the Opry."

Gradually costumes, waved-in applause, and other such trappings began to appear. In 1934, about the time the Opry moved to the Hillsboro Theater, the station founded the Artist's Service Bureau to schedule road performances for Opry acts. It was begun, Hay says in his history, "to book a free show for a local church to pay some of its bills."

In the fall of 1934, an ex-bandleader named Vito Pellettieri

An early WSM studio band. Future Opry stage manager Vito Pellettieri, standing, was its leader

was assigned to the Hillsboro to help with the staging of the Opry, so that Hay could concentrate on his duties as announcer and master of ceremonies. It was a madhouse, says Vito, who remained stage manager of the show for the next forty years.

After the first Saturday night on his new job, he says, "I went home, took me a big drink, and told my wife there weren't enough devils in Hell to ever drag me back there." Economic realities and his wife's opposition prevailed over this hasty decision, but he resolved to try to bring some order out of the chaos. He suggested that the show be divided into fifteen-minute segments scheduled a week in advance, so that the musicians would know exactly when they were to appear. Then, after a couple of weeks, he suggested that these segments could be sold to advertisers. As a result, he says, the first such segment was sold to the manufacturers of a product called Crazy Water Crystals.

By 1936 the Hillsboro had become too cramped and the show moved on again, this time to a sawdust-floored religious revival house in East Nashville. The Dixie Tabernacle, as it was called, contained a couple of thousand crude, splintery bench seats. There the crowds continued to grow, some members of these audiences coming from long distances, beckoned by WSM's clear-channel signal.

There still was no authorized charge for tickets, but a hustling young East Nashville fan named Vic McAlpin, who was so smitten with the music that he would get up in the middle of the night to listen to hillbilly broadcasts on an ultrapowerful Mexican border station, sold Opry tickets anyway. McAlpin would beg a couple of dozen tickets each week from different National Life agents and hawk them in front of the Dixie Tabernacle. He sold them for a quarter apiece to people who had driven into Nashville to see the show without knowing they had to have tickets. McAlpin, a successful songwriter for more than two decades, says that after he had sold all his tickets he could usually talk an attendant at the door into admitting him for free.

The evening before the first Opry performance at the Tabernacle, Dr. Humphrey Bate died of a heart attack at his home.

"Daddy knew he was going to die," says Alcyone Beasley. "He'd had angina for years. He was a doctor, and he knew when the attack came that it was a bad one. He looked down at his fingernails, because he could tell how bad it was from the way they looked, and he said, 'Uh oh.' Then he told my mother, 'Ethel, this one's going to take me away from here.'

"He was feeling his own pulse when it stopped."

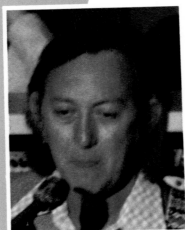

JACK GREENE

SEELY

THE STAR SYSTEM EMERGES

BOB LUMAN

While Uncle Dave Macon and the rest of the Opry's first performers were making the show a regional phenomenon, the man who would make it a national one was serving a humble apprenticeship several hundred miles east of Nashville. Roy Acuff began his professional music career with a medicine show, traveling through southwest Virginia and eastern Tennessee. His boss was a Dr. Hauer, and Acuff worked for him for more than a year.

The products Dr. Hauer huckstered were of varying quality, but at least the laxative did what it was supposed to, and that was what country people usually needed most in that day of unbalanced farm diets. And Dr. Hauer's corn remover usually cured corns, at least long enough for the show to get safely out of town.

"He'd get some man wearing old brogan shoes to come up on the stage, and he'd ask him if he was bothered with corns," Acuff recalls. "Wearing those shoes, why, of course the man would say yes, that he could hardly walk because of corns. Then Dr. Hauer would pour some of the corn remover on top of the shoes, and it would seep right through. After a moment, Dr. Hauer would put one of his feet on top of one of the man's feet and bear down with all his weight.

" 'Does that hurt?' he'd ask the man.

" 'No, it don't hurt at all,' the man would say, wiggling his foot around. Of course, the reason it didn't hurt at all was because he couldn't feel anything at all. The corn remover would take the corns off, all right, but it might take your foot off with it."

The performances the medicine show presented were free, designed to draw prospective buyers. They consisted of both music and comedy, and sometimes many hundreds of people would gather around the stage. Acuff fashioned his strong, impassioned singing style from those early days when he was required to try to reach the rear row of his audience without the aid of a microphone.

He was a complete novice. "I never saw a show 'til I put one on," he recalls.

Acuff was born September 15, 1903, in Maynardville, Tennessee, a few miles north of Knoxville. He was the son of a Missionary Baptist minister in a family that was prominent in the area. His paternal grandfather had been a lawyer and state senator, his maternal grandfather had been a physician.

As a teen-ager, Acuff was strong. On his father's farm he often amused himself by walking around while balancing shovels, axes, and even plows on his chin. He went to Central High School in Knoxville and became an impressive athlete, a three-sport star who planned a career in baseball. A New York Giants scout signed him to a professional contract after his graduation, but three cases of sunstroke wrecked his chances for a career on the diamond.

His only ambition suddenly shattered, the young man had to recuperate and readjust. Because of the sunstroke, he had to stay indoors during the heat of the day, and to pass the time he began to learn how to play the fiddle. He also started fooling around with a yoyo, a new toy that was being sold in the novelty stores.

The young Acuff, genial and—for him—somewhat dandified

"I started yoyoing just to kind of pacify my mind from throwing a baseball," he recalls.

"In the evenings after the sun'd go down I could go down and stand around on the corner and yoyo and talk."

He had moved permanently to Knoxville by this time, and he soon acquired the two-fisted reputation of a good old boy. "Roy would fight you in a minute and then give you the shirt off his back in the next minute," says Grand Old Opry comedian Archie Campbell.

When he went off with Dr. Hauer's medicine show, young Acuff did as much comedy work as singing, sometimes dressing up as an old woman or blacking his face with charcoal. This was valuable experience for his next job, a radio spot on WNOX in Knoxville with a group called the Crazy Tennesseans.

At first, Archie Campbell was a member of this group.

Campbell recalls that Acuff complained to the management after a while that the Crazy Tennesseans were not being paid enough, and when the management disagreed he took the group over to WROL, a rival station. Campbell stayed at WNOX and got a raise.

The Crazy Tennesseans came down from WROL to the Grand Ole Opry in 1938, while the show was playing at the Dixie Tabernacle. The group was not an overnight success.

"I was like all the others who come to Nashville," Acuff says. "I had spent all of what money I had, and I was just barely eating. I spent most of my time on the road, and I slept in cars. I'd just married, and when I joined the Opry we moved here and lived four years in a house trailer. Trailers then were smaller than they are now, but it was good enough for sleeping and cooking and bathing. We lived in it, just the two of us."

As they had done in Knoxville, he and his group began putting on shows in schoolhouses, theaters, and any other place that would allow them inside. Mildred, his new bride, often took on the job of collecting the money at the door.

When they first arrived in Nashville, the Crazy Tennesseans resembled other Opry bands in some ways. Acuff was the leader, the fiddler, and the most prominent singer, but most of their songs—with the exception of a few distinctive solos like "Wabash Cannonball" and "The Great Speckled Bird"—were the usual trio- and quartet-style numbers. Acuff became a full-time soloist almost unintentionally, in response to a demand.

The demand was a crying need, although nobody realized it until afterward. The best the early Opry broadcasts could do was convey the rhythm and spirit of the performances; the mechanical equipment available, according to Aaron Shelton, was too primitive to be able to transmit a very clear sound from an undisciplined live show. In the din, Acuff's brief and impassioned solo spots stood out like gunshots at midnight.

"I think I brought a different voice to the Opry," he says now.

"Most of the people on the show back then were crooners. They sang soft, and they sang harmony, where I would just open my mouth and fill my lungs with air, and let it go with force. I wasn't

One of the early publicity pictures has Acuff as the principal passenger on this wagon loaded with Smoky Mountain Boys, with girls, and with other musicians

conscious at the time of being different, because I was just doing it in my own natural way, but I knew I wasn't crooning.

"I didn't realize how different my singing was from the rest until my mail started coming in. The letters I got would mention how clear I was coming through, and how distinct my voice was, and how they could understand my words. The others, they couldn't distinguish the words."

After a few months, Harry Stone and Judge Hay asked Acuff to join the Opry. At the same time they asked him to change the name of the band.

"They thought Crazy Tennesseans was a kind of a slur name," he recalls. "They thought a change would be best, and it was. They knew that I knew about the Great Smoky Mountains and could possibly answer any question about them, so Judge Hay suggested that I call the band the Smoky Mountain Boys."

The Crazy Tennesseans had not been the Smoky Mountain Boys long when, in 1939, a new group called the Blue Grass Boys came into Nashville with Bill Monroe, a stony-faced Kentucky mandolin picker.

As Acuff was to be the prototype for a kind of country musician who picks an easy kind of music and grins to the crowd, Monroe would become the stern father of another kind of country music, a hard-driving hill sound played in utmost gravity, with somber contempt for deviations from its traditionalism.

Bill Monroe's music came by its funereal trappings honestly.

OPPOSITE PAGE:
ABOVE: Roy Acuff with his Knoxville group, the Crazy Tennesseans. From left they are Acuff, Red Jones, Jess Easterday, and James C. (later Cousin Jody) Summey, Hawaiian guitar.
BELOW: One of Acuff's early Opry groups. From left, Oswald Kirby, Jess Easterday, Acuff, Little Rachel Veach, and Lonnie (Pap) Wilson

BELOW:
One of Bill Monroe's first Blue Grass Boys groups—from left, Art Wooten, Monroe, Billy Borum, and Jim Holmes

The youngest son in a large family whose parents died young, Monroe was born with weak, crossed eyes and was raised in what today would be called poverty. He took to music as an almost providential respite from back-breaking farm work and the painful shyness caused by his physical abnormality.

"We worked hard back in that country," Monroe recalls now, speaking of Rosine, Kentucky.

"We farmed and worked in timber, drove cross-ties to the railroad and hauled coal from a coal mine we had on our farm. You worked from Monday morning 'til Saturday afternoon, then you had Saturday evening off. There might be a baseball game or something on Saturday, but there wasn't hardly nothing going on back in that country. Of course, there was church on Sundays and prayer meeting on Wednesday nights."

His Uncle Pen Vanderver, his mother's brother and probably the most important influence on Monroe, took him in after his parents died. In the evenings, after the day's hard work and a supper of fatback and cornpone, Uncle Pen would play the fiddle. The instrument's impassioned ring never failed to stir young Bill, and soon he began trying to play his uncle's music on a mandolin they had.

Pen Vanderver died when his young charge was eighteen. Bill Monroe left Rosine for Chicago, where he joined his brothers Charlie and Birch and got himself a job in a Sinclair refinery. He held it for five years, sometimes supporting his brothers.

The Monroe Brothers made their first professional music appearance in 1932, as square dancers on the WLS National Barndance. By 1934 they had their own program on radio, first in the Midwest at Shenandoah, Iowa, and Omaha, later in the South at Columbia, Charlotte, and Raleigh.

They became the rage of the Carolinas. Other old-time performers from the same era recall that the Monroes practically owned that area of the South, sometimes playing three or four shows in the same schoolhouse or theater in a single evening to accommodate the demand.

By 1936, Bill Monroe recalls, he was making enough money to be able to save some. In that year, he and his brothers made their first recording, "What Would You Give in Exchange for Your Soul?" and "This World Is Not My Home."

For their last year and a half together, the Monroes broadcast over a powerful clear-channel station in Raleigh. Then, in 1939, Bill became tired of being treated as the younger brother and quit Charlie and Birch to form his own group. He passed briefly through Asheville, Little Rock, and Greenville before arriving in Nashville in the fall.

At the Opry things were steadily changing, onstage and off.

In what seems to have been an uncharacteristically severe action, Judge Hay fired his harmonica wizard, DeFord Bailey, after Bailey had been on the show for a decade. His reason, he explains in his history, was that Bailey knew only "about a dozen harmonica numbers, which he put on the air and recorded for a major company," and "he refused to learn any more." Some Opry old-timers point out that

Bill Monroe picks his mandolin onstage at the Opry

many longtime Opry acts play the same two or three numbers every time they appear, and this has been standard practice for many since the early days. However, the Judge was adamant. He ordered Bailey to learn some more tunes, giving him a year to do so. When he did not, he was fired. There may be a glimmer of prejudice in the Judge's observation that Bailey, whom everybody on the show seems to have liked, was lazy.

There were other changes.

Sometime in the late thirties, Sam and Kirk McGee had brought an electric guitar down on Saturday night and Sam had played it on the show. When he came off the stage, Judge Hay had a little talk with him.

"The Judge said, 'Sam, that's purty but it's too modern,'" Kirk recalls. "He said, 'What we want to do is keep the show down to earth.' So we took the guitar home and never brought it back again."

That did not end the discussion of electrification, however; it only started it. A while later, Western bandleader Bob Wills and the Texas Playboys came in for a guest appearance and also used an electric guitar. Then Pee Wee King brought one down from Louisville with his Golden West Cowboys during his second stint on the Opry, beginning in 1941. Ernest Tubb had one in his band when he joined the Opry in 1942.

"After the Golden West Cowboys came, everybody started

trying to out-loud everybody else," Honey Wilds says.

Ernest Tubb's reasons for switching to the electric guitar were those that made the instrument a hillbilly phenomenon in the early forties. The jukebox was taking hillbilly music into the honky-tonks at that time, and some honky-tonk operators wrote Decca Records complaining that Tubb's recordings could not be heard over the roar when their crowds were large. So Tubb asked his guitarist to attach an electrical hookup to his conventional guitar, and when the results proved favorable, he acquired an electric guitar.

A number of changes were made in the original conception of the show to try to achieve national prominence for the Opry.

Republic Studios in Hollywood sent an associate producer to Nashville in 1938 to investigate the possibilities of shooting a motion picture about the Opry. WSM was amenable to the proposal.

"We discussed the show and its history with that very intelligent young man," Hay says in his history, "and took him out to Uncle Dave Macon's farm for a dinner which consisted of Tennessee country ham, fried chicken, and ten or twelve other items designed to satisfy the appetite of a senator."

The "intelligent young man" returned to Hollywood, doubtless pleasurably belching. Nothing more was heard from him.

During the following winter, however, a significant success was achieved. Through the William Esty advertising agency in New York, WSM sold a half-hour segment of the Opry to the R. J. Reynolds Company, manufacturers of Prince Albert Smoking Tobacco.

That sale turned out to be the most important in the Opry's history. As a result of it, Judge Hay writes, Dick Marvin, the radio director of the Esty agency, "got an idea in the back of his head to put the Opry on the NBC network."

"His idea was considerably off the beaten track used by advertising agencies in the metropolitan areas of our country, and he came in for much ribbing by members of his profession."

It took Marvin a year to get his offbeat idea off the ground, but he ultimately succeeded. In October 1939, the same month Bill Monroe joined the show, Prince Albert began to sponsor a thirty-minute network broadcast of the Opry over a limited number of stations that had agreed to carry it. These stations were scattered all the way from the southeastern zone to the West Coast.

The first night of the broadcasts, a large group of NBC executives came to Nashville to watch.

"Heretofore, we had not made any attempt to produce the show, in the accepted sense of the word," Judge Hay notes. "We had to be snatched off the air at the end of our thirty minutes, but with that exception, the half hour went over pretty well. Before the next week rolled around, we had timed our opening and closing and had no further difficulty."

When the Opry went on the network, it did so from better surroundings than those in which it had been located for the past few years. In July 1939 it moved from the Dixie Tabernacle to War Memorial Auditorium, a fashionable hall in the center of town and just

Ernest Tubb in the early sixties

across the street from the National Life home office building. An admission fee of a quarter was instituted.

The insurance company's willingness to let the Opry return to a spot so close to the one from which it had been forcibly evicted just a few years earlier may have been a concession to the show's increasing national importance.

When NBC picked up the Opry in 1939, it was by no means WSM's first network show. Network productions had been emanating from WSM for some time, under the supervision of Jack Stapp, a former CBS producer in New York.

Stapp, a Nashville native, had moved to Atlanta as a child. He became involved with radio in his teens, and by the time he was twenty-one had done two important things: he had become program director of an Atlanta radio station, and he had hired Bert Parks, now the well-known television master of ceremonies.

Stapp and Parks became close friends and eventually went to New York together to work for CBS. Establishing a bachelor apartment, they set to work and moved up quickly in different jobs. Parks became one of the better-known CBS voices, and Stapp worked his way into a position as the network's acting production manager. After they had been there five years, however, Parks was transferred to California and Stapp's affection for Manhattan cooled. WSM offered him a job as second in command of the station under Harry Stone, and Stapp took it.

Before he left New York, Stapp called officials at NBC and told them he hoped to feed them some programs from Nashville. They encouraged him to try. Within a few weeks he assembled an eighteen-piece orchestra at WSM and began producing sophisticated, hour-long musical programs, and NBC began accepting them whenever they needed them. These programs gave national airing to such pop-style singers as Dinah Shore and Snooky Lanson. The first, irregularly scheduled groups of programs were done on Sunday afternoons. Stapp named them "Sunday down South."

George Hay's Saturday night down South was considerably different from Stapp's Sunday afternoon, but its homely fare proved powerful when the limited-network broadcast of the Opry began.

One result was another call from Republic Studios.

After the "intelligent young man" who had eaten Uncle Dave Macon's ham and chicken returned to Hollywood, the Opry project was pigeon-holed for more than a year, Judge Hay relates, but it was revived when the Opry "went network" and was carried by one of the Los Angeles stations.

An agreement was negotiated with WSM, and the station and the studio picked a cast of Opry performers that was fairly evenly divided between old-timers and new ones: it included Uncle Dave and Dorris Macon, the Solemn Old Judge, and Roy Acuff and the Smoky Mountain Boys.

Grand Ole Opry, as the first movie featuring the Opry was called, was shot in Hollywood in two weeks during the spring of 1940. In a community development that seems to have surprised Hay, the

Jack Stapp in his early days as a WSM executive

During the premiere festivities, Opry announcer Louie Buck interviews the nation's best-known World War I hero—Sergeant Alvin C. York of Pall Mall, Tennessee

film was premiered in gala fashion in Nashville later that year. Sergeant Alvin C. York, Tennessee's famed World War I hero, and Governor Prentice Cooper attended the festivities.

Such diversions were few, however.

Even successful Opry performers faced an almost endless cycle of work. There had always been the little schoolhouses and movie theaters in which a hillbilly show could charge a quarter apiece for adults and fifteen cents for children; now, if a man was really successful, there were such added chores as recording sessions and tent shows.

One of Roy Acuff's first recordings had been produced in the late thirties in the old Gayoso Hotel in Memphis, in a room rented by Art Satherly. It was made in the bathroom, because the bathroom's acoustics were better than those in the rest of the suite.

"We had his band in there and everything," Satherly recalls. "We put the recording machine on a tripod in the bathtub. We didn't have headphones and all that business to judge our sound with, the way they do these days. All we had was our ears."

The recording sessions were no more primitive than the tent shows. The first major tent show operated by Opry performers began its fitful travels about 1940, presided over by Jamup and Honey. In ten trucks, including nine tractor-trailers, it straggled across the land like a starving army.

"The tent was 80 feet wide and 220 feet long, big enough to sit down 1,600 people under the canvas," Honey Wilds recalls.

"It took 25 roughnecks to move it, and we moved it every cotton-picking day, feeding the roughnecks three hot meals a day in the process. With salaries, lot rent, advertising, and licenses, our daily operating expenses fluctuated between $550 and $600 a day. In other words, we had to make $600 a day before Jamup and I would make a nickel. Everybody said we were crazy."

The cast of performers the first year included Uncle Dave Macon and Roy Acuff, and the crowds were "monstrous," Wilds says.

Macon and Acuff and the other Opry members who worked with the show returned to Nashville each Saturday for the Opry, but Jamup and Honey had permission from Harry Stone to stay out most of the time the tent show was out, so that they could keep it operating. It was not easy.

"We'd always have one or two trucks broke down that we'd have to overhaul," Wilds says.

"Lord, I've laid on the road a many a time, with it anywhere from 95 to 100 degrees, and put a transmission in a Chevrolet truck,

OPPOSITE PAGE, ABOVE:
Roy Acuff and the Smoky Mountain Boys sit in the back seat of a suitably antique automobile. They are surrounded by the rest of the cast of the 1940 motion picture *Grand Ole Opry*. Uncle Dave Macon tips his hat in the front seat, beside driver Frank Weaver. Others are, from left, Leon Weaver, Allan Lane (smoking cigar), June Weaver, Loretta Weaver (with hand raised), Rachel Veach (head partially hidden on other side of auto), George D. Hay, Lois Ranson, and Dorris Macon.
BELOW: A majorette struts past a band gathered in front of Nashville's Paramount Theater at the premiere of *Grand Ole Opry*

laying flat on my back to get it in there. Not to mention wrecks. We came off a mountain over in North Carolina one time, and the trucks were tailgating and five of them crashed. The front one went haywire, and then the first four behind him hit him. We had roughnecks, trucks, and seats thrown all over the place. We wound up with sixteen men in the hospital."

By this time the nation was mobilizing for World War II, and it was difficult to get tires, parts, or anything else.

"A many a time I've gone down a little old country road and seen a truck setting, and stopped and asked the farmer what he'd take for that truck," Wilds recalls.

"I'd buy the truck, jack it up, take the tires off of it and leave the truck setting."

It was a hard business, but a lucrative one if the show drew crowds. After learning with Jamup and Honey how it was done, Acuff started a tent show of his own the next year. His place with Jamup and Honey was taken by Bill Monroe and the Blue Grass Boys.

Soon after the close of the first Opry tent show season, a new star was born on the stage at War Memorial Auditorium. The birth was inauspicious at best.

It was November, Minnie Pearl remembers, and even the twenty-five-cent admission fee did not keep many homeless drunkards and other derelicts from joining the Opry crowds so they could sleep in the rear rows.

"It was just a warm place to get into," she says.

Sarah Ophelia Colley was her name then; it is Mrs. Henry Cannon now. Then she was a twenty-eight-year-old old maid with high theatrical ambitions and not much else except a $50-a-month recreation job with the Works Progress Administration. She did not at all want to do comedy, but she was willing to use any possible avenue to get to the Broadway stage. Even the Grand Ole Opry.

Thus she found herself one Wednesday in the studios of WSM, auditioning a comedy routine in front of Harry Stone, Jack Stapp, Judge Hay, and announcer Ford Rush. After she finished, Ford Rush came over to give her the verdict. Grudgingly he told her they would try her on the Opry the following Saturday evening. He was not enthusiastic.

"He told me that they had done a little investigating about me," she recalls, "and he wasn't sure those people out there wouldn't think I was a phony. 'A phony!' I said. 'Why would they think that? I come from the country—you can go down there where I was raised and look at it for yourself if you think I'm a phony.' "

Rush said he knew where she was from, but he also knew she had gone to a girls' school. Acknowledging that this was true, she told him that she had gone there only two years and had not really belonged there in the first place.

"Well, he said that I was to get there at ten-thirty that Saturday night and be ready to go on the Crazy Water Crystals Show at eleven-oh-five," she says.

"He also said that there normally weren't that many people

Art Satherly, left, and one of his many discoveries, Roy Acuff

ABOVE: Sara Ophelia Colley as Minnie Pearl, doing a
routine on the Opry's nationally broadcast Prince
Albert Show. RIGHT: Sara Ophelia in civilian attire in
her first days at WSM

listening to the Opry at that time of night anyway, so if they didn't like me it wouldn't harm things very much."

Properly cowed, she arrived punctually on Saturday evening in her Minnie Pearl costume. She introduced herself to Hay, who was clad in his famous black coat and black hat and was carrying his steamboat whistle. He was very gracious, she says, telling her where to stand, out of the way, until he could get back to her to tell her about the show. Then he went about his business, putting on other acts and generally running the performance.

"I was twenty-eight," she says, "but I might as well have been sixteen. I had never been on the radio, and I was frightened completely out of my gourd."

After a few minutes, Judge Hay returned. He told her that the eleven o'clock show would open with another act—she does not remember who—and she would go on second. Then he looked down at her and noticed that she was shaking.

"Why, you're scared, aren't you?" he said, very kindly.

"Yes, sir, I'm scared absolutely and utterly to death," she acknowledged.

The Judge smiled encouragingly, and then gave her one of his many theories about the mechanics of the operation of the Grand Ole Opry.

"You just go out there and love 'em, honey," he said, "and they'll love you right back."

When her time came, she went out and did her three minutes. She received no encore, nor even any very great applause. When she came off, the Judge told her—sympathetically, she thought—that she had done all right, and that they would probably get in touch with her later.

She went out and found her mother and brother-in-law, who had come down with her and had watched her debut from the audience. The three of them stepped out into the street together, and nobody said anything at first.

Finally, Sarah Ophelia asked them how they thought she had done. There was a pause, and then her mother made an objective assessment.

"Several people woke up," she said.

GEORGE JONES

JIMMY DICKENS

THE SHOWCASE OF STARS

JEAN SHEPARD

he first triumphant times—the times of the ascendance of Acuff, Monroe, and Pee Wee King, and the promise of other stars to come—must have been troubled ones for George D. Hay. An extremely uncommon man who never seems to have thought of himself as one, Hay had had a dream early in his life and had seen it come to fruition. But by 1940 the Opry was already attracting a million letters a year from its listeners, and change was inevitable. Business principles had to be instituted, bringing a more disciplined atmosphere to which Hay was temperamentally unsuited. The Judge "had no love" for the humdrum detail that is the soul of good management, David Stone recalls. Harry Stone and Jack Stapp, better businessmen, were making the principal decisions, while Hay remained the titular head.

Edwin Craig, the man who had brought Hay to Nashville fifteen years earlier because he had been captivated by the dream, was no happier than Hay about the changes being made.

"Harry Stone and Mr. Craig really fought," Irving Waugh remembers. Waugh, a Tidewater Virginian brought to Nashville through the influence of Jack Stapp, joined WSM in 1941. Within a year he had become aware of the hot disagreement over the role of the Opry.

"Mr. Craig felt very close to the Opry, and his position was that it was being endangered. He wanted to keep it the way it had been in 1935, with a cast made up primarily of instrumental string bands. He believed that the Elizabethan folk songs would survive, and he disagreed with the star system as it evolved.

"Harry was very near the same age as Mr. Craig, and they had worked together when they were younger. Harry would sometimes raise his voice in disagreement with Mr. Craig, which none of the rest of us would ever do."

Most of the people at the station appear to have agreed, at least privately, with Stone rather than Craig. Waugh, an almost patrician actor-turned-announcer who was now becoming a tough and sophisticated salesman, cared nothing for the Opry's music at first but was struck by the same commercial possibilities Stone had recognized. Even DeWitt, Craig's young protege, disagreed with Craig.

"Harry was more progressive, and I sided with him on that to a certain extent," DeWitt says.

"I felt that you shouldn't restrict the Opry too much. You had to let it grow and take its own natural course. I never thought you should permit trumpets onstage or anything as radical as that, but you should not set a lot of arbitrary limits on what it could become."

Craig seems to have been an enlightened ruler. Rather than order his employees to do his bidding, he tried to persuade them that his way was the correct one. When he was unable to do so in the case of the Grand Ole Opry, the changes went ahead.

The Opry's performers had begun wandering the map like pioneers. Almost every week, one or another of them would play some hamlet, town, or city that no Opry act had ever played before. Following the WSM clear-channel signal, they covered the central South and the Midwest like a blanket and began moving outward from there.

Jamup and Honey, those pioneers in so many things, opened up the state of Florida in the late thirties, not long before they started their tent show. Like most discoveries, that of Florida was completely unintentional.

"Jamup and I wanted to go fishing," Honey Wilds recalls.

At that time Silver Springs, the Florida resort, was owned by two Opry fans, Wilds says, and anytime an Opry cast member wanted to go there, everything was on the house. After one particularly grueling siege of work, Harry Stone decided to let Jamup and Honey off to go to Silver Springs for a week. He also decided to go with them.

Stone made the decision on a Friday, Wilds recalls. The following night at the Opry, the three of them happened to meet a musician named Hugh Jernigan. Jernigan came from Jay, a small town in Florida's western panhandle, and the three of them mentioned that they would be visiting Silver Springs the next week on a fishing trip. Jernigan suggested that they stop Saturday in Jay on their way back to Nashville and play the school there.

"Why, we wouldn't have enough people to start a fight," Wilds protested.

"I believe you will," Jernigan told him. "Everybody listens at you on the radio."

When Harry Stone agreed to let them miss the Opry the following Saturday evening, Jamup and Honey decided to perform in Jay. They spent a relaxing week at Silver Springs and arrived in Jay about four o'clock on Saturday afternoon.

The village consisted of a huge consolidated school, a large general store across the road from it, a couple of smaller stores, and a post office.

"There wasn't a soul around when we got there," Wilds says.

He tried to talk Stone into heading on toward Nashville immediately, but Stone said no, that they had promised Jernigan they would be there at the school that night, and after all, somebody might show up after a while.

Sure enough, after a while somebody did. Through arrangements Jernigan had made with the school officials, people from areas for miles around were brought to town in the schoolbuses. Hundreds more came in automobiles.

"I have never seen the like of people in all my borned days," Wilds says.

"We turned 'em away that night, and the traffic was so bad that two people got killed in it. One poor old man was coming down the road on a bicycle and got run over, and there was a car wreck right in front of the school that killed another man."

Jamup and Honey had other obligations that kept them from going back to Florida immediately, but at that time Roy Acuff had only the Saturday Opry shows to do in Nashville. Wilds told him to go to Florida.

"It'll be hard on you, driving down there and back every week, but I believe you'll do well," he said.

OPPOSITE PAGE:

FROM THE TOP: The Solemn Old Judge, George D. Hay, right, appears to be studying this proffered scroll naming him an honorary Kentucky Colonel; Edwin Craig during his middle years; Harry Stone, right, and Jack Stapp, WSM's principal decision-makers during the era in which the Grand Ole Opry became a national phenomenon; Irving Waugh, now WSM president, shortly after he joined the station as an announcer

Honey and Alexander (Lee Davis Wilds and Jim Alexander)

127

Dave Akeman, who called himself Stringbean,
the Kentucky Wonder

Acuff soon went down on a five-day swing. When he returned, he told Wilds he had never seen anything like Florida.

He and the Smoky Mountain Boys spent much of their time in the Sunshine State from then until they signed on with the Jamup and Honey tent show for a year in 1940. In 1941 they bought their own tent, and Bill Monroe and the Blue Grass Boys took their place with Jamup and Honey. Then, in 1942, Bill Monroe started yet another tent show.

"When there got to be three," Wilds says, "each one would pick out a route and stick to it all summer. They called us the number one tent show because we were first, and we'd pick where we wanted to go. Then number two would pick, and number three would get whatever was left."

Those days hold old Oswald Kirby's fondest Opry memories. He and the other musicians in the various bands would disperse into the rest of America each week and then meet back at the Opry on Saturday nights, gathering to tell tales of their travels.

"There'd be talk like you don't ever hear anymore," he says.

"Talk like, 'How'd you do last week? Do you need any money? I made a little bit last week if you need it. You're sure you didn't lose none, now? I've got some I could loan you if you need it.'"

For a year or more, Acuff concentrated his prodigious energies on Florida. Then he crossed the Mason-Dixon Line into Pennsylvania and worked parks from one end of that state to the other. After the opening of a seaside stage show called the Los Angeles County Barndance in California in the early forties, he set that show's attendance record: eleven thousand, one hundred, and sixty persons.

"I guess I was the first to really go into the business and start going out and drawing tremendous crowds," Acuff remembers.

"Somehow or another, people just flocked by the hundreds or more to see our show. I could play in any town and then go twenty or thirty miles the next night and play, and half the people that had been there the night before would follow me over to the next town. I played every night, went fifteen years without ever missing one that I know of. I had to make it, I had to make the payrolls."

Back in Nashville Harry Stone and Jack Stapp gradually, in a variety of ways, were assembling a legion of performers that would completely change the face of the Grand Ole Opry.

In 1941 Bill Monroe, searching for a distinctive sound with which to accompany his old-style songs, hired a tall, skinny banjo player named Dave Akeman. Akeman called himself Stringbean, the Kentucky Wonder. Lanky Texan Ernest Tubb had the huge hit record "I'm Walkin' the Floor over You" in 1941, and joined the Opry the following year. A group called Paul Howard and the Arkansas Cottonpickers joined the show in 1942, bringing with them an electric mandolin player named Rollin Sullivan. Rollin and his brother Johnny later became, and for many years remained, the Lonzo and Oscar comedy team, with Rollin performing Oscar.

Performers who had been popular on other prominent shows began to join the Opry cast. One of the most important of these was

Stringbean in later years, in the comic garb he wore onstage

Paul Howard, second from left, and his Arkansas Cottonpickers

Benjamin Francis (Whitey) Ford, the Duke of Paducah, a former WLS National Barndance comic who was hired in 1942 to fill a spot on the Prince Albert show with Acuff and Minnie Pearl.

The most significant of the developing "stars" of this period, both literally and symbolically, were probably Pee Wee King and the Golden West Cowboys.

The Western image had already invaded rural music with a rush, spurred by the surging popularity of Western movies in the thirties and the increasing reputation of some Southwestern music groups whose cowboy heritage was genuine.

Whitey Ford, who began his career in 1922, says that the first widely popular Western group was Otto Gray and the Oklahoma Cowboys, which was founded in 1923. Gray's popularity led to the rise of other such acts in the thirties. By the early thirties cowboyism was represented on the Opry by such groups as Zeke Clements and the Bronco Busters and a group, led by Ken Hackley, which is credited with being the show's first Western-dressed band. The new look grew more prominent as the decade wore on. By 1940 Bob Wills and the Texas Playboys, a landmark electrified Western swing band, had become so popular that Bing Crosby recorded their "San Antonio Rose" and had great success with it.

There is said to have been some discussion of whether accepting the "Hollywood influence" of Western dress was advisable for the Opry, but the topic does not seem to have become controversial until Pee Wee King's Western act became popular.

King and the Golden West Cowboys first came to the Opry in the late thirties, shortly before the arrival of Acuff. They brought with them Western garb and a promising vocalist named Smiling Eddy Arnold. Their initial stay on the show lasted only a couple of years. When they returned in 1941 they brought along electric instruments as well as the Hollywood dress. Almost immediately they embarked on one of the most important series of tours in the Opry's history, taking along Minnie Pearl for comic relief.

The Camel Caravan, as it was called, was organized in late

OPPOSITE PAGE:
Pee Wee King with his "original" Golden West Cowboys. Standing are Curley Rhodes, Jack Scaggs, and Abner Sims. Seated are King, Texas Daisey (Curley's sister), and Milton Estes

Whitey Ford, the Duke of Paducah, at left, looks down the barrel of a six-shooter brandished by Western movie comic Smiley Burnett

1941 by representatives of the R. J. Reynolds Company, Harry Stone, and a prominent promoter named J. L. Frank who was Pee Wee King's father-in-law. The Caravan toured stateside military installations crammed with support troops and trainees awaiting reassignment overseas. These entertainment-hungry soldiers and sailors included many fans of rural music, of course, but they also included thousands of Northern and Eastern boys who had never heard it before. World War II was to take hillbilly music and many of its fans to places they had never been, and the Camel Caravan was a major attempt to help this process along.

If Western dress was resisted by some traditional Opry fans,

BELOW: Pee Wee King's Golden West Cowboys and Harry Stone greet visitors with the "official" Caravan car.
BOTTOM: Eddy Arnold sings for service personnel

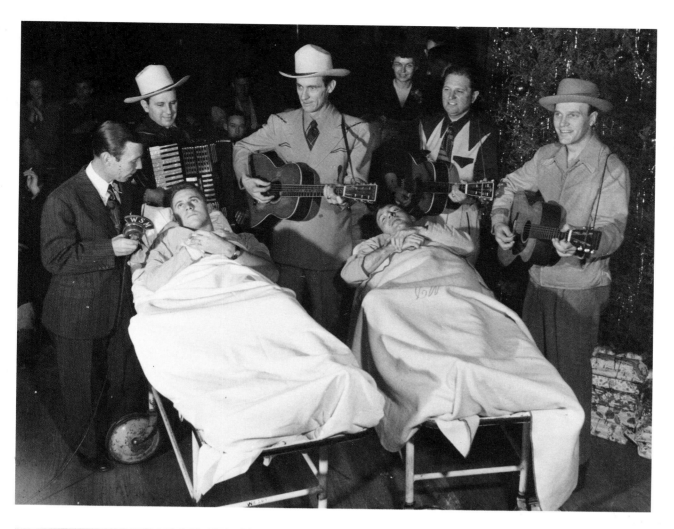

ABOVE: Pee Wee King (with accordion), Ernest Tubb (center), and Arnold (on the right) visit a veterans' hospital. LEFT: The regulars on the Opry's network radio broadcast in the late forties —Red Foley, left, Minnie Pearl, and Rod Brasfield—wave from the steps of a military transport plane

it was not unattractive to shrewd advertisers. Cohen Williams, chairman of the board of Martha White Foods, says an example of Western advertising in Texas prompted him to buy his first block of country music time on WSM.

"I got the idea from Burrus Mills, a Texas light crust flour company," Williams recalls.

"When I first got into the flour business, Burrus was sponsoring a Texas radio program by Pappy Lee O'Daniel and the Light Crust Doughboys. Later on, Burrus and Pappy had a disagreement, and Pappy decided to get him a flour of his own. He got him one called Hillbilly; the front of the package had a picture of a goat on a hill and was the worst-looking brand advertisement you ever saw.

"Anyway, Pappy went back on the radio with a group called the Hillbillies, and he got a lot of mail. One day he got a letter from a guy who said, 'Pappy, you ought to be governor.' Pappy read it on the air and said, 'Well, you folks know I'm an honest man, and politics never did interest me, and I don't know if I'd ever be interested in this governor thing, but if a lot of you folks think I should, well, write to me.'

"The mail just poured in. Pappy ran for governor and got elected. Then he went on to the Senate. And I thought, 'If he could do all that in Texas with Hillbilly Flour, what could I do in Nashville, Tennessee, with Martha White Flour and the Grand Ole Opry.'"

Unlike many advertisers who respected the Opry's pulling power but scorned its music, Williams loved hillbilly music. He remembers Saturday evenings when his children invited company to the house and he would take his radio into the bathroom to listen to the Opry.

Still, he was a little cautious about connecting the name of Martha White with the images of other Opry advertisers. Some were respectable enough, like Jefferson Island Salt, Warren Paint, and Wall-Rite, a manufacturer of a brown building paper that was used as insulation in cheap frame houses. There were others, however, that were pretty zany, like the southern Illinois company that advertised mail-order baby chickens.

"And there was a guy who sold fruit trees," Williams remembers. "He got to selling so many fruit trees that he couldn't raise them fast enough, and he started shipping weeds and everything else. They threw him off the Opry."

The example of Pappy Lee O'Daniel, however, was too powerful to resist. Williams initiated Martha White's long association with WSM by buying a fifteen-minute morning country music show. He recalls that it featured a group advertised as "Milton Estes, the Old Flour Peddler and His Musical Millers." As soon as he could afford it, Williams bought a fifteen-minute segment of the Opry.

With its network exposure, the Opry was becoming a national, even if homely, radio phenomenon.

The success of the limited-network broadcast sponsored by R. J. Reynolds attracted the attention of another national advertiser, and by January 1943 the Ralston Purina Company had begun to sponsor a similar network broadcast of an Opry half hour, feeding it to stations in the South and Southwest. Then, in October 1943, NBC began carrying the Prince Albert half hour on the entire coast-to-coast network of more than 125 stations.

"As a result of these network broadcasts," Judge Hay's history says, "it has become necessary to produce the show somewhat, which has changed the old Opry much as the advanced models of automobiles have been streamlined."

And, liking the old-fashioned better than the streamlined, he adds a veiled note of caution: "This is only right and proper, as long as we keep the show in the groove of homespun entertainment, presenting American folk music and comedy."

In 1943 the crowds attending the show were still homespun enough to make themselves unwelcome in the plush War Memorial Auditorium. Apparently because of the destruction of some seats, or similar misbehavior, the State of Tennessee evicted the Opry from the War Memorial, and it moved to the Ryman Auditorium, a picturesque former tabernacle which had wooden pews for seats.

Meanwhile, a showcase of stars began to develop, its ranks

ABOVE LEFT: Martha White Foods executive Cohen Williams started advertising on the Opry after seeing a musical flour peddler—Pappy Lee O'Daniel, leader of the Light Crust Doughboys—elected governor of Texas. ABOVE: Milton Estes, center, and the Musical Millers, one of the first groups Cohen Williams sponsored on WSM radio. LEFT: With both hat and cigar at a jaunty angle and steamboat whistle in the crook of his arm, Judge George D. Hay prepares for one of the Opry's early national network performances

swelled by new performers brought in by Stone and Stapp as they sought to make the Opry preeminent over the nation's other live-broadcast country music shows.

In 1944 Bill Monroe hired a former tenor singer and mandolin player named Lester Flatt, who had worked earlier for Charlie Monroe. The Poe Sisters, who frequently appeared with the Ernest Tubb show, joined the Opry. The next year, a well-known National Barndance star named Bradley Kincaid was hired away from Chicago, and Monroe hired a banjo player named Earl Scruggs. Pee Wee King brought in a vocalist named Lloyd (Cowboy) Copas to replace Eddy Arnold, who left the Golden West Cowboys to become the "Tennessee Plowboy"; Arnold was now making records and appearing as a featured Opry star.

The gathering of these men reflected the Opry's steadily growing national popularity. So did some musical business ventures that were being started in Nashville.

In 1942 Roy Acuff had approached songwriter Fred Rose, who was then working at WSM, about forming a publishing company. What Acuff wanted to do was to publish his songs himself, so that he could retain the rights to them. Rose, who had worked in Chicago and Hollywood, knew the mechanics of the music-publishing business.

"Everybody in New York was trying to buy my songs, offering me a lot of money for them," Acuff recalls. "I just decided that if a song was that valuable to them, it must be valuable to me." Rose laughed off the idea at first, but after a week or so he came back

ABOVE: The Poe Sisters worked with Ernest Tubb in the forties. BELOW: Dobro guitarist Buck (Uncle Josh) Graves performs at center with Lester Flatt and Earl Scruggs's Foggy Mountain Boys. From left are Paul Warren, Scruggs, Graves, and Flatt

around to talk. He told Acuff he had no money to invest. "I said, 'I'm not looking for you to make the investment,'" Acuff says. "I said, 'You just run it and handle it, and I'll make the investment.' I put up the money, and he put up the ability." In that way, Acuff says, the present huge Acuff-Rose combine was born. Acuff is a modest man.

Near the end of World War II, Aaron Shelton and two other WSM employees, studio supervisor George Reynolds and engineer Carl Jenkins, opened the Castle Recording Studio in a former dining room of Nashville's Tulane Hotel. They did so, Shelton says, because they believed that "with the pool of talent gathering here, it would be a natural. We knew that it would be easier and much less expensive for one arrangements-and-repertoire man to come here to record the talent than it would be to take the talent to New York or Chicago," he explains.

It was, indeed, a natural. Almost from the beginning, Castle's business was so heavy that the three partners had to persuade other WSM engineers to help them with their moonlighting at times.

Cowboy Copas on an early WSM television show

By the early forties, the mold had been firmly set: the Grand Ole Opry was to seek much wider popularity than just the predominantly rural audience at which it had originally been aimed. After this goal was established, managing the Hay-Craig dream became a more difficult matter of following the fitful courses of increasing popularity. As the stars multiplied, so did the prizes and problems of success.

Roy Acuff left the Prince Albert portion of the Opry in 1946 in a contractual dispute with R. J. Reynolds. Clyde (Red) Foley, a Kentucky-born baritone who had been one of the most popular stars of the National Barndance, was brought in to replace him on the network segment. There seems to have been some resentment among the Opry musicians, at first, toward this New York-dictated invasion by a Chicago star. Foley was well received by the audience, however, and Acuff's wail began to be rivaled by newer, less traditional, generally softer Opry voices, especially those of Foley and Eddy Arnold.

Grant Turner, a young announcer who came from Texas by way of Knoxville, joined the show as one of Hay's assistants in 1945. The next year, the Oklahoma-born Willis brothers, Guy, Skeeter, and Vic, joined the show as the Oklahoma Wranglers, working for Eddy Arnold. Dot and Smokey Swann, a group that worked frequently with Ernest Tubb, came in. Red Foley brought with him a lanky East Tennessee guitarist named Chester Atkins. Atkins left the show a few months later when the Esty agency deleted his guitar solo spot from the network half hour, but he reappeared in Nashville a few years later.

The demand for personal appearances by Opry stars had become staggering.

WSM's staff was booking and promoting road appearances by Opry acts, charging 15 percent for the service. The Artist's Service Bureau organized by Hay in 1934 to book talent for a church social had charge of these tasks. In 1946 the Bureau was put under the direction of Jim Denny, an enterprising former clerk in the National Life actuarial department. Denny first became connected with the Opry

Red Foley

ABOVE: Fred Rose, left, and Roy Acuff, partners in Nashville's first music publishing firm. BELOW: Announcer Grant Turner at his zenith as an Opry network voice and personality

when he was assigned an overtime job of answering telephones and helping with concession sales on Saturday nights. He eventually became house manager of the show, and then head of the Artist's Bureau.

Not all of the Opry's quests for national prominence were successful, of course. There was a memorable summer-long disaster in 1947 at the Astor Hotel in New York, where Opry shows had been booked into the famous supper club on the roof. Hillbilly music and fashionable dining did not seem to go with each other; at any rate, the show did not draw many patrons.

Stage shows in New York appear to have done well in the late forties, however. Two performances in Carnegie Hall on consecutive nights in the autumn of 1947 were solid successes, Hay reports. Ernest Tubb headlined these first Opry forays into the nation's best-known concert hall, accompanied by Minnie Pearl, Dot and Smokey Swann, and some other acts from the East, Minnie Pearl recalls. "At the time, Ernest was quoted as saying of Carnegie Hall, 'This place'd hold a lot of hay'—although whether he actually said it, I don't know," Minnie says. "There wasn't much press coverage of it, I remember. We were reviewed in *Variety* and panned, and I was pretty down about that."

A success was scored about the same time in Constitution Hall in Washington, D.C., where 4,500 seats were filled twice in one evening for performances by a roster of stars that included Eddy Arnold, Minnie Pearl, comedian Rod Brasfield, the Oklahoma Wranglers, Lonzo and Oscar, and the Solemn Old Judge. The Washington show seems to have been a particularly memorable one for Hay, who notes in his history:

Chet Atkins as an Opry guitar soloist

"The Judge opened the show with a little talk about the Opry and told the audience that 'We are not going to tell any jokes about Congress tonight—Congress has a much better show than we have.' That broke the ice, and away we went to a very appreciative audience. Americans are swell people."

The Constitution Hall show was one of Hay's last appearances with a road troupe from the Opry. That fall he suffered a serious emotional breakdown, and although he remained with WSM for another decade, his work was mostly limited to three spots on each Saturday-evening show and a short weekly radio broadcast in which he talked about stars of the Opry. One of those Saturday spots was the closing, a whimsical and nostalgic ritual he had devised many years before. In Hay's failing years it must have had great poignance for the show's old-timers when he signed off with his deep, slow, yet strangely charged phrasing:

> That's all for now friends,
> Because the tall pines pine,
> And the pawpaws pause,
> And the bumblebees bumble all around.
> The grasshoppers hop,
> And the eavesdroppers drop,
> While, gently, the ole cow slips away ...
> George D. Hay saying so long for now.

Jim Denny succeeded Judge Hay as manager of the Grand Ole Opry in 1947.

Judge Hay blows his steamboat whistle in his later days on the Opry

Jim Denny, who became manager of the Opry in 1947

Another, equally important administrative change was made that same year. Jack DeWitt, Edwin Craig's longtime protege, returned from World War II service and was soon named president of the station. This placed DeWitt above Harry Stone, whose outspoken disagreement Craig had endured in discussions of the Opry.

DeWitt now discovered, to his amazement, that "Grand Ole Opry"—the unmatchable name Hay had pulled out of the air that night in 1927—had never been copyrighted. He quickly remedied the oversight.

This action, one of DeWitt's first after he returned from the war, shows how much importance the station now attached to the show that had so long been a torture to announcers and engineers. WSM was determined to stay in the forefront of the local "music business" that was growing up around the Opry.

This was not always the easiest thing to do. Eddy Arnold had replaced Roy Acuff as the leading country recording star. In 1948, Arnold threatened to leave the Opry unless he received a percentage of the gate receipts. WSM refused to make such an arrangement. All Opry stars were paid the same amount—the "scale" set by the musicians' union for pay to a leader of a group in Nashville—although some received special pay from advertisers on whose portions of the show they appeared.

Arnold's manager, the same Tom Parker who now manages Elvis Presley, enterprisingly sold a series of transcribed Arnold half-hour shows to Ralston Purina. These were then offered to WSM for airing on Saturday nights. WSM refused to take them because doing so would mean breaking up the Opry broadcast. The shows were then offered to another Nashville station for use on Friday nights.

By now Irving Waugh had become WSM's sales director. When he heard about the offer to the other station, he flew to St. Louis to the Ralston Purina vice-president in charge of advertising.

"Looking back on it, I don't know how I ever had the gall to do it, but I told them that if they put the Eddy Arnold show in this market it had to go on WSM, because we were the country station," Waugh says.

The Purina executive pointed out that the show had already been offered to WSM, but that WSM would not clear its regular programming to receive it.

"I told him that if he went on the other station on Friday night, we would put a live country music show against him, and in front of him, and behind him," Waugh recalls.

"I said, 'I hate to say this, because it sounds as though I'm threatening you, but this means that much to our company.' He did react as though I was threatening him, and he was a very important chap in an important job for a major corporation. But he finally said, 'You can have it, but you'll have to do what you say you would do if the show went on the other station—you'll have to build a live show in front of it and behind it.'"

Thus, in 1949, the Friday night Opry show was born. But Edwin Craig was in no mood to pass out cigars.

Rod Brasfield, left, tells Ray Price—and
the Opry audience—one of his zany stories

George Morgan became an Opry member in 1948

Johnny Wright, left, and Jack Anglin,
one of the Opry's most popular duos

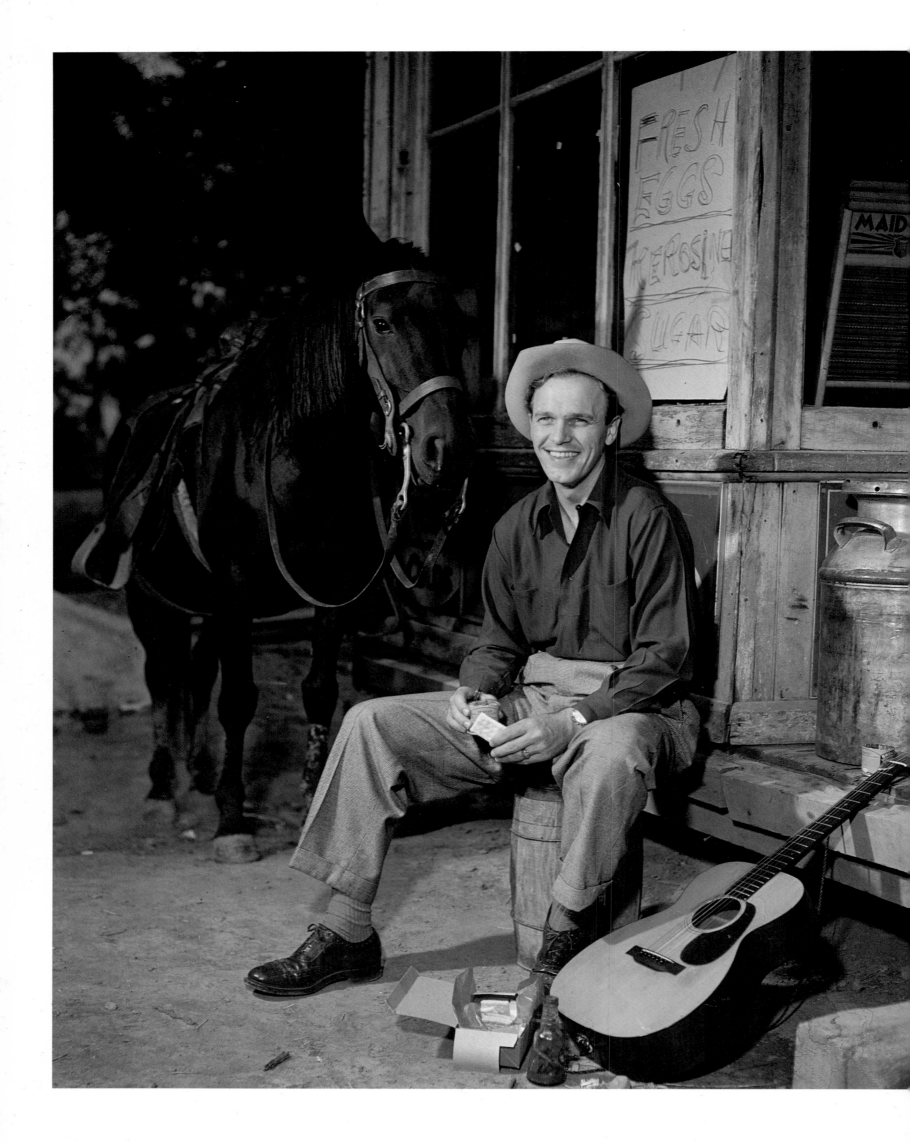

ABOVE: Eddy Arnold in his days as the Tennessee Plowboy
OPPOSITE PAGE: Grandpa Jones came to the Opry from the National Barndance

ABOVE: Little Jimmy Dickens, the Opry's smallest star. RIGHT: Kitty Wells, who came to the Opry as part of the Johnny and Jack troupe

LEFT: Mother Maybelle and the Carter Sisters, June, Anita, and Helen.

BELOW: About 1950, a group of Nashville performers got together with WSM executive Harry Stone and George Rosen, the radio editor of *Variety*. From left are Hank Williams, Milton Estes, Red Foley, Minnie Pearl, Rosen, Stone, Eddy Arnold, Roy Acuff, Rod Brasfield, and Lew Childre. Kneeling in the foreground is Wally Fowler

"Mr. Edwin kept me upstairs for three and a half hours one day about it," Waugh remembers.

"He said that this was too much exposure, that having the Friday night show would damage the Opry. He wanted me to take the Friday night show off, but he wouldn't order me to take it off. I told him that this was in keeping with what he had always told us to do: to try to make friends for the parent company, deliver the biggest audience we could deliver, and if possible to make a dollar. I said, 'This will do all of those things.'"

Every time Waugh felt completely backed into a corner, he would remind Craig that Craig was of course the boss, and that if he ordered the Friday night show off the air it would certainly be taken off. But he kept insisting that this would be the gravest of mistakes.

As in the arguments with Harry Stone, Craig declined to issue an order.

"We stayed up there until it was time for him to go to dinner—he had a party or something at home—and he never asked about it again," Waugh says, "so we kept it on."

The next year, 1950, marked the Grand Ole Opry's first quarter century of existence. By now the concept of the showcase of stars was fully formed.

Grandpa Jones had arrived from the National Barndance in 1947. That same year two duet singers, Johnny Wright and Jack Anglin, joined the Opry; they brought along Wright's wife Muriel, who had taken the stage name Kitty Wells. Rod Brasfield, who was to become the funniest man in country comedy, had joined the show, along with a piano player named Moon Mullican, a crooner named George Morgan, a pint-size novelty singer named Little Jimmy Dickens, and a gaunt balladeer from Alabama named Hiram (Hank) Williams. In 1950, through the efforts of Ernest Tubb, a little Nova Scotian named Hank Snow arrived for a lengthy tryout. Chester Atkins returned, coming in from Knoxville with Mother Maybelle and the Carter Sisters.

The Opry had become so influential that Roy Acuff was persuaded to run for governor of Tennessee in 1948. He lost, but one of the reasons for his defeat was that he remained loyal to his East Tennessee heritage and ran on the Republican ticket, which had elected a Tennessee governor only twice since Reconstruction.

Compared to its original size the Opry had come to resemble a colossus. Bigger and bigger columns of faithful queued up in front of the Ryman's old doors to see it, and it was reaching an ever more diverse audience.

MINNIE PEARL

...ZO AND OSCAR

THE GREAT COMEDIANS

JERRY CLOWER

Typical folk music sung and played by the people of the hills and countryside carries a bit of the sadness and longing for the next world on the one hand and a rollicking sense of comedy on the other.

GEORGE D. HAY

MINNIE PEARL: Rod Brasfield, do you know they're having just the grandest party down at Grinder's Switch tonight? How would you like to go to it with me?

ROD BRASFIELD: Well-by-Ned-Miss-Minnie-you-know-I'd-just-love-to-go-to-the-par-ty-with-you. But-I-cain't-to-night. I-al-read-y-prom-ised-Lem-Puck-ett-I'd-help-him-get-his-pigs-back-in. They've-root-ed-out-of-the-fence-Miss-Min-nie.

PEARL: Oh, Lem Puckett's pigs! Come on and go to the party. You'll have more fun there than you will chasing a bunch of hogs.

BRASFIELD: Bud-I-al-read-y-prom-ised-Lem-Miss-Min-nie.

PEARL: Rodney, what do you care about Lem's pigs? Why, do you know there's talk they may even play a game of post office at the party?

BRASFIELD: (pausing, mugging raptly. Then, confessionally): Miss-Min-nie-I-ha-ven't-sent-a-let-ter-in-years.

Wild applause goes up in this particular one of the innumerable halls they have played in their time. It is the kind of applause the former Sarah Ophelia Colley describes as "beautiful, rising and rolling across the auditorium from one section to another as one part of the audience catches it and then some other part, and then rolling back as one group's laughter sets another group off again." Finally it lessens, then dies out.

BRASFIELD: (after the echo of the last laugh): Not-even-a-post-card-Miss-Min-nie.

Sometimes in her mind it is 1929 or 1930 again, and she is in an old tent somewhere around Centerville, Tennessee, against her parents' wishes, watching a crazy slapstick show. Sarah Ophelia Colley's parents did not think tent shows were good places for a young girl to hang around, and her parents were undoubtedly correct. But Sarah Ophelia was stagestruck. She had been since childhood.

The fire of her ambitions was stoked by the tent show players. Her imagination was captured particularly by two of them, one a rube in a red wig, blacked-out front teeth, and baggy pants, the other a flashily dressed hero. The two were brothers, Boob and Rod Brasfield.

"Boob was the comic then, and Rod was the hero," recalls Minnie Pearl's creator, who is now Mrs. Henry Cannon.

"I thought Rod was just the handsomest thing I'd ever seen. He played the hero in a tuxedo that was green with age, and between acts he would have to rush down to play the drums, but I was about seventeen or eighteen at the time and had never had a chance to see anything much. I thought it was the most glamorous thing."

Rod Brasfield and Minnie Pearl, doing what
Minnie characterizes as "double comedy"

Boob, whose real name was Lawrence, was the elder of the Brasfield brothers. Rod was a youngster about Sarah Ophelia's age, who had quit high school and gone on the road with his brother. Eventually joining a group named Bisbee's Comedians, they played Alabama, the Carolinas, Georgia, and Tennessee, setting up in a new town each week and staging hackneyed "dramas," doing a different show every night.

Miss Colley followed the tent shows around when they were in the Centerville area, much to the dismay of her father, who was a rather prominent lumberman, and her college graduate mother. One night, in a flush of stage fever, she even went backstage and confessed to the Brasfield brothers that she wanted to go into show business.

"No, you don't," Boob Brasfield said.

"Yes, I do," Sarah Ophelia said.

"No, you don't," Rod Brasfield said.

"Yes, I do," she repeated. "And I'm going to."

Whenever she hung around after that, they probably referred to her between themselves as "that brat," Mrs. Cannon suspects.

But the brat, if that is indeed what they called her, was determined. Hers was not just an idle dream. She worked at it. She got into every available dramatic production in high school and college, then began directing dramas in schools around the South. She stuck to it even as passing years returned nothing for her diligence. Husbandless then, she was regarded in her hometown as a twenty-eight-year-old failure when she worked the Grand Ole Opry that night in the late fall of 1940. And she felt like a failure for several days afterward.

"The next morning was Sunday, and I went to Sunday School and church," she remembers.

"A few people said, 'What's this I hear about you bein' on the Grand Ole Opry?' Two people said they'd heard me, but that's all they said, just that they'd heard me. So I figured that I'd lost another one, but I'd lost so many jobs it didn't make much difference. Daddy was dead by then, and Mama and I were living down in that little town of Centerville, and I said to myself, 'Well, I've lost it, but I couldn't have lived on ten dollars a week anyway.' So I went on about my business."

Wednesday, the telephone rang. It was Ford Rush again, the WSM announcer who had told her she could work the Opry the first time. He told her they were going to let her do it again, but they wanted her to come up on Friday and let them hear what she was going to say.

The material she had used the previous Saturday night was all she had, but she did not tell Rush that. By Friday her sister, a teacher at Sullins College in Bristol and the only one in the family who had really encouraged her obsession for the stage, had mailed her some new routines.

"When I went back up there to let Mr. Rush and Judge Hay see what I was going to do, I had this great big box of fan mail, three hundred and seventy-five pieces of it," she recalls.

"That's why they asked me to come back. I read every letter and answered it. I spent a fortune on postcards. Most of the mail said something like, 'We knew you were scared, but you just hang in there, because we think you're sweet, kid.' And she is. I'm not, but Minnie Pearl is. She's sweet, and kind, and honest, and a lady. The only thing that's saved her through the years is that she's picked up very few of my bad qualities."

One reason Sarah Ophelia did not realize how well she had done that first Saturday night was that she really felt as scared as she sounded, which was part of her charm. But another reason was that she had never cared much for hillbilly music and was uncomfortable in its atmosphere. Her father used to listen to the Opry on the radio, but Sarah Ophelia, aspiring to the Broadway stage, "just never could see it," she says.

The kind of work she was getting into was specialized and colorful. Country comedy was a world of cousins and uncles and the folks next door, people with whom smalltown Americans, who constituted the majority of the population then, could identify. Country comedians were part of a "cult of the twenties, thirties, and forties," she says. They played to an open, hospitable America still made up of good neighbors.

Opry comedy was considerably different then than it is now.

Sarah Colley entered it long before Archie Campbell defied the Opry management one night in the late 1950s by strolling onstage in a suit instead of a costume. It was even before Lonzo and Oscar temporarily revolutionized country comedy in 1947 by selling a million and a half copies of a recording titled "I'm My Own Grandpa," briefly making hillbilly musical comedy a lucrative recording proposition. (Briefly, because airplay tended to discourage the hillbilly comedy record, making its humor an old joke long before customers could find it in a record store.)

In 1940 the rules about what kind of material could be used were stringent, but there was a wealth of practitioners of the art. Each prominent Opry troupe employed at least one comic character and sometimes as many as three. Lonnie (Pap) Wilson, Clell (Cousin Jody) Summey, and Bashful Brother Oswald Kirby all worked with Roy Acuff at the same time.

"And there used to be a big barrel full of iced-down cold drinks on the Opry stage every Saturday night," Oswald remembers. "A Saturday night never went by that I didn't get picked up by somebody and set into that ice cooler during one of the commercials."

One of the few Opry acts still carrying a dressed-up comic now is traditionalist Porter Wagoner, who retains Speck Rhodes.

There are, however, several Opry performers who are musician-comics in the great tradition of Uncle Dave Macon. The most prominent today is Louis M. (Grandpa) Jones, who combines a dry wit—which is demonstrated weekly on the Hee Haw television show— with a highly traditional and historically important style and repertoire of country and folk singing. Bill Carlisle is another prominent Opry musical comedian, as was Dave (Stringbean) Akeman until his untimely death in 1974.

The first full-time comedians on the Opry were actually comediennes—Sarie and Sally (Mrs. Edna Wilson and Mrs. Margaret Waters) from near Chattanooga. Roy Acuff says they were "some-

Speck Rhodes of the Porter Wagoner Show, one of the few men still practicing country comedy on road tours, prepares to launch one of the classic routines—a telephone call to a girlfriend

Johnny, left, and Rollin Sullivan, brothers
long known as "Lonzo and Oscar"

154

Archie Campbell, who gave Opry comedy a new image one night in the late 1950s when—without permission—he went out on the stage in a tie and sport coat instead of what he calls "rube garb"

Cousin Jody, one of the Opry's comic characters from the late
thirties into the early seventies, came to the Opry with Roy Acuff
as James Clell Summey, a member of the Crazy Tennesseans

Lonnie (Pap) Wilson, a long-time musician and
comic figure with the Smoky Mountain Boys

Cousin Jody hits a hot lick on his Hawaiian guitar
in one of his typical Opry appearances

Sarie and Sally entertain an audience in the thirties

Jamup and Honey had as many black fans as white ones, Honey recalls today

what like Minnie Pearl, except that there were two of them." One played a disagreeable older woman and the other a scatterbrained younger one, and their standard act was to sit and talk about their friends and relatives.

The Opry's first great road comedians were Jamup and Honey. Honey Wilds had come into Nashville as the partner of the prominent minstrel Lasses White. When White left to become a Hollywood motion picture actor, Wilds found himself a new partner whom he called "Jamup." The late Tom Woods, Bunny Biggs, and Harry LeVan each put in stints as Jamup. Wilds also teamed with Jim Sanders in a blackface partnership called Honey and Alexander.

Both Wilds and Lasses White came from Texas. The blackface kind of comedy they did had been popular all across America since the nineteenth century. In the racial reforms of the 1960s it was popularly assumed that blackface comedy poked fun at black people, and the form died. Wilds claims, however, that if black people find blackface demeaning, they do it in retrospect.

"We didn't think we were making fun of them, and evidently they didn't think we were making fun of them," he says.

"Half of the people we drew were Negro. They filled the balconies up at almost every show. And we didn't get along too well with some of the managers of theaters we played because of it, because they didn't care too much for the fact that Jamup and Honey were as popular with blacks as whites."

In 1942 NBC imported Whitey Ford, the Duke of Paducah, a former star of Chicago's National Barndance. The Duke was slick, polished, citywise. His humor, which he still keeps cross-indexed in vast volumes at his Nashville home, was crafted through lengthy experience in big-time entertainment. A Missourian who is somewhat like a sober W. C. Fields, Ford started a Dixieland jazz band in 1922, toured as a banjo player, worked with Otto Gray's Oklahoma Cowboys, and fronted a road show for Gene Autry before he joined the WLS Showboat, forerunner of the National Barndance. He was on network radio three years with a "Plantation Party" show from Chicago before joining the Opry.

"I'm goin' back to the wagon, these shoes are killin' me," was his trademark farewell, and it became a standard observation among hillbilly music fans after Ford joined the Prince Albert segment of the Opry in 1942.

The unquestioned king of country comedy, however, was a hawk-nosed little man with bad teeth, a rheumatic heart, and a fondness for the bottle. He joined the show around the end of World War II.

"One night I was dressing, getting ready to go out and do the network show in a few minutes, when I heard this outlandish laughter from the audience out there," Minnie Pearl's creator recalls.

"Well, whenever I heard any laughter like that, by Ned I had to get out there. Duke worked a different kind of comedy from me, and I knew from the laughter coming up out there that somebody was doing my kind of stuff, and I wanted to find out who in the Sam Hill it was. I started walking toward the stage, and before I ever got to the wings I thought all of a sudden, 'That's Boob.'"

Rod Brasfield, a small man, wore a stage costume that made him look even smaller

Rod Brasfield in his early days as a country comedian

Minnie Pearl singing and dancing onstage at the Opry

OPPOSITE PAGE:

Rod Brasfield doing a routine on the Prince Albert network show. At right is the network show's singing star during the late forties, Red Foley

Her guess was close. In the decade and a half since she had seen the Brasfield brothers, Boob had become ill with emphysema and a form of arteriosclerosis. Rod, the youngster who had looked so handsome in the tent show's ancient tuxedo, had become a comic.

"I got out to the wings, and there he was," she remembers.

"He was wearing baggy pants and the old, funny sidebutton shoes with the white bottoms and the black upper part. He had on a suit that was five times too big for him, with galluses and an old coat and a little tiny hat. And he was just raking the audience over the coals, tossing them around anyway he wanted to. When he came off the stage I grabbed him and hugged him and told him I was so glad. I found out that by that time he knew Minnie Pearl was the dumdum who used to bug him and Boob."

Brasfield had been discovered by Judge Hay, who ran into Bisbee's Comedians on a tent-show tour through Alabama and offered Brasfield a job.

"Brasfield was the best comedian I ever saw, in country or any other kind of comedy, at getting an audience into his pocket," Mrs. Cannon says. "The women loved him, the men loved him, everybody loved him.

"He could get by with the rankest, bluest material, and these old fat ladies would just laugh themselves to death. When he got into this old, clean-living, Bible Belt comedy on the Grand Ole Opry, he never said anything bad—it was just that he couldn't keep from intimating things with the tone of his voice or with his face, which was like a piece of rubber.

"He was just a funny old boy, the kind that would stand on the corner on Saturday night down in his hometown of Smithville, Mississippi, and make cracks about the girls. But if he actually spoke to one of them he would be a perfect gentleman. *Everything* was risqué to Rod, just naturally. He'd lived on the street too long. He'd played those old tent-show audiences where it was so hard to get a laugh with those old dumdum shows they had. And he'd have to invent all this—I don't know, innuendo—to get the laughs."

ROD BRASFIELD: Miss-Min-nie-I've-a-got-to-be-a-goin'-now. I'm-a-goin'-o-ver-to-my-girl-friend-Su-sie's-to-night.

MINNIE PEARL: (with great womanish interest): Oh! Is Susie entertaining?

BRASFIELD: Ohhhhhhh, not-ve-ry-Miss-Min-nie.

When Mrs. Cannon imitates her onetime stage-mate, the result is almost ghostly. Brasfield is there. The simple ultrasincerity. The machine-gun-like snapping of the jaws, keeping the loose false teeth in, which gives the words the effect of a stammer, except that no word is ever repeated. The resultant phrasing places careful, almost equal emphasis on each word. And the timing is exquisitely slow.

I-came-down-here-today-on-na-train-yes-sir-came-down-on-na-train. An'-I-had-me-a-berth-on-na-train. A-berth-by-Ned. One-of-them-shelf-like-things-that-hangs-there-on-the-wall-of-the-train-one on-top-of-the-o-ther-one-'cept-they-ain't-shelfs-they're-beds-by-Ned. An'-it-come-time-to-go-to-sleep-an'-I-climbed-up-to-my-berth-an'-by-Ned-they-was-two-women-in-my-berth. An'-I-said-well-by-Ned-one-of-y'uns-is-a-gon-na-have-to-leave.

Minnie Pearl doing a monologue

Minnie Pearl with her trademark, the hat with the price tag still attached

The laughs would come up to him then, not so much for the joke as for the way he had told it, the way he let them savor it. And at the way he was standing there now, looking patiently out at them, an almost pitifully sincere-looking little creature—the country fool.

Rod Brasfield went on the Prince Albert network portion of the Grand Ole Opry in 1948, as the result of a disagreement between the sponsor and the Duke of Paducah. The three regular stars of the segment thus became Minnie Pearl, who had been on it since 1942, Brasfield, and Red Foley. For the next ten years, Minnie and Rod worked together much of the time. On road shows, Rod would come on first; then Minnie would come out and do ten or fifteen minutes alone; finally she would introduce "my best friend, Rod Brasfield," and they would do "double comedy" together. Double comedy seems to be her own term.

"Like Burns and Allen, Laurel and Hardy," she says, "where each one had to be as funny as the other one or it was no good. The straight man played the comic like you were catching a fish: he'd roll him out and then he'd reel him in, and the comic would flap on the end of the line, knowing exactly how much to flap before he let himself be

Minnie Pearl clowning

caught. I've never felt funny, *that* funny, to anybody since then. Rod thought funny, and I thought funny when I was around him because I knew what the fool was thinking."

Minnie was the "straight man" most of the time, and Rod the buffoon. It scared her badly sometimes when they did it on the network show, because she could never be sure what Brasfield was going to do, especially if he had had a drink.

"He was so much smarter than me that he could just run rings around me, and he knew it," she says.

"Sometimes on the network he would get me way off the routine we were supposed to be doing, just for the fun of gradually pulling me back into it again."

Rod Brasfield was funny onstage or off, and like most people who are that way he was an intensely private person. Excellent at making other people happy, he was unable to do it for himself. He was obviously unhappy in much of his private life, but he and Mrs. Cannon never talked about things like that. With them, it was only the funny things. Her husband, Henry, says he was as happy to drive his wife and Brasfield to a show as to see them onstage, because they were funny anywhere.

One of the ingredients of Brasfield's prodigious comic abilities was a poignance that communicated itself to the audience, however subtly—perhaps even prompting them to laugh all the harder to try to make him happy. Smaller than Minnie Pearl, he played the classic fall guy, the little man for whom nothing ever seemed to work. He was "Chaplinesque," she says.

In one of their road routines, Brasfield would come out and ask Minnie Pearl to sit down beside him. She would refuse, pointing out that there were no chairs. He would then run offstage and get two chairs for them. Seated with her, he would ask her to let him put his arm around her, and after protesting his foolishness she would eventually consent. Then he would ask her for a kiss. Protesting mightily, she would finally tell him to close his eyes and promise not to look, and he would do it, a look of delirious joy on his face. Then she would get up from her seat beside him, get a stocking-clad wooden leg from just offstage, and stick it through the crook of his arm. Warning him not to open his eyes, she would creep offstage.

Brasfield would sit out there alone in the middle of the stage with his eyes closed, the audience convulsed in laughter at him. He would touch the leg and be suspended between delight and shock. "Miss-Min-nie!" he would say in alarm. "This-ain't-like-you-Miss-Min-nie! What's-got-in-to-you?" He would carry it on for minutes, registering more and more simultaneous delight and unspoken disappointment in his longtime confidant and respected friend. Finally he would touch the top of the wooden leg and it would dawn on him that the leg was only wooden, connected to nothing.

"And I'd come out to the edge of the stage where they could see me then, and I'd just be cackling up a storm at him," Mrs. Cannon says. "He would slowly open one eye then, and peek over there at me. Then he would open both eyes wide and holler '*Oh-Miss-Min-*

nie!'" as if he were embarrassed and glad at the same time.

Then the fast music would start up, and he would run around the stage picking up the two chairs and the leg and scurry offstage, the house coming down behind him.

A little man of perhaps five-foot-six, who had a way of making himself look smaller, Rod Brasfield died in 1958 at the age of forty-eight. Most of his other Opry colleagues say that he drank himself to death, but Mrs. Cannon prefers to say that he just wore himself out.

"He had bad teeth and finally had them all pulled, and his new ones didn't fit," she explains.

"He never enjoyed his food after that. Henry and I have talked about how he didn't eat enough to keep a bird alive. In the later years he didn't weigh a hundred pounds, I don't guess."

He died after a lengthy hospitalization. She went to see him many times, thinking each would be the last. On one of those visits he spoke the only really serious words that seem ever to have passed between them. He told her that he was sure most people would never realize that he had sometimes been hard to work with, but that he loved her and wanted her to know that. But then she had already known that.

The only gift he ever gave her was his hat, the piece of homely headgear, several sizes too small, that had helped make him look ridiculous. He left it to her, and she gave it to Nashville's Country Music Hall of Fame, on the condition that it be placed beside Minnie Pearl's own chapeau, the price-tagged straw one.

Mrs. Henry Cannon is an elegant lady who now lives down the street from Tennessee's governors' mansion, frequently playing tennis with its occupants. But a little hatchet-faced man with ill-fitting teeth who used to run around frantically applying denture adhesive substances before the Opry shows still lives in her mind. That is evident from her meticulous impersonations, her careful renderings of his wit. Rod Brasfield remains as real to her as does her own creation, the scatterbrained country girl from Grinder's Switch. Both of them, Minnie and her late friend, are classics of a kind neither the Opry nor any other show will see again.

"That second night I went back to the Opry, Judge Hay said, 'Are you still scared, honey?'" Mrs. Cannon remembers.

"I said, 'Yes, sir, and I'll stay that way.' Later on, when I got to know him real well, he said to me one time, 'Honey, when you get to the point where you're not scared, when that adrenalin isn't running anymore, you're out of luck, because you're out of business.' And he was right. Because I've worked shows where I didn't get up for them, you know, where I just fluffed them off.

"And Minnie Pearl just scurries away into a corner. And then it's just this other false something that gets up and puts on her costume and acts smart. It's not Minnie. When you hear the real Minnie Pearl, she's still scared. And she's still singing at church socials, and it all matters very much. She still knows that the very next day she's going to be seeing some of those same people she talked and sang to, that those are the people she'll always live her life with."

ABOVE: Minnie Pearl—or Mrs. Henry Cannon—at home.
BELOW: Mrs. Cannon concentrates on her backhand

HANK WILLIAMS

HANK WILLIAMS

WILLIS BROTHERS

Clothes often seemed to hang limply
on Hank Williams's tall, bone-thin frame

A cheaply dressed, unimpressive-looking young man rode into Nashville on a bus from Montgomery, Alabama. His tall, thin frame was wrapped in a much-worn coat, and he kept his large, dirty cowboy hat rammed down on his head for most of the two or three days he was in town. Hank Williams was probably balding even then, in December of 1946, at the age of twenty-three.

"You couldn't forget him, because of his appearance," says Vic Willis, now one of the Opry's Willis Brothers and then one of its Oklahoma Wranglers.

"He was a skinny, scrawny guy. Bobby Moore, who is a bass player here in Nashville, used to say Hank Williams was the only guy he ever saw who could sit back in a chair and cross his legs and still put both feet on the floor."

At that time Guy, Skeeter, and Vic Willis had just come to Nashville and the Opry from Chicago. They were making guest appearances on the Purina Checkerboard Jamboree radio show at the downtown Princess Theater when Fred Rose came to them with a proposition. He asked if they would be interested in a flat-fee, no-royalty recording deal with a New York company named Sterling Records.

"Sterling was looking for a Western-sounding band, which was what we were, and a country singer," Vic recalls.

"For the country singer Fred said he already had a fellow from Montgomery named Hank Williams. Fred wanted us to make some records on our own and then back up Hank instrumentally and vocally on his." This fellow from Montgomery, Rose told the Wranglers, wrote all his own songs but sang "a little bit out of meter.'

"That means if he hit a note he liked he might hold it a little longer than he was supposed to," Willis explains.

The flat fee was probably about $200, he recalls, and that was enough to interest the Wranglers. They agreed to do it.

The recording session was held in WSM's studio B a week or two after Rose approached them. "When I saw him, I remembered I'd seen him once before," Vic Willis recalls. "It had been at the Princess about two months before that. He had been trying to pitch a song to Ernest Tubb."

A lot of Nashville performers had seen him before, especially the prominent ones like Tubb and Acuff. Whenever they played the Montgomery area he would go to their shows and then go back to their dressing rooms, squatting on his heels against the wall until they invited him to play them a couple of the latest songs he had written.

The Oklahoma Wranglers, polished pros who had worked on the popular "Brush Creek Follies" show in Kansas City before going to Chicago, ran quickly through the songs they were to record in the Sterling session. There were four by the Wranglers and four with the Wranglers backing up Williams.

They rehearsed one day and came back for the actual recording session the next, according to Willis's memory, and the Wranglers cut their songs first.

...liams buckles his knees in a distinctive mannerism that
...ted feverish responses from his audience

ABOVE: The Oklahoma Wranglers, now called the Willis Brothers, were the first group to record with Hank Williams. From left, they are Vic, Skeeter, and Guy Willis and their bass player, Cherokee Chuck Wright. BELOW: The hottest star of his time, Williams drew record-shattering crowds

"While we did ours, Hank just hung around the control room," Willis says. "He was nervous, the way you'd expect anybody to be before they made their first record."

After the Wranglers successfully finished their recordings, everybody took a break for lunch. Williams and the Willises walked down the block to the restaurant of the Clarkston Hotel, where they talked a little as they ate.

Williams showed no particular optimism about his upcoming session. Someone, perhaps one of the Willises, asked him if he would like to have a beer with his meal. He shook his head.

"You don't know old Hank," he said. "Old Hank don't just have *one*."

They went back to the studio, and for one afternoon the Oklahoma Wranglers became the Drifting Cowboys, the name of the band Williams had in Montgomery. They did four songs written by Williams: three fundamentalist religious hymns and a country blues.

When Williams boarded the bus back to Montgomery late that afternoon, the Willises quickly dismissed him from their minds. They had liked him well enough during their brief association those two days, but they were unimpressed with his music. His singing was unprofessional and his songs seemed so amateurish as to be almost in bad taste.

"We hadn't been used to hearing a country singer who was as country as he was," Willis says.

In a Williams hymn titled "Wealth Won't Save Your Soul," there was a place where the Willises were supposed to sing along with Williams on the line, "My friend, it won't save your poor wicked soul." After many tries and an explosion by Rose, the pronunciation had to be changed a bit.

"Hank couldn't say 'poor,'" Willis says. "Every time he sang it, it came out 'purr.' Fred, who had a low boiling point sometimes, finally said, 'Damn it, Wranglers, just sing it the same way he does.' And you can hear it on the record like that today. We sang it 'purr.'"

The "hillbilly Shakespeare," as he came to be called, was not much more than half-literate. The music he knew consisted principally of a few technical rudiments, most of them picked up in boyhood from an elderly black street singer.

Hank Williams hardly had the luxury of a childhood; during most of his early years he had to try to be a man. From the time Hank was seven, his father spent most of his time in various Veterans Administration hospitals for treatment of psychological and physical damage incurred during service in World War I. Hank's mother ran a succession of boardinghouses and Hank himself spent much of his youth selling peanuts on the streets of the various southern Alabama towns in which they lived. He began his brief career before most boys start high school.

The twenty-three-year-old who rode the bus into Nashville for his first recording session had already been a professional musician around Montgomery for a decade. If he was less than starry-eyed about it, as Vic Willis's account suggests, it was because he just was not the starry-eyed type.

"He was just a country hick like me," says Vic McAlpin, the Nashville songwriter, who became one of Williams's few friends. "The kind of hick that comes from so far back in the country that you're like a damn whipped dog people kick around in this business. You don't make friends too easy because you got your own thing, and you don't trust nobody very much, and to hell with 'em. A backwoods cat, that's what I call 'em. That's kinda the way he was."

His first real step out of the backwoods was made when he was signed by Acuff-Rose and put on a $50-a-month songwriter's draw a few months before the Sterling session. The next step was the material, however amateurish, that he recorded for Sterling. Something about the very harshness and raw power that had repelled the polished Willises aroused the interest of Fred Rose. Perhaps he recognized it as a different form of the same kind of honest emotion so successfully merchandised by his partner Acuff, a man who could literally soak his shirt in tears on a sad song.

Rose negotiated a contract for Williams with Metro-Goldwyn-Mayer, which had just gotten into the recording business, and in 1947 he began to bring him into Nashville regularly to record for MGM at Castle Studio. During this period Williams first met McAlpin, who hung around the Acuff-Rose office because it was the only music business in town.

In 1947 Hank Williams was just country—authentically so, without any of the romanticism that later attached to him.

Williams was part of one of the Opry's tours of the U.S. military installations. Shown here, from left, are Rod Brasfield, a soldier, Red Foley, another unidentified figure, Little Jimmy Dickens, Minnie Pearl, Williams, and two more soldiers

"We called him 'Gimly-ass,'" Vic McAlpin recalls.

"He was one of these guys who was so thin that he didn't have no ass at all, so that one back pocket would hit against—and even lap over—the other one. Like Porter Wagoner maybe, except thinner. There were several of us that called him 'Gimly' all the time. We'd leave the 'ass' part off around the public."

Hank Williams moved to Nashville in 1949. He joined the Opry in midyear, coming up from the Louisiana Hayride show in Shreveport.

The night he arrived is legend. His performance of the magnetic, half-sung and half-yodeled "Lovesick Blues"—a new recording on its way to becoming a million-seller—brought down the house and stopped the Opry show dead. With a continuous standing ovation, the Ryman audience refused to be denied at least a half-dozen encores. Finally Red Foley, by then the most prominent star on the Opry, had to come out and make a speech to settle down the crowd and get things moving again.

"I never saw anybody have an effect on the Opry crowd the way he did when he was here," says Ott Devine, then an announcer and later a manager of the Opry. "Nobody could touch Hank Williams and the only one who came close was Foley."

Williams had a mannerism that was somewhat controversial then. In faster songs like "Lovesick Blues," he would hunch over the microphone with his back bent, close his eyes, and hit his almost painful-sounding yodel notes while dipping his knees forward together in time to the music. This rhythmic action moved him up and down in a fashion that was at least arousing, if not downright suggestive, especially to his lady fans.

He learned quickly that he could wield unusual power over crowds, and he liked to do it.

"He liked to watch the friends and neighbors cry," McAlpin says. "On the Friday night Opry show he did a thing for Duckhead Overalls every week, and I'd go up there and sit on the stage waiting for him to finish so we could go fishing. He'd be singing one of his songs and you'd see some of the people out there kind of dabbing at their eyes. But that wasn't enough to suit him.

"He'd turn around to Don Helms, his steel player, and say, 'Take it at the turnaround—there ain't enough cryin' goin' on in here.' And he'd sing half of the song over again."

Williams quickly became country music's hottest performer. "Lovesick Blues" was the first of eleven consecutive gigantic sellers for him. Through an arrangement Fred Rose and his son Wesley made with New York arranger Mitch Miller, pop singers were recording Williams's songs as soon as they had had a good run in the hillbilly field. "One time he had five of the top twelve pop songs at the same time," McAlpin recalls. "He wore that *Billboard* chart out carrying it around in his pocket and showing it to people."

McAlpin says that Williams's sudden affluence never went to his head, at least in terms of his practical view of things. That seems to be borne out by a story told by Willis S. (Bill) Graham, who was

Williams chats with a young military fan

then vice-president of a Nashville public relations firm that handled the Friday night Duckhead Overalls show. Graham recalls that he was standing outside Studio C one evening when Williams approached him and asked if he could speak with him a minute.

"I said, 'Sure, Hank, what's on your mind?'" Graham says.

"He said, 'Mr. Bill, my boys are all right here. Why don't we just step around the corner?' I said okay. I figured I was about to hear a musician's sad story, of which there are endless varieties. When we got around the corner, he said, 'Mr. Bill, I'm sure you don't know what Duckhead's paying me to do this show. I'm sure you wouldn't let it go on if you knew.' Well, I knew, but I said, 'What do you mean, Hank?' He said, 'Well, Mr. Bill, money doesn't mean a thing to me, you know —I made $400,000 in the last three months. It's just that my boys are giving me such an awful time about it. Red Foley's getting paid $50 to do the 7 o'clock show, and Duckhead's only paying me $35 to do the 6:30 show. My boys are giving me all sorts of trouble about me not being worth as much as Red Foley.'"

Graham, who says he himself was making about $300 a week at this time, when Williams was earning more than $100,000 a month, quietly arranged for Williams to get a $15 raise.

The fishing trips with McAlpin, unlike many such outings engaged in by amateur sportsmen, were not primarily an excuse to drink. McAlpin cannot drink, having had a rheumatic heart since the age of eleven, and he does not like to associate with people who are drinking. "Drunks bug me," he says simply. A few times Williams took a couple of bottles of beer along, but not often. The two of them got together just to fish, talk about the music business, and sometimes write a song. The most famous one they wrote was "Long Gone Lonesome Blues."

"I'd drive his limousine down to Kentucky Lake, which was where he kept his boat and stuff, and he'd usually sleep on the back seat," McAlpin says.

"This particular morning he was saying that he needed another song like 'Lovesick Blues.' Every once in a while he'd sing a few words of something, like 'I've got those long gone blues.' We got down to the boat, and he was fooling with his plugs but I could see his mind wasn't on it. Finally I said, 'Are you going to fish or just watch the fish swim by?' He said, 'Hey, that's the first line.'

"We wrote it in ten minutes, with him beating the time on the boat seat."

As with most of the other half-dozen songs they wrote this way, McAlpin sold his half of it to Williams.

With "Lovesick Blues," Hank Williams came into more money than he had known was in the world. He began spending it, sometimes showering lavish gifts on his wife Audrey. Many times he gave it away, trying to erase the dismal memory of the poverty of his youth. But there were some things that could not be erased.

"He had a bad disc in his back that caused him to drink," McAlpin says. "That's what got him. He told me once that it was caused by malnutrition, from eating peanuts a week at a time when he was a kid, when he didn't have nothin' else. He said that's what the doctor told him."

The disc had been injured in a childhood fall from a horse, and the condition worsened, finally requiring surgery at Vanderbilt Hospital in Nashville. It remained painful, and on fishing trips it even bothered McAlpin, because it made Williams unable to sit comfortably for very long.

"After ten minutes, he'd be up walking around in the boat," McAlpin says. "He'd worry the hell out of you."

The constant pain which McAlpin says finally "got" Williams seems to have been combined with a profound conviction that is summed up in a line he often repeated: "Nothing ain't going to be all right nohow."

As it is with all tragic characters, his greatness carried the seeds of his destruction. The very raw countriness that Fred Rose had recognized as distinctive probably also made it impossible for Williams to deal with the complexities of stardom and his own personality. The pain and the turn of mind that could transform trivial incidents into musical classics also produced prolonged depression and a thirst for alcohol that was just held in check when he first came to Nashville.

The high style of life made possible by his money and fame contributed to, if indeed it did not cause, the breakup of his stormy marriage. When his wife Audrey divorced him early in 1952, Hank Williams fell apart completely. His drinking, which had been increasing during previous months, became obsessive and self-destructive. In a series of incidents that became more and more publicized, he arrived drunk at some performances and entirely missed others. His image rapidly became one the Opry, with its family appeal, could not afford to tolerate.

After a lengthy meeting of WSM officials and following various conversations with Fred Rose in mid-1952, the Opry dismissed the most prominent country music star of his time.

Fred Rose sent him back to the Louisiana Hayride in Shreveport to see if he could straighten himself out, and not long afterward he married a beautiful nineteen-year-old telephone operator named Billie Jones. A little later, needing money, he married her twice more on the stage of a New Orleans auditorium, charging admission to the spectacle.

"He told me the wedding made him $30,000," Vic McAlpin says, "$15,000 for each show."

The last time McAlpin saw him was in mid-December 1952 —six years, perhaps to the day, after he rode the bus into Nashville from Montgomery to record with the Willis brothers.

This time he had come to town to talk to Jim Denny, and afterward he and McAlpin walked down to the Clarkston Hotel restaurant in which he had eaten lunch that day with the Willises. Over a cup of coffee, he told McAlpin about the wedding in New Orleans. He also said he was moving back to Nashville and going back on the Opry after the first of the year.

The likelihood that his return to the Opry had been arranged is questionable. Wesley Rose says that Williams told the truth, that the whole purpose of Williams's return to Louisiana was to see if he could get himself in shape to return to Nashville. But no one at WSM can confirm this. It may be that Jim Denny promised Williams that he would see what he could do about getting him back on the show in 1953. Whatever Jim Denny may have said, there was nothing to be done for Hank Williams in 1953. On the first day of the new year, from the bleak little town of Oak Hill, West Virginia, the first paragraphs of his obituary reached the world.

No one knows exactly where he died. He had been scheduled to sing New Year's night in Canton, Ohio, and when his flight to Canton was prevented by a snowstorm, he hired an off-duty taxi driver to chauffeur him there from Montgomery. He had a bottle with him on the back seat of his white Cadillac when they started out, and they stopped once in Knoxville for some kind of injection, presumably for the pain in his back. Somewhere between Knoxville and Oak Hill, he died of a heart failure that has been attributed to various things: sustained consumption of alcohol over a long period; mixture of alcohol and drugs in his system at the same time; general debilitation.

He was twenty-nine.

Guy, Skeeter, and Vic Willis did a show that day in Wichita, Kansas. They had hardly seen Williams since that 1946 recording session, but the news of his death blared from every radio. Vic Willis recalls feeling "just awful."

"I guess I felt that way because I realized that Hank had come up out of the worst kind of poverty, the kind some stars nowadays claim to have come from and didn't," he says. "I remember wondering then whether anybody else who had come from what he had come from, into all he finally came into, could have taken the pressure any better than he did."

Hank Williams's funeral, held in Montgomery, was probably the biggest in country music history. Three of his former idols—Acuff, Tubb, and Foley—sang his eulogy, and 25,000 people tied up traffic on the streets from which he rose to fame.

Mostly, his mourners were the little people.

They were the rural and industrial workers Judge Hay says

Williams's coffin is carried by his pallbearers, who include Wesley Rose, second from left on the near side, and Fred Rose, wearing glasses

The Cadillac in which he died

the Opry was founded for. Some were drunk but most were sober: grieving, unabashedly sincere people who had come down to Montgomery respectfully clad in whatever was their best.

More than anyone else in his business before or since, Hank Williams captured the imagination of hillbilly music fans, particularly of the working class. In his tall, frail frame he embodied their neighborliness, generosity, and striving for Heaven on the one hand and, on the other, their underlying bitterness about their lot.

"Old Hank" gave them something that can never be forgotten. Universally acclaimed a "genius," he proved beyond a shadow of doubt that even a red-neck can be one.

Showing a visitor around their former home, where she has lived since the 1952 divorce, Audrey Williams points to a portrait of her late ex-husband

TRADITIONAL GRAND OLE OPRY SONG FAVORITES

The tunes of the Grand Ole Opry and of country music in general have sometimes been referred to as "heart songs." The term is apt, for although country music contains some satire and a lot of humor, it rests on a solid foundation of reality. Although its themes are often lofty—love, faith, work, death—they are almost always dealt with in terms of the average person.

There are millions of country songs by now, and hundreds of older songs that still exert a powerful influence today, either in their own right or as part of the musical heritage of today's country songwriters. The sixteen printed here have been chosen as examples of the best old-time country songs.

The first three—"Just a Closer Walk with Thee," "I'll Fly Away," and "The Great Speckled Bird"—are religious songs, each rooted in the belief that the spiritual rewards of the next world will make up for the pain and tribulation of the present one. The next three songs—"Turkey in the Straw," "Old Joe Clark," and "Cripple Creek"—are sprightly airs that lend themselves to being performed as instrumentals on fiddle and banjo; they illustrate the week's-end joy of Saturday night, when the farmer-musicians who were country music's first exponents would get together to try to make the present world a little happier.

Country songs are often story songs. One of the archetypal ones, "John Henry," also exhibits country music's kinship of subject—if not audience—with the black man and his blues; "Wildwood Flower" can be traced to nineteenth-century Caucasian roots. Train songs like "The Wabash Cannonball" and "The Wreck of the Old 97" illustrate the country musicians' interest in modern subjects. Songs like "Muleskinner Blues" and "Nine Pound Hammer" illustrate the profound interest country musicians have always had in the way people make their livings, while "Old Rattler," which is about a hunting dog, and "Rye Whisky," which is self-explanatory, address themselves to more leisurely activities. "Salty Dog" and "Roll in My Sweet Baby's Arms" convey a rollicking, rakish masculinity—the lighter, worldlier side of country music's classically melancholy approach to love.

These songs have all been, and still are, part of the historic repertoire of the Opry cast, and some are closely identified with a particular star. "Just a Closer Walk with Thee" was a favorite of the late Red Foley. "The Great Speckled Bird" and "Wabash Cannonball" were Roy Acuff's first hits, and his group and others still sing "I'll Fly Away" on Friday and Saturday nights at the Opry. "Cripple Creek" is still a favorite of devotees of the bluegrass banjo; Bill Monroe's version of "Muleskinner Blues" can still be heard practically any time he performs, as can Grandpa Jones's version of "Old Rattler." "Rye Whisky" was a regular with the late Tex Ritter until his death in 1974, and Lester Flatt still performs his classic versions of "Salty Dog" and "Roll in My Sweet Baby's Arms."

Old music, these songs continually become new again—through new variations and through their influence on the songs that are written today.

Just a Closer Walk with Thee

Traditional Version

Arranged by George N. Terry

Just   a clos-er walk with Thee,   grant   it Je-sus if you
Through the days of toil that's near,   if   I fall dear Lord who
When   my fee-ble life is   o'er,   time   for me will be no

please. _____   Dai - ly walk-in' close to Thee,   let it
cares. _____   Who with me my bur-den shares,   none but
more. _____   Guide me gent -ly, safe-ly on,   to Thy

be,   dear Lord, let it be.
Thee,   dear Lord, none but Thee.
shore,   dear Lord, to Thy   shore.

The Great Speckled Bird

Traditional Version

Arranged by George N. Terry

I'll Fly Away

Traditional Version

Arranged by George N. Terry

Moderato

Some bright morn - ing when this life is o'er ____
When dark sha - dows of this life are nigh ____
Just a few more wear - y days and then ____

I'll fly a - way
I'll fly a - way
I'll fly a - way

to a land on
like a a bird, far
to a land where

God's ce - les - tial shore. —
from these pri - son walls. —
joys will nev - er end. —

I'll fly a - way.
I'll fly a - way.
I'll fly a - way.

Turkey in the Straw

Traditional Version

arranged by George N. Terry

Moderately fast

As__ I was a - go - ing down the road tir - ed team and a
went out to milk and I did-n't know how I milked a goat in -
met Mis-ter Cat - fish com-in' down stream, says Mis - ter Cat - fish "What

heav - y load, crack my whip and the lead - er sprung; I
stead of a cow A mon - key sit-ting on a pile of straw I a -
does you mean?" Caught Mis-ter Cat - fish by the snout And

says "day - day" to the wag - on tongue.
wink - in' his eyes__ at his moth-er - in - law.
turned Mis-ter Cat - fish wrong - side out.

Tur-key in the straw

Came to the river and I couldn't get across
Paid five dollars for an old blind hoss
Wouldn't go ahead, nor he wouldn't stand still
So he went up and down like an old saw mill.

As I came down the new cut road
Met Mr. Bullfrog, met Miss Toad
And every time Miss Toad would sing
Ole Bullfrog cut a pigeon wing.

Oh, I jumped in the seat, and I gave a little yell,
The horses run away, broke the wagon all to hell;
Sugar in the gourd and honey in the horn,
I never was so happy since the hour I was born.

Old Joe Clark

Traditional Version

arranged by George N. Terry

Moderato, not too fast

Old Joe Clark, the preach-er's son, preached all o-ver the
used to live on a moun-tain top but now I live in
When I was a lit-tle girl I used to play with

plain, The on-ly text he ev-er used was
town I'm board-ing at the big ho-tel
toys Now I am a big-ger girl I

"High, low, jack and the game."
court-ing Bet-sy Brown.
rath-er play with boys.

REFRAIN

Round and a-round, Old Joe Clark,

When I was a little boy,
I used to want a knife;
Now I am a bigger boy,
I only want a wife.

Wish I was a sugar tree,
Standin' in the middle of some town;
Ev'ry time a pretty girl passed,
I'd shake some sugar down.

Old Joe had a yellow cat,
She would not sing or pray;
She stuck her head in a buttermilk jar
And washed her sins away.

I wish I had a sweetheart;
I'd set her on the shelf,
And ev'ry time she'd smile at me
I'd get up there myself.

Cripple Creek

Traditional Version

Arranged by George N. Terry

Moderato

I got a gal at the head of the creek
Girls on the Crip-ple Creek 'bout half grown
Crip-ple Creek's wide and Crip-ple Creek's deep

go up to see her 'bout the mid-dle of the week.
jump on a boy like a dog on a bone.
I'll wade old Crip-ple Creek a-fore I sleep.

Kiss her on the mouth just as sweet as an-y wine
Roll my britch-es up to my knees I'll
Roads are rock-y and the hill--side's mud-dy and

wraps her - self a - round me like a sweet per - ta - ter vine.
wade old Crip - ple Creek when I please.
I'm so drunk that I can't stand stead - y.

REFRAIN

A7 A9 D

Go -in' up Crip-ple Creek go -in' in a run go -in' up Crip-ple Creek to

A7 A9 D

have a lit -tle fun. Go -in' up Crip-ple Creek go -in' in a whirl

1. 2.
A7 A9 D

3.
A7 A9 D

go - in' up Crip-ple Creek to see my girl. see my girl.

John Henry

Traditional Version

arranged by George N. Terry

Hen-ry's ham-mer ring, Lord, Lord,— you can hear John
be the death of me, Lord, Lord,— ham-mer's gon - na

1.

Hen-ry's ham-mer ring._____
be the death of me."_____

2. *Fine*

When John man"..._____
Well, the
etc.

A7   D

Well, the captain said to John Henry,
"Gonna bring me a steam drill 'round,
Gonna bring me a steam drill out on the job,
Gonna whup that steel on down, Lord, Lord,
Gonna whup that steel on down"...

John Henry said to his captain,
"A man ain't nothin' but a man,
And before I let that steam drill beat me down,
I'll die with a hammer in my hand, Lord, Lord,
I'll die with a hammer in my hand"...

John Henry said to his shaker,
"Shaker, why don't you pray?
'Cause if I miss this little piece of steel,
Tomorrow be your buryin' day, Lord, Lord,
Tomorrow be your buryin' day"...

John Henry was driving on the mountain
And his hammer was flashing fire.
And the last words I heard that poor boy say,
"Gimme a cool drink of water 'fore I die, Lord, Lord,
Gimme a cool drink of water 'fore I die"...

John Henry, he drove fifteen feet,
The steam drill only made nine.
But he hammered so hard that he broke his poor heart,
And he laid down his hammer and he died, Lord, Lord,
And he laid down his hammer and he died...

They took John Henry to the graveyard
And they buried him in the sand.
And every locomotive comes a-roaring by says,
"There lies a steel-driving man, Lord, Lord,
There lies a steel-driving man"...

Wildwood Flower

Traditional Version

Arranged by George N. Terry

pale am - a - ni - ta and hys - sop so blue. Oh, he wild - wood flow-er.
(etc.)

Oh, he promised to love me,
He promised to love,
And to cherish me always
All others above.
I woke from my dream
And my idol was clay.
My passion for loving
Had vanished away.

Oh, he taught me to love him,
He called me his flower,
A blossom to cheer him
Through life's weary hour.
But now he is gone
And left me alone,
The wild flowers to weep
And the wild birds to mourn.

I'll dance and I'll sing
And my life shall be gay,
I'll charm every heart
In the crowd I survey;
Though my heart now is breaking,
He never shall know
How his name makes me tremble,
My pale cheeks to glow.

I'll dance and I'll sing
And my heart will be gay,
I'll banish this weeping
Drive troubles away.
I'll live yet to see him
Regret this dark hour,
When he won and neglected
This frail wildwood flower.

The Wabash Cannonball

Traditional Version

Arranged by George N. Terry

Moderato, not too slowly

long and she's tall and the hand - some,   yes, she's loved by one and
might - y   rush of the en - gine   hear the lone - some ho - bo
the hills of Min - ne - so - ta   where the rip - pling wa - ters
earth - ly   race is o - ver   and the cur - tain 'round him

all,   she's a mod - ern com - bi - na - tion   called the
squall,   no   rid - ing through the jun - gle   on the
fall,   we'll   car - ry him to glo - ry   on the
fall,   no   chanc - es can be tak - en   on the

1. 2. 3.

Wa - bash Can - non - ball.
Wa - bash Can - non - ball.
Wa - bash Can - non - ball.
Wa - bash Can - non -

4.

Now the

ball.

The Wreck of the Old 97

Traditional Version

Arranged by George N. Terry

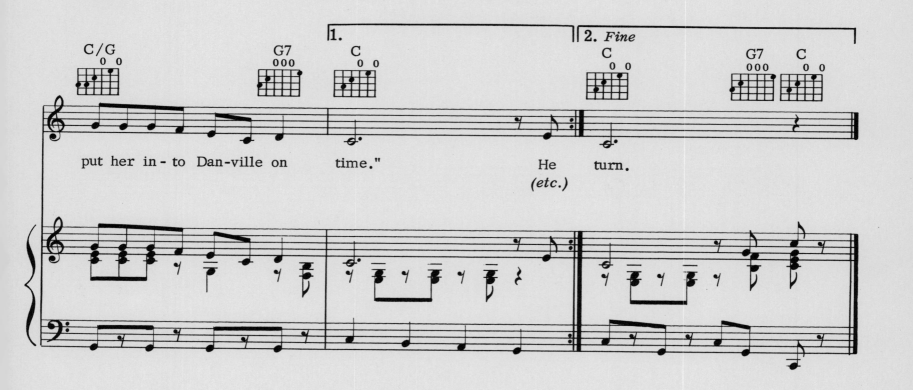

put her in-to Dan-ville on time." He turn.
(etc.)

He turned and said to his black greasy fireman,
"Just shovel on a little more coal,
And when we cross the White Oak Mountain
You can watch old 'ninety-seven' roll."

It's a mighty rough road from Lynchburg to Danville,
On a line on a three mile grade,
It was on this grade that he lost his average,
You can see what a jump he made.

He was going down the grade makin' ninety miles an hour,
When his whistle broke into a scream,
They found him in the wreck
With his hand on the throttle, he was scalded to death by the steam.

Now, ladies, you must take warning,
From this time now on learn,
Never speak harsh words to your true loving husband,
He may leave you and never return.

Muleskinner Blues
Traditional Version

Arranged by George N. Terry

Well, I like to work — I'm rolling all the time.
Well, I like to work — I'm rolling all the time.
I can pop my initials right on the mule's behind.

Well, it's hey little water boy, bring your water 'round.
Well, it's hey little water boy, bring your water 'round.
If you don't like your job set that water bucket down.

I'm a-working on the new road at a dollar and a dime a day.
I'm a-working on the new road at a dollar and a dime a day.
I got three women waiting on a Saturday night just to draw my pay.

Nine Pound Hammer

Traditional Version

Arranged by George N. Terry

207

Old Rattler

Traditional Version

Arranged by George N. Terry

Old Rat-tl-er was a good old dog, As blind as he could be.

Ev - 'ry night at sup-per-time, I be-lieve that dog could see.

REFRAIN

"Here Rat-tl-er, help, help, Here Rat-tl-er, help." Call Rat-tl-er from the barn —

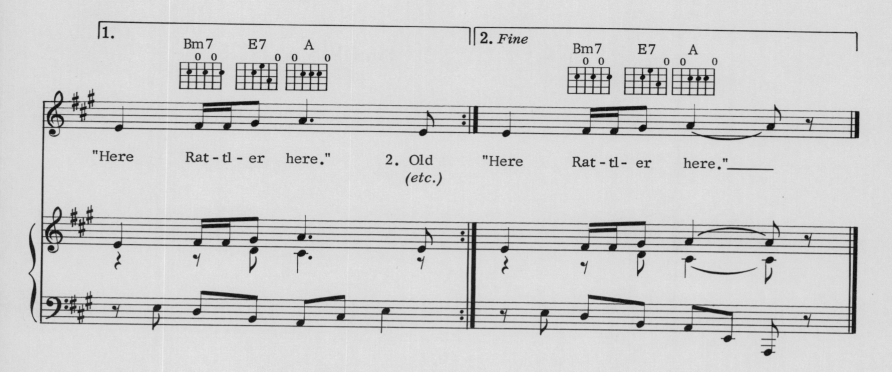

"Here Rat-tl-er here." 2. Old "Here Rat-tl-er here."____
(etc.)

Old Rattler treed the other night,
And I thought he treed a coon.
When I come to find out,
He was barkin' at the moon.

Well, Grandma had a yeller hen,
We set her, as you know.
We set her on three buzzard eggs
And hatched out one old crow.

Grandpa had a muley cow,
She's muley when she's born.
It took a jaybird forty years
To fly from horn to horn.

Now, if I had a needle and thread
As fine as I could sew,
I'd sew my sweetheart to my back
And down the road I'd go.

Old Rattler was a smart old dog,
Even though he was blind.
He wouldn't hurt one single thing
Though he was very fine.

One night I saw a big fat coon
Climb up in a tree.
I called Old Rattler right away
To git him down fer me.

But Rattler wouldn't do it
'Cause he liked that coon.
I saw them walkin' paw in paw
Later by the light of the moon.

Now Old Rattler's dead and gone
Like all good dogs do.
You better not act the dog yourself
Or you'll be goin' there too.

Roll in My Sweet Baby's Arms

Traditional Version

Arranged by George N. Terry

Ain't gon - na work on the rail - road,_____

Ain't gon - na work on the farm,_____

Lay 'round the shack 'til the mail train comes

back   then I'll   roll   in   my   sweet   ba - by's

arms. _____   bail. _____

Refrain:

Roll in my sweet baby's arms,
Roll in my sweet baby's arms,
Lay 'round the shack 'til the mail train comes back,
Then I'll roll in my sweet baby's arms.

Can't see what's the matter with my own true love,
She done quit writing to me,
She must think I don't love her like I used to,
Ain't that a foolish idea.

Sometimes there's a change in the ocean,
Sometimes there's a change in the sea,
Sometimes there's a change in my own true love,
But there's never no change in me.

Mama's a ginger-cake baker,
Sister can weave and can spin,
Dad's got an interest in that old cotton mill,
Just watch that old money roll in.

They tell me that your parents do not like me,
They have drove me away from your door,
If I had all my time to do over,
I would never go there any more.

Now where was you last Friday night,
While I was locked up in jail,
Walking the streets with another man,
Wouldn't even go my bail.

Rye Whisky

Traditional Version

Arranged by George N. Terry

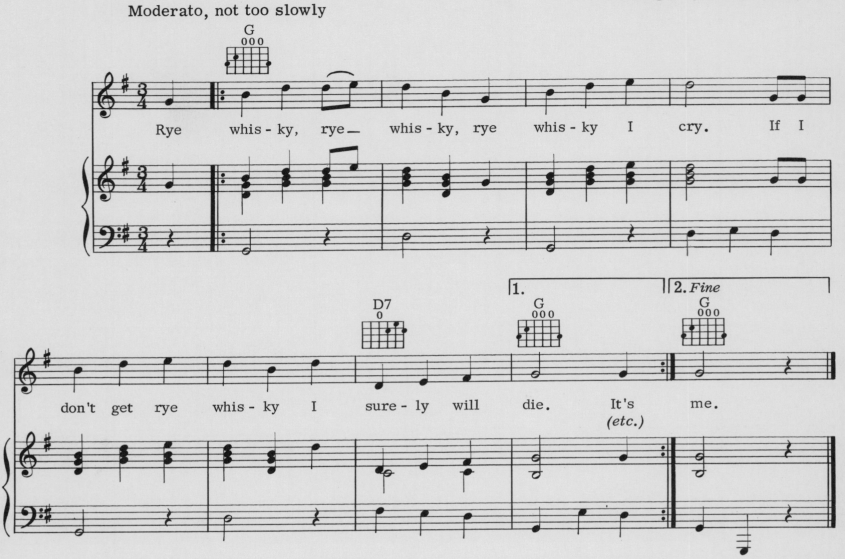

Moderato, not too slowly

Rye whis-ky, rye— whis-ky, rye whis-ky I cry. If I
don't get rye whis-ky I sure-ly will die. It's me. *(etc.)*

It's whisky, rye whisky,
I know you of old,
You robbed my poor pockets
Of silver and gold.

It's beefsteak when I'm hungry,
Rye whisky when I'm dry,
A greenback when I'm hard up,
Oh, Heaven when I die.

I go to yonder holler
And I'll build me a still,
And I'll give you a gallon
For a five-dollar bill.

If the ocean was whisky
And I was a duck,
I'd dive to the bottom
And never come up.

But the ocean ain't whisky,
And I ain't a duck.
So I'll play Jack o' Diamonds
And trust to my luck.

Her parents don't like me,
They say I'm too poor,
And that I am unfit
To darken her door.

Her parents don't like me,
Well, my money's my own,
And them that don't like me
Can leave me alone.

Oh whisky, you villain,
You're no friend to me,
You killed my poor pappy,
God-damn you, try me.

Salty Dog
Traditional Version

arranged by George N. Terry

10

CONNIE SMITH

BOBBY LORD

THE FIRST BAD TIMES FOR THE OPRY

DEL WOOD

Wesley Rose had been chasing Mitch Miller, head of Columbia Records, all over the country. He had flown to Chicago to see him only to be told that Miller had gone to New York, then to New York only to learn that he had returned to Chicago, then back to Chicago for more of the same. When Rose finally caught up with Miller in 1949, he played him Hank Williams's recording of "Cold, Cold Heart," and Miller listened.

"Wes, have you shown this to anybody?" he asked.

"Anybody?" Rose said. "I've shown it to everybody!"

"You mean if I don't get somebody to do it, it won't get done."

"That's the way it looks," Rose acknowledged.

"Well," Miller asked, "what do the others say about it?"

Wesley Rose had not been a song plugger for too many years. Before that he had been an accountant for Standard Oil in Chicago, and he had never tuned his radio to the WLS Barndance show during the whole time he lived in its listening area. Hillbilly music did not suit his ear.

Fred Rose, right, and his son Wesley, standing before a display of their company's music

He came to Nashville in 1945 because his father, Fred, who had formed a publishing company with Roy Acuff, needed somebody to balance the books and run the business so that he would be free to write songs and produce records. But then Wesley Rose had started liking the stuff.

When Mitch Miller asked him what the others had been saying about "Cold, Cold Heart," Wesley told him the truth.

"They say it's nothing but a hillbilly song." Then, however, he added his personal demurrer. "But I don't buy that. Because I like it, and I don't think I'm a hillbilly."

This could only have sounded like a challenge, and Miller must have noted by then that Wesley Rose in no way fitted the hillbilly stereotype. If anything, he seemed more like a pipe-smoking, rather pedantic young professor.

Miller mulled it over for a moment. "Great," he finally said. "Let's show 'em."

In the early 1950s Mitch Miller and Wesley Rose did just that. Starting with a big hit on "Cold, Cold Heart" with a young popular singer named Tony Bennett, they followed it with other Williams songs recorded by such other pop stars as Rosemary Clooney, Frankie Laine, and Doris Day. All of them were on Miller's Columbia label, and virtually all became hits. The track record was so good that Miller began to let Rose decide which of Columbia's stars should sing each tune.

Rose recalls that Miller was particularly taken with "Jambalaya," the Williams lyric dealing with such seemingly divergent themes as Creole cuisine, partying, and love.

"It had all these Cajun words like 'pirogue' in it, you know," Rose remembers, "and when I played it for Mitch the first time he said, 'What the hell does all that mean?' And I said, 'I'll be damned if I know.' And he said, 'Great! Great!'"

Rose picked Frankie Laine for "Jambalaya," and took a copy of Williams's recording of it to California, to a recording session in which Miller was cutting Laine and Jo Stafford in a duet on Williams's "Hey Good Lookin'." Miller, anxious to see what Laine's reaction to "Jambalaya" would be, took Laine into a corner of the studio and played the record for him during a break in the middle of the session.

"Well, while this is going on, I can see Stafford starting to lose her cool," Rose remembers.

"I start to get worried when Stafford goes over and starts talking to Mitch. After a while, he calls me over and whispers to me, 'Jo Stafford would like to do it.' Well, I wasn't too crazy about this because I'd never had a Jo Stafford record on anything, but Mitch had backed himself into a corner. So we made the deal.

"But Mitch was such a diplomat that he came back to me about a half-hour later and said, 'We'll cut it with Jo, and if it doesn't get high in the charts in six weeks, I'll cover it with Frankie Laine.' Well, how can you miss on a deal like that?"

It turned out that Rose did not need the insurance Miller had so graciously promised him. Jo Stafford's recording of "Jambalaya" made it into the Top Ten in no time.

The Top Ten—the *pop* Top Ten—became almost the private property of Acuff-Rose material in the early fifties. In one week during this period, Rose recalls, the firm had nine of the Top Ten songs in the nation, along with Number Eleven. Once Rose even bet a New York friend $20 that Mitch Miller and he could make any song in the Acuff-Rose catalogue a hit within six weeks. As part of the bet, the friend was allowed to choose which song Rose and Miller would have to make a hit; he picked "Too Old to Cut the Mustard."

Rose told Miller about the bet the next day, and Miller agreed to go along if he could have half of the $20 bet for himself. Then he asked whom Rose wanted to sing "Too Old to Cut the Mustard." Jo Stafford, Rose said. She could do a comedy record somewhat similar to a recent, very popular comedy recording by another female singer of the song "Temptation." Miller said fine, that he would get in touch with Jo Stafford about it. When a couple of weeks went by and nothing further happened, Rose called Miller.

"There's something funny going on," Miller said. "She said she'd do it."

There was indeed something going on, although it may not have been terribly funny at the time. Jo Stafford finally confessed that she did not want to do the song, and why.

"Apparently she was trying to get an annulment of her marriage through the Pope right then," Rose says, "and she didn't think he would like some of the lyrics to 'Too Old to Cut the Mustard.'"

Rose was crestfallen. He told Miller that their chances of collecting the $20 bet were dead, since they had only four weeks left to get "Too Old to Cut the Mustard" into the charts.

"No, we're not dead yet," Miller said. "You think about it all night, and I'll think about it all night, and we'll talk tomorrow." He called Rose early the next morning. "I thought about it until three o'clock," he said, "and I've got it: Rosemary Clooney and Marlene Dietrich. A duet. What do you think?"

"Marlene Dietrich can't sing her name, and you don't even have her on Columbia anyway," Rose said.

"Man," Miller told him, "those are just details."

Remembering it now, Rose still wonderingly shakes his head. "I'll be damned if he didn't go out and sign Marlene Dietrich," he says. "He cut the record, and it made the Top Ten, and we won our $20."

Growing accustomed to triumphs such as these, the Grand Ole Opry entered the 1950s, its most trying decade, almost entirely unaware that grave troubles lay ahead. There seemed no reason to expect any slowdown in the steadily increasing popularity of both hillbilly music and its live-performance Mecca, the Opry. There had hardly been an interruption in the growth of the Opry's success.

Eddy Arnold, a huge star, had left in the late forties, to be sure, but during the same period Opry star Red Foley had scored a break-through with "Chattanoogie Shoe Shine Boy," the first pop hit by a hillbilly star since the days of Vernon Dalhart in the twenties. There had been the disastrous attempt to book hillbilly music into the fashionable Astor Hotel in Manhattan, but there had also been successful Carnegie Hall shows in New York the same year, and the Opry's guiding minds—cosmopolitan men like Jack Stapp—were convinced that New York acclaim is merely the recognition, and not the cause, of national popularity. And there was solid evidence to support such a conclusion: In 1948, in one of the first national radio surveys ever made, WSM startled its industry by reaching a total of ten million

Marty Robbins, appropriately attired, croons his "White Sport Coat" in the late fifties

Ray Price, the Cherokee Cowboy, emerges from a rear door
of the **Ryman Auditorium** in the early sixties

ABOVE: Webb Pierce, one of the Opry's biggest stars of the fifties, revisits the show. RIGHT: Faron Young was one of the most appealing of the younger Opry stars

homes at least once a week. "This, of course, was the Opry influence," Irving Waugh notes.

The Opry entered the 1950s continuing to enlarge its already vast showcase of stars. In mid-1949 it had added Hank Williams, and now it quickly brought other attractive newcomers in to join him. Most of these were younger than the stars of the forties; some, like Webb Pierce and Marty Robbins, were born in the same year the Opry was; others, such as Carl Smith, Ray Price, and Faron Young, were even younger.

By now, virtually none of the new stars were coming in without serving an apprenticeship on one of the other country music shows over which the Opry had achieved predominance. An unusually large number of them came up from Shreveport.

"The Louisiana Hayride worried us a little," Waugh recalls. "They were developing a lot of talent down there. So as soon as they developed it, we went after it. We started using them as a sort of minor league feeder."

By the mid-fifties, the Opry cast even included a square-dance troupe, the Cedar Hill Dancers. Such a development might have occurred even earlier had not the cause of square dancing received a decided setback on the stage of the Ryman one Saturday night in the late forties. Oswald Kirby remembers the incident well.

"A bunch of us were dancing out there on the stage in the middle of the show one night, just having fun and acting the fool, when this short stocky fellow from Louisville, Kentucky, jumped up onto the stage with us from out of the audience.

"This fellow started dancing right along with us. I guess he thought it was open to anybody, and I suppose he'd had him a little something to drink. Anyway, Roy [Acuff] could have stopped it by just going over to the boy and putting a hand on his shoulder and telling him quietly that members of the audience weren't supposed to be on the stage. But before Roy could do anything, Jim Denny went over to the boy and popped him one on the chin. It started the awfullest fight you ever saw. That boy whipped Jim Denny all over the stage, then he whipped six policemen and half the musicians, before they could get him hauled off to jail."

In the new decade the Opry ran into some surprises as unexpected and unpleasant as the one Jim Denny rushed into that night. The show's leadership awoke one day in 1951 to the realization that radio was no longer in the vanguard of the communications industry.

"Television, which was new, was the dramatic thing," Irving Waugh recalls.

Waugh had moved into sales from news in 1947, and he was gravely concerned about the impact of television on the Opry. Searching for ideas, he asked his staff to come up with a promotion that might help keep attention focused on the Opry. A girl in the advertising department suggested that the disc jockeys around the nation who were playing the Opry stars' recordings might be invited to Nashville the weekend of the Opry's twenty-fifth birthday. The station decided to do this, as a one-time promotion. Fewer than fifty radio announcers came, but when Waugh saw how impressed the guests were, and how hon-

The Solemn Old Judge, George D. Hay,
flanked by Alcyone Bate Beasley and
irrepressible Uncle Dave Macon, cuts the
Opry's twentieth-birthday cake in 1945

ored they felt at being invited, he persuaded Stapp to make the anniversary celebration an annual thing. The "Grand Ole Opry Birthday Celebration," as it is called, has become the centerpiece of a great autumn country music festival in Nashville.

This "birthday celebration" was not very big at the start, however, and suddenly nothing else looked very big, either. By 1953, attendance at the Opry was beginning to sag noticeably. The Opry leadership, increasingly worried, began to look at the other country music shows, to see if the same thing was happening to them. It was. Some people may have begun to wonder if, with the ushering in of a new day, the Opry's time had passed.

"We began to say to ourselves, is this softening of attendance due to television?" Waugh remembers. "Or is it due to the world's becoming more accustomed to air conditioning? That was another one of the big new things in those days. We wondered if we had a problem at the Ryman because of it."

Whatever the problem was, a solution was going to have to be found. This had been decreed by Edwin Craig, up at National Life.

Waugh says, "Mr. Craig took the position that we had made a mistake by going to the star system rather than keeping the Opry the way it had been in 1935, but that we were going to have to keep it going, come hell or high water."

Attendance levels at the other country music shows continued to worsen as mid-decade approached, but about 1955 the Opry's attendance figures stabilized at acceptable levels, Waugh says.

He adds that he does not know why the Opry's troubles were not as great as those of some of the other shows, except that perhaps some of these others panicked and began to reduce their schedules. The Opry's lot may also have been improved by its almost immediate attempts to get some national television exposure. During this period the Opry was featured on four twenty-five-minute segments of the Kate Smith network show, and later it produced one live hour a month from the Opry stage, alternating with the new Ozark Jubilee show in Springfield, Missouri. The other country music shows, having less prestige than the Opry, could not achieve this kind of exposure.

Meanwhile, hillbilly music had begun to fight for something it had never had: respectability. As a first step, its leaders began to urge that the term "country" be used instead of "hillbilly," arguing that the latter word insults rural people. In 1954, a small group formed the Country Music Disc Jockeys Association to try to gain general radio acceptance of their kind of music. By the end of the decade, the Disc Jockeys Association became the Country Music Association.

The stresses from outside the country music industry were no more powerful than those from within. The brilliant victories scored by Wesley Rose in the pop field were ominous indications that the

This picture of the Pointer Sisters performing at the 1974 Opry Birthday festivities dramatically illustrates country music's changing times

OVERLEAF:
The Opry cast
in 1965

223

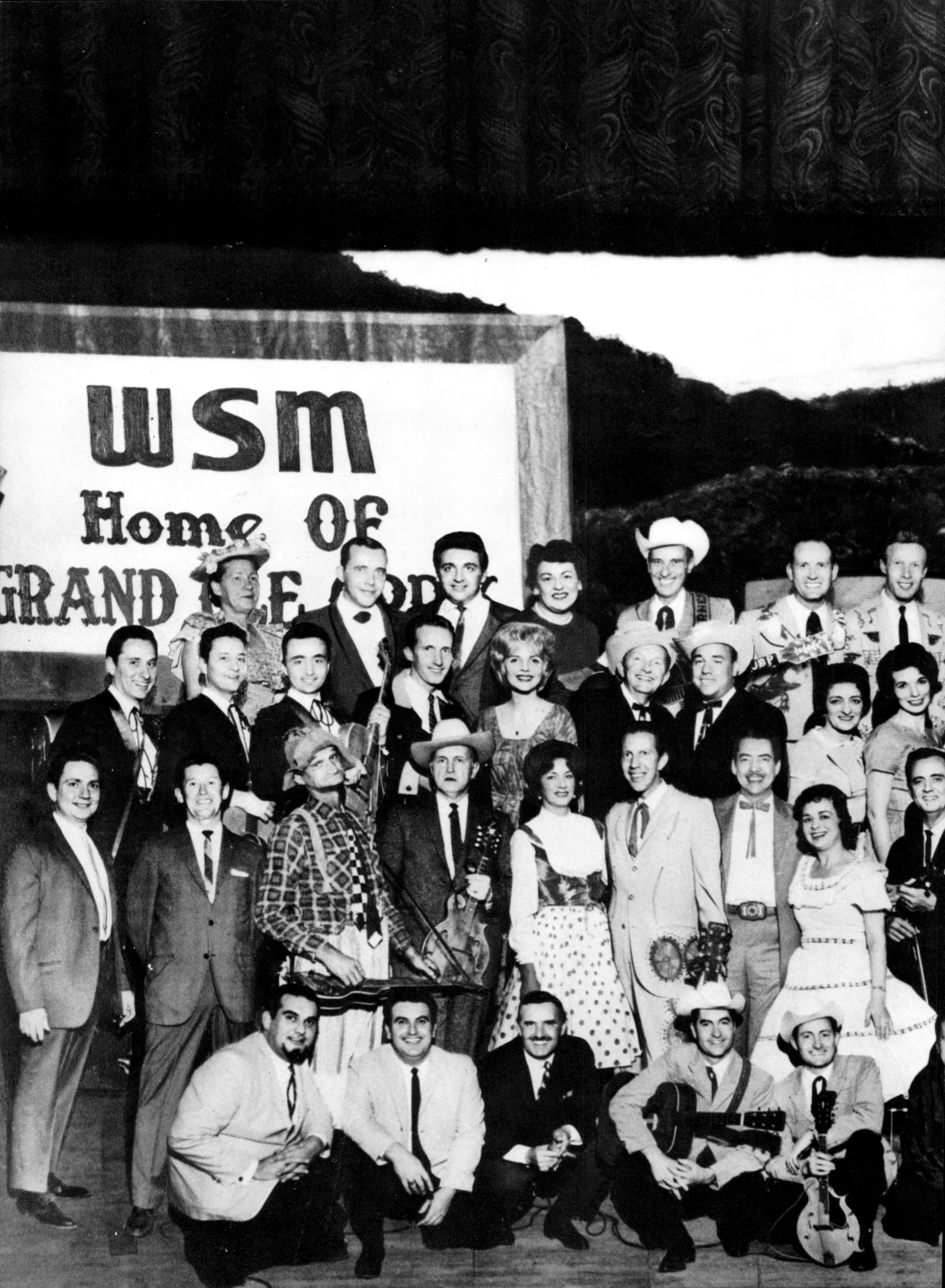
WSM
Home Of

The Coopers, one of the Opry's staunchest traditional groups. From left are Stoney, daughter Carol Lee, and Wilma Lee. As a small girl in the late thirties, Wilma Lee and her family recorded for the Library of Congress after winning a statewide folksinging competition in West Virginia

Dee Kilpatrick

Nashville music phenomenon that had been born with the Opry was getting far too big to be housed under the same roof with it any longer. The industry's growing pains were to cause many problems within the WSM power structure in the next several years.

One critical problem was outside interests. To what degree should the station, and the Opry, be connected with the other businesses beginning to grow up in country music? Should the station allow its employees to work part-time in music businesses which could conceivably be in conflict with the interests of WSM?

In the early fifties, one potential such problem was avoided when Aaron Shelton, George Reynolds, and Carl Jenkins decided to close their Castle Studios and limit their activities to WSM. But there were a number of fierce personality clashes. Jack DeWitt, elevated to the presidency of the station in 1947, began to try to assert control over Harry Stone and eventually ousted him.

A similar clash occurred a few years later between DeWitt and Jim Denny.

Denny, who had come up as house manager of the Opry, also later directed the Opry and the Artist's Service Bureau, which booked the Opry stars on the road. It was a huge business; one pamphlet distributed from Nashville in 1955 claims that in the previous year Opry acts made 2,554 personal appearances, entertaining nearly eight million people.

Denny already had formed his successful Cedarwood Music publishing company, in partnership with Carl Smith and Webb Pierce. When DeWitt told him he would have to give up his outside interests or leave the station, Denny left and opened a talent bureau. Before long he became one of the most prominent bookers of any kind of talent in the world. A future member of the Country Music Association's exclusive Hall of Fame, he was unquestionably one of the men most instrumental in Nashville's rise to national prominence in the fifties and early sixties.

Not everyone at WSM was in favor of DeWitt's hard line. Waugh says he thought it would remove WSM from the forefront of the Nashville music business, a course Waugh did not favor at all. When Denny left, in 1956, some stars went with him, refusing to appear on the Opry; among them, understandably, were Pierce and Smith. Even Minnie Pearl left for a time, but she eventually returned.

DeWitt decided to go outside WSM's personnel roster for an Opry general manager to replace Denny, and chose the Nashville representative of Mercury Records, a North Carolina-born ex-Marine named Dee Kilpatrick. The WSM officials who interviewed Kilpatrick acknowledged that the show had problems. By this time, the rock and roll revolution that had begun with the first recordings of Elvis Presley in 1954 was beginning to hit country music hard.

"They asked me what I thought was wrong," recalls Kilpatrick, who now operates several large Nashville fabric stores.

"Well, back in the days when I was working with Mercury I was at the Opry every Saturday night I was in town, and I could look at the audience and see what was wrong. The Opry didn't have the

Carl Butler displays the impassioned singing style
that has prompted some to compare him with Roy Acuff

ABOVE: Johnny Cash looks to his style-setting guitarist, the late Luther Perkins, far left, for an instrumental assist. RIGHT: A sober-faced Porter Wagoner in the late fifties, soon after he came to the Opry from the Ozark Jubilee show in Springfield, Missouri

OPPOSITE PAGE:
ABOVE: Jim Reeves, the Opry's most popular exponent of softer styling in the late fifties and early sixties, backed on the bass by Buddy Killen. BELOW LEFT: Roy Drusky, another of the Opry's smoother, more modern stylists. CENTER: Guitarist-singer Billy Grammer is accompanied by the late Junior Huskey. RIGHT: Bobby Lord came to the Opry in the late fifties, when the show was seeking to capture younger audiences

Visiting one of the farthest outposts of country music's international popularity, Ferlin Husky appears on a show called the Tokyo Grand Ole Opry

appeal to the younger audience that you have to have if you're going to keep growing. All I could see there were older people and little teeny kids. There weren't any teen-agers."

Kilpatrick thought the show needed some new acts and some new promotion techniques.

He and Stapp brought in some new performers. Some of these, like Wilma Lee and Stoney Cooper, Carl Butler, and Porter Wagoner, represented no departure from the Opry's traditional music. Others, like Johnny Cash, the Everly Brothers, and Rusty and Doug Kershaw, were influenced by the revved-up beat of the newer sound.

Kilpatrick says he tried to go after the younger audience, rather than waiting for it to come to him.

"I noticed that we had a lot of Arkansas stars on the Opry, so I wrote every high school senior class in the state of Arkansas," he recalls. "I offered them a special rate to bring the whole class down to see the Opry. I did that with several states. Before you turned around, I had the Ryman filled with kids."

During this period, the Opry leaders seemed to try to emphasize the newness of their old show. In a long article that appeared in the *Nashville Banner* on March 30, 1957, Roy Acuff cited an expanded cast which was the biggest in history and represented "the highest quality of entertainment since I have been with the show." The article cited the popularity of Marty Robbins, Ray Price, Johnny Cash, and Ferlin Husky, pointing out that Husky was soon to appear on the Ed Sullivan Show and that Cash would make an appearance on the Jackie Gleason Show. The article added:

"Not only have new stars been added, but veteran greats have perfected new routines and arrangements, and the cast totals almost one hundred seventy persons. For instance, June Carter is a 'changed

Ferlin Husky was one of the Opry's most popular performers during the middle and late fifties

person,' a beautiful and glamorous brunette who teams with comedian Smokey Pleacher in a new act that has stopped the show every night since it was first presented four weeks ago."

While the Opry subtly courted a younger audience in these several ways, Kilpatrick staunchly refused to make any concessions to the popularity of rock and roll on the stage itself. He refused to allow drums, although he acknowledges that he had problems with some performers who wanted to do rock and roll-style songs.

"The drum was the principal instrument in rock and roll music," he says. "Why take the thing that's killing you and start giving in to it? I figured if we allowed drums then, with all the antagonism that there was between country music and rock and roll, we would lose the traditional audience that we had always had."

Kilpatrick had strong opinions. A man who uses profanity with the familiarity one might expect of a former Marine, he nevertheless regarded the lyrics to many rock and roll songs as morally unfit for anybody to listen to, especially young people.

"I thought rock and roll was devil's music," he says simply.

Kilpatrick lasted less than three years at WSM. DeWitt says he could not seem to get along with people very well, especially some of the stars. Waugh and Kilpatrick both acknowledge that one of the people he did not get along with was Waugh, who regarded him as somewhat of an outsider who did not "belong" at WSM.

In any case, in 1959 Kilpatrick left. By that time Waugh's friend Stapp had been gone almost a year and was now devoting his full energies to building his Tree Publishing Company into an empire.

"Those were hard times," Waugh says. "Once during that period I even went over to WSIX (another large Nashville radio and television station) for about a week myself."

Yet during this troubled decade, the Opry added many more stars. They included Lester Flatt and Earl Scruggs, the Carlisles, Ferlin Husky, the Jordanaires, Don Gibson, Billy Grammer, Ira and Charlie Louvin, Teddy and Doyle Wilburn, Kitty Wells, Jean Shepard, Justin Tubb, Margie Bowes, Bobby Lord, Hank Locklin, Hawkshaw Hawkins, Del Wood, Jim Reeves, Jimmy Newman, Roy Drusky, Archie Campbell, Stonewall Jackson, Patsy Cline, Bill Anderson, George Hamilton IV, and Skeeter Davis.

By the end of the fifties, "country" music was beginning to assimilate some of the beat and some of the audience of rock and roll. It also began to grow, stimulated by the gradual death of network radio, which encouraged activity by local stations. Jack Stapp points out that this gave radio listeners a reachable local disc jockey and prompted them to ask for the music they wanted.

This change could help the Opry only indirectly, of course, by having the playing of the records focus attention on the individual stars. The old show itself remained on one part or another of the NBC network into the sixties, long after almost all the rest of network radio had gone the way of the Amos and Andy show.

In the late fifties June Carter (now married to Johnny Cash) strikes a much more glamorous pose than country comediennes had been allowed to until that time

ABOVE: Justin Tubb, Ernest's son, became an
Opry star in his own right. RIGHT: The
Jordanaires, Opry stars and also background
singers for Elvis Presley

OPPOSITE PAGE:
ABOVE LEFT: Don Gibson, writer of "I Can't Stop
Lovin' You" and one of country music's most
original stylists. RIGHT: Jean Shepard was one of
the new stars of the fifties. BELOW LEFT: George
Hamilton IV, a quiet North Carolina college
graduate who became one of country music's
most popular performers in Canada, England,
and Scandinavia. RIGHT: Jimmy C. Newman,
currently the Opry's sole member from
Louisiana's Cajun country

OPPOSITE PAGE:

ABOVE: Charlie Louvin, right, and his late brother Ira were one of the Opry's most traditional groups in the fifties and early sixties. BELOW: Patsy Cline, the first female Opry singer to craft a softer, more universal sound, singing at the Ryman in the early sixties

RIGHT: Stonewall Jackson, the last performer to become an Opry star simply on the strength of an audition, joined the show in the late fifties with virtually no professional experience. BELOW LEFT: Skeeter Davis in the late fifties. RIGHT: Kitty Wells, "Queen of Country Music"

Margie Bowes in a 1970 appearance

Lester Flatt, Earl Scruggs, and the Foggy Mountain Boys perform at the 1963 Opry Birthday ceremonies

Archie Campbell today

Doyle, left, and Teddy Wilburn, one of the Opry's
best-known brother duet teams

OPPOSITE PAGE:
ABOVE: Pianist Del Wood (born Adelaide
Hazelwood) pounds out her always popular
"Down Yonder." BELOW: Backstage at the
Ryman Auditorium, Hawkshaw Hawkins clowns
as he helps June Carter into her slipper

Hank Locklin

A recent picture of Bill Anderson
on his syndicated television show

Doug Kershaw, right, the Cajun singer and fiddler who is presently a particular favorite of college audiences, was an Opry member in the late fifties and early sixties. He is seen here with his brother Rusty. Together they had a huge hit recording in Doug's song "Louisiana Man"

The Everly Brothers—Phil, left, and Don—when they were Opry stars

The Carlisles, with Bill at center, perform one of their vintage stompers

LESTER FLATT

THE RISE OF BLUEGRASS

STONEWALL JACKSON

Sometime in 1953 Efford Burke, a Martha White Flour salesman, came to see Cohen Williams, the head of Martha White Foods. Burke was carrying a small poster. It was not much more than a handbill, just a cheap advertisement for a schoolhouse show that Burke had attended in the little town of Livingston, Tennessee, but the show had impressed him so much that he tore down the poster and took it with him so as not to forget the names of the performers. His interest was more than casual. By this time Martha White was sponsoring both a portion of the Opry and a fifteen-minute morning radio show on WSM, and Burke was aware of Williams's personal and financial interest in hillbilly music. So he showed him the poster with the large letters that spelled out a homely but somehow stirring name:

LESTER FLATT, EARL SCRUGGS, AND THE FOGGY MOUNTAIN BOYS.

"I went to see these boys the other night," Burke told his boss. "I think this is who we need to sell flour."

These were of course magic words to Cohen Williams. He decided to drive up to Knoxville, where this group was working daily on the WNOX Mid-Day Merrygoround, and have a look for himself.

"I went to see the radio show and liked what they did," Williams recalls, "so I went backstage and introduced myself and told them I'd like to talk with them. They didn't have any idea what I wanted to talk to them about, and they were pretty distant, you know. They said they'd been out all night on an appearance and had just gotten in barely in time to do the Merrygoround, and they were tired. I said, 'Well, what about seeing you this afternoon?' They said, 'Well, we were planning on going home to get a little rest.' I said, 'Well, what about tonight?' and they said, 'Tonight we're going up to Harlan, Kentucky, to put on a show.' I said, 'Could I ride up there with you?' They thought that was a little strange, I guess, but they said it was all right."

They picked him up in front of the Andrew Johnson Hotel late that afternoon in a 1934 Ford with a bass fiddle tied to the top of it, and at the show that night they took in probably $65, Williams says. On the way back to Knoxville late that night, he told them he wanted them to become regulars on his early morning radio show on WSM. After discussing it a little, they said they wanted to come over to Nashville the following Saturday and talk with him about it some more. Williams said that would be fine.

When he returned to Nashville, Williams discovered that WSM did not look upon Flatt and Scruggs with much favor at all. They were pupils of Bill Monroe, whose Blue Grass Boys they had left to form their own band in 1948, and WSM officials thought it would not be fair to put them on the Opry to compete against Monroe.

"They were doing many of the songs that Monroe did, and in those days, when there were fewer performers on the Opry, that would have made a lot more difference than it might today," Irving Waugh says.

Flatt acknowledges that they were doing a lot of Monroe's material then, although he and Scruggs also were writing some original material. Perhaps as important as the material was the fact that both men had played significant parts in the crystallization of the bluegrass form when they were with Monroe. Both had gotten wide exposure in their Opry work then, with Scruggs becoming recognized among musicians as the fastest banjo picker in the world and Flatt serving as a primary vocalist who was featured often in solo Opry singing spots.

What today is called bluegrass was still evolving when Flatt joined Bill Monroe in 1944 after having worked a little while with Bill's brother Charlie. At that time, Flatt recalls, the instrumentation of the Blue Grass Boys included such foreign-seeming components as an electric guitar like the one Charlie Monroe used, and an accordion.

With the addition of Scruggs's fiery five-string banjo in 1945, however, Monroe molded a distinctive musical genre made up of many important elements. They included a five-string banjo picked with the individual fingers; a mandolin picked the same way, for melody rather than just rhythm; a fiddle played in the fast and yet eloquently mournful style of Monroe's Uncle Pen Vanderver; chillingly high, tight harmony sung by Monroe and Flatt together; a relentless, hard drive like that used by Bill and Charlie Monroe in the thirties, except that this time there was no electrification; and, finally, when done to perfection, a stern, uncompromising reverence in keeping with the grave visage of Bill Monroe.

No one man can be said to have invented bluegrass, but Bill Monroe was the boss of the people who did. When Flatt and Scruggs left his organization in 1948, only the bands of Ralph and Carter Stanley and Jim and Jesse McReynolds, both in southwestern Virginia, were experimenting with the kind of string music that would one day evolve into forms of bluegrass.

Flatt and Scruggs seem to have tried to innovate rather than merely to copy. They gradually made changes in Monroe's formula, and Flatt acknowledges now that they consciously tried to present "a little different sound from Bill." In the mid-fifties they dropped the mandolin altogether and replaced it with a dobro guitar played by Buck (Uncle Josh) Graves, whom they hired from Wilma Lee and Stoney Cooper's Clinch Mountain Clan. Flatt also pitched his voice much lower than Monroe's high sound, even though Flatt himself had always sung tenor until he joined Monroe's band.

That Saturday in 1953 when Flatt and Scruggs came over to Nashville to see Cohen Williams, Williams told them that nothing was going to be easy and that they were not going to be allowed to go on the Opry. Their minds seemed to be made up, however.

"They wanted to know what kind of a contract I wanted, what kind of a take they were going to have to kick in to me," Williams recalls. "I said, 'You aren't going to have to kick in any take, and there isn't going to be a contract. When I want to get rid of you I want you to go, and when you get tired of me I'll quit.' And that's the way it was. We never had a contract."

As Williams had warned them, it was not going to be easy.

Williams had to do some talking just to get them on his own

Earl Scruggs

OVERLEAF:
LEFT: Lester Flatt. RIGHT: Lester Flatt dances a jig as Earl Scruggs, left, and the Foggy Mountain Boys supply the music

fifteen-minute WSM morning radio show, finally having to get it cleared through Jack DeWitt. That done, Flatt and Scruggs took up where they had left off in Knoxville, doing the daily radio show and making schoolhouse appearances throughout middle Tennessee, southern Kentucky, and northern Alabama. At every appearance they made commercial announcements just the way they did on the radio, hawking Martha White Flour, and people who brought labels cut from Martha White packages were admitted at reduced rates.

"They worked the territory real hard," Williams says.

After a year or so, Williams expanded the territory. In a bold move, he got them a weekly WSM television show, and soon afterward he got them similar shows on different days of the week in Jackson, Tennessee; Atlanta and Columbus, Georgia; Florence, South Carolina; and Huntington, West Virginia.

Since this was before videotape came into widespread use, they had to do every one of these television shows live, traveling a frantic 2,500-mile-a-week circuit by automobile. But it was not to be a permanent thing.

"Cohen told us, 'I'm going to set you up on these stations for thirteen weeks, then I'll get you some more stations lined up and we'll move you,'" Flatt remembers.

"He said, 'You can't stay in one place too long—you'll burn yourself out.' I told him, 'I've never argued with you about anything yet, and I'm not going to argue with you about this, but we aren't going to be burned out anywhere in any thirteen weeks.'"

That turns out to have been one of the larger understatements in the history of show business. Flatt and Scruggs and their Foggy Mountain troupe made their weekly 2,500-mile treks until videotape came in two years later, and never missed a television show in any of their six cities.

It was a killing but rewarding pace.

On the television show in Huntington Flatt mentioned, just once, that they would "have a songbook off the press next week, if anybody would like to be one of the first ones to get one." When they arrived back in Huntington a week later to do the show, they were greeted by 1,400 orders for the songbook.

Their exhausting journeys were more important for them, for bluegrass music, and for the Opry than anyone could possibly have imagined at the time.

As the Opry suffered through the mid-1950s and the on-slaughts of television and rock and roll, Flatt and Scruggs used the new medium to go out and capture a tremendous following, mean-while playing schoolhouse dates in every area in which they were appearing on television.

"I know the Opry people were really hurting at the time, but we did some of our best business while rock and roll was at its peak," Flatt recalls.

"TV was hot, and rock and roll was hot, and it just about shut radio out."

WSM's leaders soon had a change of heart. More accurately, it must have been a change of mind.

"The mail started coming in," Cohen Williams remembers. "WSM always paid a lot of attention to that. So I got together a great big sack of it one day and went up there. Finally, they agreed to put them on the Opry."

That was in 1955. There was no wholesale throwing open of arms. The other Opry acts treated the newcomers pretty coldly, "steering around us as if we was a bunch of outlaws," Flatt says amusedly now. "But after we was there a few weeks things changed, and they started coming around and patting us on the shoulder."

Not everything changed, however, even then. Dee Kilpatrick remembers that although they were known far and wide as the down-home diplomats of Martha White Flour, they were not permitted to emcee the Martha White portion of the Opry until Kilpatrick took over as general manager. Monroe, their former boss, remained implacably opposed to them, declining even to speak to them. The atmosphere between the bluegrass patriarch and his two former assistants became so unpleasant that Kilpatrick refuses to discuss it even today.

The role of television in the dramatic national rise of Flatt and Scruggs was probably considerably more important than their own intricate musicianship.

In their bus, emblazoned with the name of the advertiser they made famous, Flatt, Scruggs, and their Foggy Mountain Boys prepare to depart on a tour

Foggy Mountain Boy Josh Graves is featured on the dobro guitar in this picture from the early days of the Flatt and Scruggs television show

The first Martha White television shows filled the same kind of need on television that the Opry filled in 1925 on radio, but on a larger scale. In addition to making Flatt and Scruggs idols of the traditional country music audiences in the cities in which they were carried, these shows also entered the homes of many more sophisticated Southerners who would probably never have gone out to see a live performance—at least at first.

When videotape came into general use in the late fifties, Cohen Williams syndicated the show in many more cities, multiplying the original viewing audience.

Almost simultaneously, fanned by the popularity of such pop-folk groups as the Kingston Trio, an intense interest in folk music began to sweep the nation's college campuses, perhaps in reaction to the immature teeny-boppery expressed by early rock and roll. The syndicated television exposure of Flatt and Scruggs allowed them to be compared with the popular New York and West Coast folk imitators, and the comparison made them instantly recognizable as authentic.

Dee Kilpatrick, who marketed some of the early Flatt and Scruggs recordings when he was working for Mercury Records, thinks he knows when the college craze for bluegrass began. Kilpatrick, manager of the Opry then, received a telephone call from Louise Scruggs, Earl's wife, who was handling the books for the troupe.

"She said Davidson College over in North Carolina had called and wanted to schedule them for a performance on the campus, and she wanted to know whether they should do it," he says.

"I said, 'What do you mean, *whether?*' She said, 'Well, we don't want anybody laughing at us.' I said, 'Laughing at you? They're not going to laugh at you.' She said. 'Well, what should I ask?' In those days, $500 for an appearance was a real big lick to them, but I said, 'Twelve and a half.' She said, 'Why, they'll never buy that.' I said, 'You keep on fooling with me, and I'm going to tell you fifteen.'

"I believe she wound up getting thirteen, and the news traveled fast. It wasn't three months until they were over at Duke University. Then, before long, that *Esquire Magazine* article came out on them."

The *Esquire Magazine* article, written by the prestigious folklorist Alan Lomax, appeared in late 1959 and formally established their reputation with a college crowd that had never given any serious attention to ordinary country music. In December 1962 they played Carnegie Hall, although not without a little concern.

The Earl Scruggs Revue, the new group formed by Scruggs. To his left is his son Randy. To his right, in blue jeans, is son Gary

"Dorothy Kilgallen, who was one of the critics in New York then, put a write-up in the paper the morning of the day of our show," Flatt remembers.

"In it she said something about 'the hicks from the sticks are coming to town, and this is to warn you in time to get out.' But that night we had a hall full of people who evidently hadn't got the word."

When they went onstage that night, they did so under the added pressure of knowing that the concert was being recorded. There turned out to be no cause for worry. The audience reaction went far beyond anybody's wildest hopes, becoming more and more enthusiastic as the performance went on. One zealot began to shout for them to sing the Martha White commercial jingle that they did regularly on their radio and television shows. Others took up the cry, and halfway through the performance Flatt finally consented to sing it. It received a tremendous ovation, and Flatt said after the show that he would have done it earlier had he not suspected that it was Cohen Williams who started the hollering.

By this time, Williams was selling flour all over the South and even outside its borders. And he was doing it through good times and bad times .

One night Earl Scruggs got word that a relative had had a heart attack, and he and Louise left immediately for North Carolina, Scruggs's birthplace. On the curving roads through the Smoky Mountains they became involved in a head-on crash that broke both of Scruggs's hips. The news was on radio and television the next morning, and Lester Flatt reached Cohen Williams's office not long after Williams did. He told Williams sadly that he guessed the band was going to have to quit.

"I said, '*You* might quit, but *I* ain't going to quit selling flour, and you don't *have* to quit, either,'" Williams recalls.

"Lester said, 'What do you mean?' I said, 'Get you another banjo picker and go right on.' So he did, and we went on TV and told the folks all about old Earl's accident. We said, 'Pore old Earl's laying up there in that hospital, and we want all you folks to write to him.' Why, in a couple of days we had to take Earl's mail out there to him in a truck, and we sold more flour on the strength of him being sick than we did with him well.

"A little bit later, Lester had a heart attack that was going to lay him up about two months. Earl wanted to quit, but I told him, 'No, just get you another emcee, and go right on.' We did. This time we went on TV and told the folks about pore old *Lester* laying up there in the hospital, and this time we had to take *Lester's* mail out there to him in a truck."

Williams often says that Flatt and Scruggs and the Grand Ole Opry built his Martha White Mills. That is probably accurate, but by shrewdly merchandising the Flatt and Scruggs phenomenon he more than returned WSM any favors it had done him.

Carrying the name of the Opry with them, Flatt and Scruggs scaled dizzying heights in the early sixties. They were worshiped by such vaunted publications as the *New York Times, Saturday Review,*

Here Flatt plays with the Nashville Grass, the group he formed after he and Scruggs dissolved their long partnership

and *Time.* They played the theme song of the CBS network's Beverly Hillbillies television show and even appeared on some of its episodes.

But as they turned more and more away from traditionalism, an increasing number of folk music authorities and fans began to raise their voices in protest, contending that Flatt and Scruggs had not been the true leaders of bluegrass, that most of the credit belonged to Bill Monroe. Still, the role of Flatt, Scruggs, and their Foggy Mountain Boys in creating a climate for the resurgence of the Grand Ole Opry and the birth of a truly national popularity for bluegrass in the 1960s was highly important. They had probably done more than anyone else to forge a new, urban, intellectual popularity for an old, rural, working-class music.

In 1969 Flatt and Scruggs broke up their partnership, Scruggs and his sons going into pop music while Flatt returned to bluegrass to go it alone.

BARBARA MANDRELL

THE WOMEN

DOTTIE WEST

Johnny Wright, Kitty Wells's husband, today

As far as the hillbilly record business was concerned, before 1952 women were the primary source of the blessings or afflictions that male hillbilly stars sang about, but that was about all. The principal subjects of hillbilly song, women were people to be loved (sweethearts, mothers, or wives), complained about (wives or sweethearts), scorned (all others), or wary of (all the above). Sometimes they could add some visual appeal or comedy to the live performances of the male stars, but they were not supposed to aspire to singing stardom for themselves.

In early 1952, however, on a trip to California, Dee Kilpatrick, then with Mercury Records, signed a teen-age female drummer to a recording contract. His superiors were not particularly enthusiastic.

"What do you want to fool with girl hillbillies for, Dee?" asked Art Talmadge, a top Mercury executive and a friend. "Girl hillbillies don't sell. Everybody knows that."

"They don't sell because we don't know how to sell them," Kilpatrick responded. "The reason we don't know how to sell them is because the hillbilly record business has been too long dominated by men. If you just got one girl singer really started, look at the business she'd do, just because there wouldn't be any competition."

Talmadge was not convinced by Kilpatrick's reasoning, and he continued to argue until Kilpatrick became angry.

"If you don't like what I've done about this, I'll tell you what we can do," he said abruptly. He tore the newly signed contract into little pieces, threw it into Talmadge's lap, and walked out of the room. The little female drummer, an Oklahoma-born and California-raised high school student named Jean Shepard, would have to find another recording label to be born on.

Talmadge's opinion looks ridiculous today, but at the time it was shared by every executive of every major recording company.

In 1949, RCA had recorded eight songs by Kitty Wells, the wife of hillbilly singer Johnny Wright of the Johnny and Jack team. The songs were all religious or semireligious, and RCA later apparently had second thoughts about having recorded them at all. None of the records were ever distributed.

"Maybe the distributors and record stores were afraid of a girl singer then," Mrs. Wright says now.

"And maybe RCA didn't really push much, because a woman had never been really popular. There were only a couple of girl artists who had any reputation then. Patsy Montana sang Western songs. Molly O'Day was the only one who sang country music, and she never was nationally popular."

The hillbilly record buyers of the day seem to have been considerably more open-minded on the subject than the record companies were. Mrs. Wright recalls that a disc jockey in New Jersey managed to get one of those 1949 recordings and started playing it on the air. The song was called "How Far Is Heaven?" a mournful piece about a child asking directions to the place she has been told her parents have gone. Sung in the unforgettable Wells lilting wail, it must have been particularly striking. RCA received letters from New Jerseyans asking how they might buy it, she says, but nothing came of it.

Kitty Wells, known for years as the "Queen of Country Music,"
was the Opry's first great female recording star

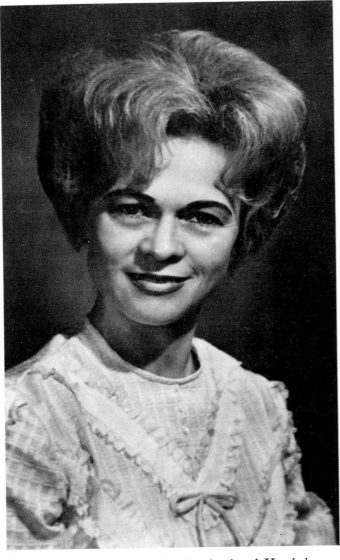

ABOVE: Jean Shepard with her late husband, Hawkshaw Hawkins, and their baby. BELOW: Jean Shepard in the 1960s

Johnny Wright believed in his wife's potential popularity. He had seen how the audience responded to her frequent appearances, primarily as a gospel singer, with the Johnny and Jack troupe.

"I used to see Johnny down at the Ernest Tubb Record Shop on many a Saturday night during the early 1950s," Dee Kilpatrick recalls. "He'd preach to me, 'Sign my wife, sign my wife.' Johnny had it figured out a long time before anybody else did."

With Wright, it was simply a musical certainty: he knew his wife had a powerful, highly appealing voice. With Kilpatrick, it seems to have been an even more elementary, logical matter of supply and demand. He explains the large number of very popular female singers on the Opry today:

"There's just as many boy hillbilly fans as there are girl hillbilly fans. It used to be that the old girl would say to her old man, 'Let's go to the Opry,' and he'd go reluctantly, because all he was going to get to listen to was old hairy-legged Ray Price, Roy Acuff, Marty Robbins, and so on. But when it got to where these boy hillbilly fans could go and hear Kitty sing a love ballad, and Jean Shepard, why naturally they were a lot more eager to go."

There had been women on the Opry, of course, ever since Alcyone Beasley played piano for the Possum Hunters with her father and Eva Thompson Jones accompanied her Uncle Jimmy Thompson. But their roles had been mostly peripheral. The star system that began to develop in the early forties did not really include them, because it was based on record sales more than anything else.

Kitty Wells was the first to really make it into the center of the hillbilly music business. It happened as the result of a gimmick.

Johnny and Jack rejoined the Opry in 1952 after having been members briefly in 1947, and Kitty, one of the few country singers who was born a Nashvillian, was home again washing dishes and keeping house. When a Hank Thompson recording on Capitol called "Wild Side of Life" began to look like a huge hit, Decca—Johnny and Jack's label—asked Kitty to record an "answer" to the Thompson song.

While Decca was recording Kitty, Hank Thompson was persuading Capitol to ignore tradition and sign the little girl drummer whose Mercury contract had wound up in small pieces in Art Talmadge's lap. Thompson had once headlined a show in California on which Jean Shepard's all-girl band had appeared, and he had been impressed with the clarity of her voice and her enunciation.

Suddenly Decca released "It Wasn't God Who Made Honky-tonk Angels," the "answer" to "Wild Side of Life." Sung in a high, forceful, lilting quaver, the recording sounded as if it had been made by a female Acuff. It was so striking that, flying in the face of all the previous theories about female hillbilly records, it quickly became the top song in hillbilly music, and led the way for many other female hillbilly classics. The next one was Jean Shepard's "The Dear John Letter," on which she was aided by a Ferlin Husky monologue.

"Dear John," hitting home to countless families with betrothed men overseas in the Korean War, stayed in the top spot in the hillbilly music popularity polls for twenty-eight weeks. Jean

OPPOSITE PAGE: Jean Shepard, now the matriarch of the Opry's female vocalists, quickly followed Kitty Wells to the top of the music popularity charts

In a short career abbreviated by an untimely death, Patsy Cline became one of the most influential stylists in country music history

Shepard cites an example of the Opry's influence on the charts at that time. "Carl Smith, who was on the Opry then, put out a song called 'Hey Joe,' which went to Number One and dropped us down to Number Two after twenty-six weeks," she says.

"Then Ferlin and I came in and did a guest appearance on the Prince Albert Show with Carl, and the next week we jumped back up to Number One. We stayed there two more weeks."

Kitty Wells reigned as the "queen of country music" for the next decade, recording a score of Number One songs. Jean Shepard, although not as prominent as Kitty, remained consistently popular. Since Kitty's husband already was a member of the Opry, it was a simple matter to add her to the roster in 1952. That same year Martha Carson, a gospel singer, joined. Jean Shepard became a member in 1955. The role of the country female vocalist was rather specialized and confined at first. The few songs that dealt with illicit love, like Kitty's "Back Street Affair," were characterized by an attitude of the deepest shame. No extenuating circumstances were even hinted. Jean Shepard was not allowed to do such songs at all.

"Capitol wouldn't let me do a triangle song unless I was on the right side of the triangle," she remembers. "I could only be the wife who was being cheated on. They said anything else wouldn't fit my image."

A woman's song was supposed to cast her in the long-suffering, motherly, wholesome role country fans of both sexes expected of wives. Woman's assigned lot was to endure, and if possible ennoble, man's cussedness.

The singers themselves, raised on this philosophy, did not struggle hard against it. Jean Shepard, for instance, remains a staunch believer in male superiority.

"The women's lib thing really doesn't turn me on," she confesses. "I can't stand for a woman to come up and say, 'I can do anything a man can do.' Maybe mentally she can, but I think it's still kind of a man's world and, to be frank, I kind of like it that way. I'd never like to see a woman president, for instance. A woman's too high-strung for that kind of job."

Two significant style-setting changes in women's country music were made at the beginning of the more sophisticated sixties.

First, Patsy Cline, a singer with a powerful voice who became a star after winning an Arthur Godfrey Talent Scouts contest, showed that country girls could sing songs in a smoother, more pop-oriented style and sell to both country and pop audiences.

Joining the Opry in the early sixties, she recorded such hits as "I Fall to Pieces" and "Walkin' after Midnight," and they briefly made her the leading female country vocalist in America before she died in an airplane crash. In 1962 most of the trade magazines voted her the "outstanding female country vocalist" of the year.

Patsy Cline's place in the forefront was taken immediately by a close friend whose approach to music was the opposite of hers. Loretta Lynn sang in the traditional, unrestrained style of Kitty Wells —but with some important lyrical modifications.

Loretta, a Kentucky coal miner's daughter, began her singing career in a Custer, Washington, Grange hall one evening when her husband Mooney, a rodeo rider, got up before an amateur-night crowd and announced that his wife could "out-sing any girl singer besides Kitty Wells."

Still a teen-ager then, at not quite fourteen Loretta had married Mooney, a twenty-five-year-old fellow mountaineer who had returned to the remote coal country around Van Lear, Kentucky, after serving a hitch in the Army. They met at a grammar school pie supper, a fundraising event at which pupils sold various dishes they had cooked.

The ex-serviceman became interested enough in Loretta to buy a pie she had baked. That pie was certainly enough to discourage all but the most dedicated admirer.

"I made a mistake," she remembers. "I put salt in it instead of sugar." Mooney Lynn was not deterred. He married Loretta Wells and eventually took her off to Custer, Washington.

After pushing her out in front of the Grange hall crowd that night, Mooney did everything he knew how to help Loretta get a recording contract, and after she got one with a small West Coast company he started driving her on long trips to radio stations to promote her recording. When the record made it into the country top ten, Loretta and Mooney made it to Decca Records and Nashville, where Loretta bought her first pair of high-heeled shoes.

Having seen a lot of life early, Loretta refused to be cowed by the limitations country music had traditionally placed on women. A recent recording titled "The Pill," in which she unabashedly and humorously describes a wife's liberation through birth control, illustrates her pet technique of approaching revolutionary subjects with a completely traditional style. The many songs she composes are written in the forthright, impassioned, and sometimes laconically humorous style she sings in. The coalminer-sharecropper-proletarian reality they convey had never really been examined by a female singer until she came along.

Loretta joined the Opry in 1962 and quickly became the most consistently prominent female star in her field. Her picture has adorned the cover of national news magazines. She was the first female Opry star to lead her own major troupe on the road, Kitty Wells having always traveled with the Johnny Wright troupe and Jean Shepard having worked mainly as a single up to then.

Jean Shepard thinks Loretta was aided by a change in the times. The sixties, she points out, were not nearly as naive as the fifties.

"People had become more broad-minded," Jean says.

"If a woman had sung a song like Loretta's 'Don't Come Home A-Drinkin' (With Lovin' on Your Mind)' twenty years ago, she'd have been taken out and tarred and feathered."

In songs like "Don't Come Home A-Drinkin'" and "You Ain't Woman Enough (To Take My Man)," Loretta Lynn made an important contribution to the image and the confidence of the country girl. Those songs and others like them that she wrote reflected her inclination to fight for her rights rather than meekly accept her lot.

Martha Carson was primarily a gospel singer in her days on the Opry

Carol Lee Cooper, daughter of Wilma Lee and Stoney

OPPOSITE PAGE: Loretta Lynn became the new queen
of country singers in the 1960s

Wilma Lee Cooper is one of the Opry's mos
staunchly traditional singers of Appalachia
mountain music. With her here are daughte
Carol and husband Stoney, leader of their grou
the Clinch Mountain Cla

The Opry today seems almost evenly divided between traditionalists like Loretta Lynn, who have followed the general pattern set by Kitty Wells and Jean Shepard, and more pop-influenced stylists who seem to be spiritual descendants of Patsy Cline.

The most traditional of all is Wilma Lee Cooper, the raven-haired West Virginian who still wears crinoline skirts and spike heels and performs authentic mountain ballads and hymns. Deep gospel roots are strongly evident in her repertoire. One of the Opry's genuine folk singers, she and her husband Stoney and their Clinch Mountain Clan rely heavily on old songs of the Appalachian Mountains and the fundamentalist churches of the hill country. They have appeared in recent years on such prestigious folk music forums as the National Festival of Folk Life and other programs of the Smithsonian Institution in Washington, D.C.

In these appearances, Wilma Lee was retracing steps she first took as a little girl in 1938, when she sang with her family on a national folk music festival sponsored by Mrs. Eleanor Roosevelt. Her family, headed by deep-voiced Jake Leary, sang gospel music. She recalls that local contests were held throughout West Virginia in 1938 to pick the performers who would represent the state at Mrs. Roosevelt's festival.

"My mother and dad and us three girls entered the one for our area, the Tygart Valley section near Elkins," she says. "We won that one, and then they brought all the winners to a state contest in a theater in Elkins. We won that one, too."

Together with winners from other states, the Learys went to Washington.

"We sang for a whole week, it seemed like," Wilma Lee recalls. "We sang at the Lincoln Memorial one day, I think, and then at an auditorium one night, and then they finally got us in a room and we recorded all one day for the Library of Congress."

She has never heard any of the recordings they made in that memorable week of her childhood. "They sent my parents some forms to fill out to get a copy of it, but they never did," she says.

Most of the recordings that Wilma Lee and Stoney have made together are to be found in the music library of Harvard University.

A younger stylist who also has been heavily influenced by authentic rural tradition is buxom Dolly Parton, a vivacious Tennessee mountain girl who wears mountainous piles of hair and gaudy clothes that accentuate her considerable physical charms. In the resultant glitter, one sometimes forgets that she is a prodigiously talented singer-songwriter who possesses a background fully as homespun and fundamentalist as that of Wilma Lee Cooper.

The fourth of a dozen children born to the family of a mountain-farmer-turned-construction-worker, Dolly says her first memories are of a farm of several hundred acres "back in the Smoky Mountains at a place that was called Webb's Mountain." Her family moved there when she was three and stayed, "raising crops and animals mainly just for our own survival, rather than to sell," for about five years. They moved another time or two in her childhood before finally

Dolly Parton developed much of the power of her style in a Smoky Mountain congregation of the fundamentalist Church of God

settling in the tiny Caton's Chapel community, a few miles from Webb's Mountain and the county seat town of Sevierville. Her raising was straightlaced. A grandfather was a backwoods minister who, according to a lyric she and a relative later wrote, "preached hell so hot that you could feel the heat."

"I was brought up in the Church of God, which is the church where they shout and sing and everything, which I love," she said in 1971. "I always loved to sing in church. When you get to singing those old gospel songs and get that good spiritual feeling, well, there's just nothing else like it."

Her voice and style have retained the powerful sense of sincerity and goodwill that are primary traits of noncommercial gospel music. Dolly sang a few times in school assemblies, and several more times on a Knoxville early morning country music television program. On the morning after her graduation from high school in 1964 she boarded a Grayhound bus for Nashville. She was to live with an uncle there for five months, until she began to make herself a place in the music business.

She met her future husband a few hours after she got there. She had gone to a laundromat with the dirty clothes she had hastily packed in Caton's Chapel. "I got me a big RC Cola," she remembered, laughing, in the 1971 interview, "and while my clothes were washing I just went out walking down the sidewalk to see Nashville. While I was walking down the street, this boy came by in this white Chevrolet. He flirted, and being fresh from the country—well, up where I come from everybody was friendly to everybody because everybody was friends, and I didn't know that you just couldn't do that anywhere." So she waved to him.

The Chevrolet passed her a couple of times more before the young man parked the car and got out to talk. "Where you from?" he asked. "I told him I was from Knoxville. I didn't figure he'd know where Sevierville was."

She and the young man in the Chevrolet, Carl Dean, a partner in his father's asphalt-paving company, began to date several days later, after he had come by her uncle's house several times to talk with her. The first time they went out he took her to meet his parents, she says, and they were married two years later, after Carl had served a hitch in the military.

While he was away, Dolly did not eat very regularly. She had signed a contract with Monument Records and Combine Music, and moved into an extremely modest apartment of her own, after staying with her uncle's family for about six months.

Speaking about those days she said, laughingly, "I couldn't afford a car or a telephone, and about the only time I ever ate was when I went out on a date, and I didn't go out on that many dates." She stopped laughing pretty quickly. "Actually, that was really about the way it was."

Recording demonstration records for songwriters to pitch to successful singers and writing songs for a small weekly salary from a Nashville publishing company, she made her first mark as a singer

with a song ironically titled "Dumb Blonde." Porter Wagoner eventually invited her to be a regular on his nationally syndicated television show, on which she stayed for several years. Now she tours with her own band and is becoming known as one of the most prolific and professional lyricists in Nashville, writing distinctively simple, fresh songs that are being recorded by many pop vocalists as well as country singers.

Jeanne Pruett, one of the newer Opry members, is another of the stars most noticeably influenced by older country music styles. A onetime Alabama farm girl, she became a star with the song "Satin Sheets," a traditional-sounding lyric about a country girl who marries a rich man but finds no solace in the luxuries he substitutes for love.

Smoother, more crafted styles show a softer touch and sometimes an obvious attempt to relate more to the younger fans. Perhaps the most dramatic current example of such a style on the Opry is that of Barbara Mandrell, the diminutive platinum-blonde Texan whose music often employs the frenetic beat of rock and roll and whose lyrics sometimes confess explicit infidelities that more traditional country singers would have thought it unseemly to discuss.

Dottie West, a smooth-singing Middle Tennessee farm girl who became a country star in 1964 with the soft ballad "Here Comes My Baby Back Again," became a national force on radio and network television in 1971 when she became the first country singer to do national advertising jingles for Coca-Cola.

"Her voice is very warm—that's what struck me when she first was brought to my attention," says Billy Davis, a New York ad man with the McCann-Erickson Advertising Agency. "She comes off as very sincere. You believe her. I was looking for somebody who had a believable sound and was currently successful and had enough songwriting ability to be able to write or co-write commercials for us."

Dottie, who has written hundreds of songs, was sufficiently multidimensional for the job. She says that writing Coke commercials is not radically different from writing country songs.

"I just write them happy," she says. "Most of the songs I sing are ballads. When I'm trying to write Coke commercials I just try to think of the happiest thing I can think of, and write about that."

The commercials, which she sometimes rewrites into country hits, are filled with images of daisies, country sunshine, and green grass.

There are many other female Opry stars whose styles exhibit considerable popular influence. Jeannie Seely, a Pennsylvania-born former secretary, joined the Opry in the mid-sixties on the strength of the sensuous ballad "Don't Touch Me." Native Kentuckian Skeeter Davis had such pop-style hits as "The End of the World" and "Last Date" after joining the Opry in the late fifties. Marion Worth came to the Opry from her hometown of Birmingham in 1963 and sang the national hit, "Shake Me, I Rattle (Squeeze Me, I Cry)." Jan Howard, a native Missourian who got her first experience by doing intricate background vocal work on some recordings by Johnny Cash, went on to write and sing such hits of her own as "My Son," written about a child of hers who died in Vietnam. Connie Smith became an overnight star in 1964 with her first recording, "Once a Day."

Jeanne Pruett is one of the Opry's newer female sta

Barbara Mandrell, a diminutive Texan with a fast-growing reputation

ABOVE: Dottie West, a former farm girl among many former farm girls on the Opry, has most successfully capitalized on the "country girl" image. RIGHT: McCann-Erickson advertising executive Billy Davis, left, and Dottie West receive an American Society of Composers, Authors, and Publishers award for "Country Sunshine," a hit that doubled as a national commercial for Coca-Cola. At right is Nashville ASCAP official Charlie Monk

Jeannie Seely

Jeannie Seely and Jack Greene

272

Jan Howard got her early training doing vocal
background work on recordings by Johnny Cash

Skeeter Davis, a Kentucky-born country girl, recorded pop hits in the early sixties

Marion Worth came to the Opry from Birmingham in 1963

The backgrounds of both Patsy Cline followers and Kitty Wells followers seem about the same. They range from lower-middle-class to poor. "One thing I always dreamed of, from childhood on, was someday to be able to have on everything new, from my shoes up, at the same time," Connie Smith says.

Connie Smith was born in Indiana, the daughter of a carpenter. Her family moved to West Virginia when she was five months old, and then to southeastern Ohio when she was ten. After her father's death, her mother married a bulldozer operator, and there were sixteen in her family in all. On the occasions when the family had a radio, she would listen to the Grand Ole Opry. When they got a television, while she was in high school, the first thing she watched on it was the Martha White show of Flatt and Scruggs.

Like Jean Shepard, but for somewhat different reasons, she believes there are things men can do better than women. She was dramatically "converted" to Christianity seven years ago, and admits to being a religious fanatic.

"I wouldn't want to compete with a man because from the Bible I'd lose, because God created woman for man," she says. She thinks men and women were created not equal but, rather, "equivalent," with the various strengths and weaknesses of the one offsetting the different strengths and weaknesses of the other. "A man can do a lot of things," she says, "but he can't have a baby."

She points out that there is slightly different treatment of men and women by the management of the Opry. Men usually host the various segments of the show, and women usually appear on them rather than hosting segments of their own. But the warmest introductions are always reserved for the women, she says.

Connie agrees with Dee Kilpatrick's observation that men have a natural liking for female performers. She says Pearl Butler, who with her husband Carl was a member of the Opry in the early sixties, once warned her that a female performer's potential enemies in an audience are her fellow women:

" 'You worry about pleasing the women,' she told me. 'You've already got the men on your side because you're a woman.' "

From her earliest recordings the small, strong-voiced singer has sounded influenced by the style of Patsy Cline. If she actually was, however, it must have been subconscious, because her favorite female singer is Loretta Lynn. Connie does not think any female country singer sounds like any other, and, like most of her feminine colleagues on the Opry, she considers herself completely country.

Any categorizing is quite arbitrary, and most of the singers in either category exhibit some attributes of the other. None of them is more of a hybrid, however, than Tammy Wynette, an Opry member since 1973.

Miss Wynette, a former hairdresser born in Red Bay, Alabama, deals with such traditional country themes as divorce and family problems. Although her enunciation is plainly country, she packages her songs as popularly as if they were television daytime

Connie Smith with two of her children

OPPOSITE: Connie Smith came from a family of sixteen. When her family bought a television set in the late fifties, the first show she recalls watching on it was Lester Flatt and Earl Scruggs

276

ABOVE: Tammy Wynette singing a
duet with George Jones before their
divorce in early 1975. RIGHT: A
pensive Tammy Wynette, singer of
dozens of songs about the institutions
of marriage and motherhood, watches
her children at play

278

drama, treating her themes in explicit but at the same time softly emotional terms.

A lot of the credit for her brilliant fusing of pop and country elements seems to be due her producer at Columbia-Epic Records, Billy Sherrill.

Sherrill is a handsomely rewarded advocate of the American Woman, who is clearly the target of every recording he produces, every song he writes. Neither coddling nor condescending, he talks to her the way a woman's magazine would, but in fewer words and with a bit more lyricism. His songs, like "I Don't Wanta Play House," "Good Lovin'," "Bedtime Story," and "Stand by Your Man," are not sweet. But they are feminine.

"Tammy speaks for every woman who's been kicked in the ass all her life," Sherrill says of his star.

"Not too long ago, somebody made a survey and found that the biggest buyers of country music are women between twenty and thirty years old. These are the kind of people who most especially identify with Tammy. They listen to her and say, 'That's me.'"

It is little wonder.

Tammy Wynette began the apprenticeship for her career in some Alabama and Mississippi cottonfields. She managed to extricate herself from the rigors of this life by enrolling in a Tupelo, Mississippi, "beauty school" and by a teen-age marriage that produced three children in as many years.

Divorcing her first husband by the time she was twenty, she took her three daughters to a government housing project in Birmingham, married a second time, and eventually made her way to Nashville, where she showed up late one afternoon in a torn sweater in the doorway of the office of Billy Sherrill, head of production for Columbia-Epic Records in Nashville. Sherrill decided to give her a chance, although it was not because he thought she would ever become a star. Actually, he says, he felt sort of sorry for her.

People have been feeling sorry for Tammy Wynette ever since, with less and less reason. George Jones physically took her away from the shambles of her second marriage, spirited her off to Mexico and married her himself. Together they became one of country music's most prominent touring acts, surviving a sometimes troubled marriage of their own until Tammy finally sued for divorce at the end of 1974.

Most of her life has been a succession of confrontations with the commonest problems of girls from unprosperous backgrounds who must scramble for survival in what is for them a man's world, enduring bad marriages—for a while, at least—and grasping for whatever honest means of income seem within their reach. Tammy Wynette first became a hairdresser and finally a country singer. Both seem like glamour jobs to young girls.

In the more than two decades of big-time female country music, there have been many small changes. For example, in "Poor Sweet Baby" in 1974, Jean Shepard finally got to do a "triangle song" in which she was on the "wrong side." Kitty Wells has recently experimented a little with pop sounds.

But perhaps the most striking thing about nearly twenty-five years of female country music is the seeming lack of really substantive change. The lyrics are much more explicit, but most of the things they say are still about the same.

Things like the belief that love and marriage remain fifty-fifty propositions. Cheating is wrong for woman or man, and the way to hang onto your partner is to care more about him than you do about yourself. Beware of the other woman. If you *are* the other woman, resolve never to act like the evil wife who made your beloved turn to you. Home and children are still the most important things, even if a marriage cannot always be kept together.

Probably the reason why the substance of women's country music has not changed very much is because the basic attitudes of the women to whom the Opry and its female singers appeal have not changed very much. Most of them are not really liberated yet, nor do they care to be.

"I'd a lot rather have somebody brag on my supper than my new record," Connie Smith says.

The others, most of them more career-oriented and less church-oriented than Connie, might not agree with her completely on that. But they would be careful about mentioning it around their fans.

MARION WORTH

TRIUMPH AND TRAGEDY

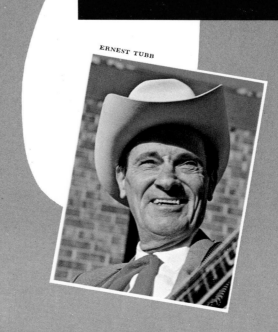

ERNEST TUBB

Television heralded a new age radically different from the radio era in which the Opry had become famous. The flood of new music businesses that began to inundate Nashville during the fifties made the country music scene much too big to be controlled by any single organization, however large and influential. In addition, the question of conflict of interest became so acute for WSM employees who wanted to be active in the music business that a number of them—like Jim Denny and Jack Stapp—left the station.

The industry the Opry had fostered was outgrowing its parent. Although most of the leaders of the Nashville music community were WSM-trained, and many felt real affection for their old employer, by the late fifties the Opry was becoming just one of many music businesses competing for attention on the Nashville scene. Sometimes, though, it received more attention than it cared for.

At five o'clock one Monday morning in the spring of 1957, Jack DeWitt was awakened by a telephone call from Bill Williams, then a WSM announcer and now the highly respected Nashville editor of *The Billboard* magazine. Williams said he was in the lobby of the National Life Building, on his way upstairs to go to work.

"Bill said, 'Jack, we've got a very serious situation down here,'" DeWitt recalls.

"I said, 'What is it?'

"He said, 'Ernest Tubb has just shot up the lobby.'

"I said, 'Oh, for God's sake!' He asked me what to do, and I said, 'Well, you've got to get Ernest home.' He said, 'Oh, it's too late for that—the police are already here.'"

Today, Williams recalls that he had just walked into the lobby of the National Life Building to go to work when a shot from a .357 Magnum pistol was fired over his head. Badly frightened, he turned and saw Tubb and shouted, "Ernest, what are you doing?" All he can remember Tubb answering is, "My God, I've shot the wrong man."

An engineer already on duty upstairs in the WSM studios called the police as soon as he heard the shot, Williams says, and they arrived almost immediately. Tubb told them he had talked on the telephone with a man whom he refused to identify, and that the man had threatened to kill him and said he would meet him here for a shootout.

Williams called DeWitt, meanwhile, and thus it came about that the man who had been shot at wound up shepherding his assailant away from the city jail a few hours later. While Williams waited for him to complete the mandatory three hours incarceration for public drunkenness, Tubb bought cigarettes for the other inmates and sang to and with them, Williams recalls.

Even after he took Tubb home, however, Williams did not learn why Tubb had shot at him. He told curious reporters for the *Banner* and the *Tennessean* that he still had nothing against Tubb. The newspapers carried front-page stories for a couple of days, but Tubb never divulged any more information about the incident and the story soon died.

Ernest Tubb today

Needless to say, the incident in the National Life lobby was out of character for Ernest Tubb. Now—and even then—one of the Opry's revered giants, Tubb was the fourth to arrive of the historic major stars who remain on the show today (the others being Roy Acuff, Bill Monroe, and Minnie Pearl).

Elected to the exclusive Country Music Hall of Fame in 1965, Tubb has had one of the most influential roles in the development of the Opry and of country music. By using the electric guitar on the Opry, he made the instrument an accepted part of country—as opposed to Western—music in the early forties, and in 1947 he became the first Opry singer to set foot on the stage of Carnegie Hall in New York City. He is also known as one of the most selfless of stars, credited with giving help to dozens of young competitors-to-be, including Hank Williams, Hank Snow, and Jack Greene. For some three decades the "midnight show" from his famous Nashville record shop has been an important and popular adjunct to the Saturday-night broadcasts of the Opry.

Years later, Williams says, Jim Denny told him that it had been he, Denny, who was on the telephone with Tubb that night.

"He said it had resulted from one of those classic bad bookings that every performer and talent manager get involved in every once in a while," Williams goes on. "Ernest had come back from it drunk and mad and had called up Denny. Jim said he finally had told Ernest to meet him in front of the National Life Building at 4:30 or so, thinking that Ernest would show up and then get tired of waiting and go home. He had forgotten that some of us would be coming to work early in the morning."

Feelings between DeWitt and Denny ran so high that to this day DeWitt actually believes that Denny engineered this incident to embarrass him and the Opry.

In the years after Denny left, DeWitt continued and perhaps even intensified his policy of separating WSM from outside interests.

"We got pretty tough about it," he acknowledges.

"When performers would go out and form a company and say they were members of the Grand Ole Opry, we'd track them down and threaten to sue them if they weren't. We made rules that they had to be on the Opry a certain number of Saturday nights to be members of the show. We were delighted for them to go out on the road and make money, but we didn't want them to be out there all the time. We couldn't afford to pay them what they could make out there—all we could pay them was regular musicians' scale. But for appearing on the Opry we felt we were giving them something very valuable in return; the right to say they were *from* the Opry."

This exchange was not considered particularly favorable by some of the younger performers, who had no reason to feel a loyalty to the Opry. Young Johnny Cash, for instance, quit after a year because he could get $350 a night on the road and did not like having to come back to Nashville on weekends for perhaps one-tenth of that.

Cash was not the only one.

In 1964, front-page stories in local newspapers reported that a dozen Opry acts had been dropped from the show's roster because they had not appeared twenty-six weekends during the previous twelve months. Those dropped included some of the Opry's most prominent performers: Kitty Wells, Johnny Wright, Faron Young, Ray Price, Don Gibson, Ferlin Husky, Stonewall Jackson, Carl and Pearl Butler, the Jordanaires, George Morgan, Billy Grammer, and Justin Tubb. WSM announced at the same time that the Opry was reducing the number of required appearances to twenty, and that several of the suspended stars had indicated they wanted to be reinstated and would make the required number of appearances during the next twelve-month period.

Down at the Ryman, things were still changing, sometimes without smooth transition. After Dee Kilpatrick's brief reign in the late fifties he was succeeded by Ott Devine, an announcer who had substituted for Jack Stapp in running the Opry when Stapp was overseas in World War II. Devine quickly countermanded Kilpatrick's policy and returned snare drums to the stage. He also instituted the policy of using a spotlight to focus more attention on the star or group who was performing, separating them from the rest of the milling mass of people on the stage. In making these changes, Devine says now, he was "not necessarily" trying to fight the influence of rock and roll but, rather, was "just trying to improve the status of the Opry."

Devine did not regard the wholesale departure of some of the stars, following the tightening of rules about weekend appearances, as a great blow to the Opry.

"It didn't seem to be," Devine says. "Things just went on as usual, and we replaced those people with younger people."

The Opry did make replacements during the first half of the sixties, and many of them were younger—like Bobby Bare, Loretta Lynn, Jim Ed Brown, the Osborne Brothers, Jim and Jesse McReynolds, Ernie Ashworth, Bobby Lord, Bob Luman, Billy Walker, Marion Worth, LeRoy Van Dyke, Sonny James, Dottie West, and the Glaser Brothers. Not all were young, however. Tex Ritter, the old Hollywood cowboy star, came down to join the show, and the Willis Brothers, who had worked with Eddy Arnold as the Oklahoma Wranglers and served as Hank Williams's first recorded Drifting Cowboys, returned.

While the Opry was attempting to continue "as usual" at the Ryman, changes which would affect it were being made in other areas.

In the late fifties WSM was split into two organizations—radio and television. Longtime WSM employee Robert Cooper was put in charge of radio, which included the Opry. Irving Waugh was promoted from his sales directorship to head WSM Television, a promotion which removed him from any direct connection with the Opry.

From his distant vantage point, Waugh disagreed with much of the handling of the Opry. He felt that DeWitt's policies built up an antagonism in the music community that the station could ill afford, and he believed that such actions as the dropping of the dozen acts because of failure to appear was needlessly damaging, especially since some of the performers on the released list no longer considered themselves members of the show and had not appeared on it for eighteen months or more.

In his new position, Waugh was able to connect himself with one aspect of the Opry that seems to have contributed greatly to the show's resurgence in the later sixties. That was the placing of some of the Opry stars on regular television shows.

"The Opry has never been an innovative thing—it has always just followed trends," Waugh is fond of saying, and that seems to have been the case with syndicated television.

Of course, the real pioneer was Cohen Williams, whose Flatt and Scruggs show was a lesson, and an object of envy, to the industry. Its success assured that others would follow.

In the latter part of 1960 Bill Graham, enterprising and multitalented former WSM publicity writer, got into the country music television syndication business. A prospective client, the Chattanooga Medicine Company, wanted to sponsor a country music show that would star the most convincing advertiser of its products that it could find. Graham set about auditioning Opry stars, arranging with

Ott Devine as an announcer

Irving Waugh today

OVERLEAF:
LEFT ABOVE: Bobby Bare today
LEFT BELOW: The Osborne Brothers
—Bobby, left, and Sonny, center—
harmonize with one of their bandsmen
RIGHT ABOVE: Jim Ed Brown and the
Cates Sisters, who are part of his
roadshow. RIGHT BELOW: Loretta
Lynn in the mid-sixties

ABOVE: Jim, left, and Jesse McReynolds, with the energy of their hard-driving music showing in their faces. RIGHT: Ernie Ashworth singing at an Opry anniversary celebration a few years ago. OPPOSITE PAGE: Bobby Lord in 1972

Bob Luman, who came to the Opry from the Louisiana Hayride with a frenetic style influenced by rock and roll, has achieved his most recent successes with slower songs

Billy Walker at about the time he became a regular member of the Opry cast

roy Van Dyke

Sonny James, one of country music's most consistent record
sellers, was a member of the Opry during the sixties

ABOVE: From left, Skeeter, Guy, and Vic Willis with
Marion Worth in 1964. RIGHT: Dottie West with
Elvis Presley

RIGHT: The Glaser Brothers in the early sixties. From left, they are Jim, Chuck, and Tompall. BELOW: Former Western movie actor and long-time cowboy singer Tex Ritter came to Nashville from Hollywood in the sixties to join the Opry

"Nobody liked us but the people," Minnie Pearl says of the first Carnegie Hall performances by Opry groups. "We didn't get much press coverage, and what there was was not very complimentary. But I remember we got a pretty good response from the audience." Minnie performed on two shows at Carnegie Hall in 1947 with Texas Troubador Ernest Tubb, Dot and Smokey Swann, and some non-Opry talent, and in 1961 she returned as a member of a full Opry troupe that included Patsy Cline, Grandpa Jones, the Jordanaires, Bill Monroe, Jim Reeves, Marty Robbins, and Faron Young. In 1961 she was presented the keys to the city by Bob Watts, deputy commissioner of New York's department of commerce and public events (as an unidentified man at the center of the picture looks on) and was photographed on the steps of New York's City Hall with, from left, Grandpa Jones, Faron Young, Bill Monroe, and Patsy Cline. The late Jack Benny was first in line to buy tickets for the show. But playing America's most famous concert hall was a frustrating experience for Minnie each time she tried it. "Having wanted so badly to be a serious actress in my youth, I was too impressed," she reflects. "Most comedy must be done slowly to be effective, and when I'm nervous about a show I tend to go too fast. I was that way at Carnegie Hall every time, and I got off wrong on my timing. Carnegie Hall overawed me." Grandpa Jones and Bill Monroe were the big successes of the 1961 show, she says.

Faron Young performs for the New York audience

Patsy Cline at Carnegie Hall

Waugh to rent studio time from WSM, once he and the medicine company found the man they wanted.

The man they settled on was Porter Wagoner. A rhinestone-studded country music traditionalist who had come to the Opry from the Ozark Jubilee show in 1957, Wagoner had had several hits, including the classic "Satisfied Mind," but he was not nearly as prominent as many of the other Opry stars until the television cameras focused on his long-jowled, companionable face. The Chattanooga Medicine Company produced such middle-class products as a heat rub, a laxative, and a female "temporary weight gain" medicine, and officials of the company marveled at the straightfaced intensity Wagoner brought to their commercial announcements. It was the same carefully crafted sincerity he brought to his frequent religious hymns and "recitation" numbers.

Just one of many good performers on the Opry stage, Wagoner made himself a legend by his skillful use of television.

"We didn't notice a whole lot of impact from it right at the beginning," he recalls. "Where we first started noticing a difference was when we went back into cities we had been in before it started running. The crowds might be two or three times as large."

Still running and apparently stronger than ever, the Porter Wagoner Show has been appearing in more than a hundred major cities for several years. It is even used as a prime-time program by a few stations in such rural states as West Virginia.

Within a couple of years after launching the Wagoner Show, Bill Graham decided that his production company, which he called Show Biz Incorporated, could sell other country music syndications—that, in fact, two or three such shows might be easier to sell as a package

BELOW: Porter Wagoner sings a duet with Dolly Parton, who was a member of his television and road show for several years. OPPOSITE PAGE: Porter Wagoner acknowledges the applause of the studio audience at one of his videotapings

ABOVE: Porter Wagoner rehearses in one of the dressing rooms at the Ryman Auditorium. RIGHT: Clad in his famous "Wagonmaster" rhinestone-studded suit, a serious Porter Wagoner accepts from Opry announcer Grant Turner a 1966 trade magazine award naming his program the favorite country television show

The Wilburn Brothers—Doyle, left, and
Teddy—followed Porter Wagoner into television
syndication. BELOW: Doyle, left, and Teddy Wilburn
harmonize with fellow Opry star Jeanne Pruett

than a single show was. His hunch turned out to be correct. A second Show Biz production featuring another traditional-style Opry act, the duet-singing Wilburn Brothers, came into being in the early sixties. Loretta Lynn was one of its cast members for several years, and the show played a large part in popularizing her nationally.

The successes of Wagoner and the Wilburns spawned a plethora of country music television shows in the later sixties and early seventies. Successful ones included two other Show Biz productions, starring Opry stars Del Reeves and Jim Ed Brown, a Show Biz weekly variety show called "Good Ole Nashville Music" that frequently features Opry stars, and two shows produced by other companies that star the Opry's Bill Anderson and Jim and Jesse. These shows all helped to bring the Opry to the attention of television audiences after the death of network radio.

The triumphs in the new medium were balanced in the early sixties by equally modern tragedies. In a grim law of averages that many performers are superstitious about, some numbers finally started coming up.

March 4, 1963, was a Sunday, and Patsy Cline, Cowboy Copas, Hawkshaw Hawkins and Billy Walker did something that day that most Opry stars do a great deal: they played a show for nothing, a benefit performance in Kansas City, Kansas, for the family of a disc jockey who had died in an automobile accident. The show raised $3,000 for the bereaved family.

At noon the next day Patsy Cline, Copas, and Hawkins boarded a Piper Comanche piloted by Copas's son-in-law, Randy Hughes, to fly home. There being only four seats in the Comanche, Walker took a commercial flight.

At about five o'clock in the evening, as darkness was falling, the private craft landed in Dyersburg, Tennessee, to refuel. While its passengers were having coffee in the airport restaurant, airport manager Bill Braese told Hughes that high winds and a misting rain were said to be developing to the east. Braese suggested that Hughes and his party stay the night in Dyersburg.

Hughes said no, he knew the route to Nashville and had already come from Kansas City. He bought twenty-seven gallons of gasoline, and then he and his three passengers reboarded the Comanche. They took off to the east, vanishing in gloom.

At about seven o'clock Sam Webb, a farmer who lived along a winding dirt road near the small Tennessee town of Camden, saw the lights of an aircraft circling his house. He said the plane sounded as if it was "revving up its motor, going fast and slow like it was trying to climb." Webb lost sight of it after a few moments, and soon afterward he heard the sound of something hitting the tops of trees.

Tuesday afternoon, searchers found what was left of the Piper Comanche and the people who had been in it.

The Camden crash was just the first installment of a two-year series of tragedies.

Next Jack Anglin, Johnny Wright's partner and half of the Johnny and Jack team, died in an automobile accident in a driving rain on his way to attend prayer services for Patsy Cline. Then Texas Ruby Owens, who had starred on the Opry with fiddler Curly Fox in the late thirties and forties, was burned to death in a fire in a Nashville house trailer. In July 1964 Jim Reeves, the Opry's (and country music's) greatest country-pop singer since Eddy Arnold, perished in the crash of his private plane a few miles from his Brentwood, Tennessee, home. In 1965 Ira Louvin, an Opry star along with his brother Charlie for several years before they broke up their duet-singing partnership in the early sixties, died in an automobile accident. Finally, in July 1965, Roy Acuff and two members of his Smoky Mountain Boys troupe nearly lost their lives in another automobile crash on a rain-slick highway near Sparta, Tennessee, as they headed toward Terrell, North Carolina, to make an appearance. Acuff, sixty-one at the time, suffered broken ribs, a fractured pelvis, and a broken collarbone. As he recuperated in the hospital, he voiced a fear that many Opry stars had come to harbor. "I think the wreck was a warning that my traveling luck is running out," Acuff told the *Nashville Banner.* "I had a premonition it was going to happen. I didn't see how I could go on riding here and there and not have some sort of an accident. Any game you play you got to lose sometime. You can't go on winning forever. I've been traveling for almost thirty years about 100,000 miles annually in all sorts of weather."

A display in an upstairs hallway of the Ryman Auditorium pays tribute to some of the Opry's deceased greats

OVERLEAF:
A moment of silence is observed on the Opry stage for Opry stars Patsy Cline, Cowboy Copas, Hawkshaw Hawkins, and Jack Anglin—all killed in accidents in 1963

In an ironic way, even the tragedies contributed to the resurgence of the Opry. As is frequently the case with talented people who meet with disaster, in many quarters the fallen stars were accorded more recognition through tragedy than their talent had ever been able to win for them.

One such quarter was Nashville, the town whose cultivated aristocrats had always prided themselves on living in the "Athens of the South" and despised the Opry for sullying what once had been a good name. Conscious of that feeling, the *Banner* and especially the *Tennessean* had virtually ignored the Opry and its stars except when they got arrested, got drunk, got divorced, got in a fight, or got caught taking a shot at somebody. Such coverage merely reinforced the town's prevailing opinion of country music people: that they were clowns, musical versions of Robert Penn Warren's Willie Stark but infinitely less worthy of study—either boobs or hypocrites, who played to the low tastes of the one-gallus, bib-overall crowd and made enough money to gold-plate their Cadillacs and shame the fine city they had taken over.

The unfriendliness of the *Banner* and the *Tennessean* had existed since the thirties, when some of the leaders of the newspapers decided that radio was a threat to print journalism. For many years neither the *Banner* nor the *Tennessean* even published the schedules of the programs of local radio stations.

Beginning with the airplane crashes and automobile accidents in the early sixties, however, the local newspapers began to reflect a gradual change in the community's conception of a country music star —perhaps because disaster sells even more newspapers than does scandal.

JIM AND JESSE

THE COUNTRY DISCOVERS BILL MONROE

BILL MONROE

One evening several years ago, when Flatt, Scruggs, and the Foggy Mountain Boys were playing an isolated village in the eastern Kentucky hills, a local musician came around during intermission. He said he was looking for work and that he had once played with Bill Monroe.

A little skeptically, one of the Boys asked the stranger his name. "Jackson," he said.

"Jackson," the cautious Foggie repeated, considering. "Hell, it's possible. I expect *Andrew* Jackson picked with Monroe at one time or another."

The story is flippant, but its message is true: the role Bill Monroe has played as a tutor in his business is overpowering.

His most celebrated pupils are Lester Flatt and Earl Scruggs, of course, but there are hosts of others. They include such vocalists as Mac Wiseman, Carter Stanley, Jimmy Martin, and Clyde Moody, such other banjo players as Ralph Stanley of the Clinch Mountain Boys, Sonny Osborne of the Osborne Brothers, and Don Reno of Reno and Smiley, and such fiddlers as Big Howdy Forrester, Chubby Wise, Gordon Terry, and Vassar Clements.

These people and others went through Monroe's Blue Grass Boys the way people in other professions go through college. They learned the intricacies of the music and then moved out on their own to make individualistic changes, but they retained most of the essential elements of the master's bedrock theory and a repertoire of his standard songs. The process was not particularly easy on Monroe, who does not seem to have set out deliberately to play the role of professor in his field. The almost continual process of producing ex-Blue Grass Boys hurt the stability of Monroe's band and his popularity for a while, but in the long run it served to spread his music and reputation far and wide.

Bluegrass music took its first firm foothold in the hills and hollows of the Southeast, a territory reached by Monroe's own powerful voice in the Opry broadcasts of the forties. The sound of that voice on the radio was an example to other men who wanted to follow in his footsteps. Even before Flatt and Scruggs were starting off in Raleigh, then moving on to Bristol and Knoxville, Ralph and Carter Stanley and their Clinch Mountain Boys, heavily influenced by Monroe, entrenched themselves in the Bristol area. That same part of southwestern Virginia was occupied in the late forties by Jim and Jesse McReynolds, who also were influenced by Monroe's style, especially in the later stages of their own evolution from an early-Opry-style string band to a bluegrass group. In 1950, Don Reno left the Blue Grass Boys to team up with Red Smiley, and then a few years after that Jimmy Martin formed his Sunny Mountain Boys.

Monroe watched with understandable chagrin as the new groups formed and moved out into the hinterlands to compete with him. A proud man whose stony manner combines a frosty near-arrogance with a deep streak of backwoods shyness, he felt that his pupils had learned from him the ability to use the weapons they could now employ to hurt him, and he did not take kindly to the wholesale

LEFT: Bill Monroe's white hat sits atop his mandolin case in a corner of a Grand Ole Opry dressing room. BELOW: The "father of bluegrass music" surrounded by some of his spiritual sons. Flanking Bill Monroe, who is seated in the center, are Don Reno of Reno, Smiley, Harrell, and the Tennessee Cut-Ups, left, and Lester Flatt, leader of the Nashville Grass. Standing, from left, are his actual son James Monroe, leader of the Midnight Ramblers; Mac Wiseman; Bill Yates of the Country Gentlemen; Ralph Stanley, leader of the Clinch Mountain Boys; and Jimmy Martin, leader of the Sunny Mountain Boys

OPPOSITE PAGE: Clyde Moody, shown here in 1974, was an early member of Monroe's Blue Grass Boys

Two of the best old-time fiddlers, Howdy Forrester, right, now a member of Roy Acuff's Smoky Mountain Boys, was an early member of the Blue Grass Boys. At left is Paul Warren, long-time fiddler for Lester Flatt and Earl Scruggs's Foggy Mountain Boys and Flatt's Nashville Grass

desertions. Monroe was not really the kind of man who could have been expected to.

"I've worked on the farm for him," Monroe's son James, 33, a singer himself, said in 1972. "I cut hay and shucked corn. He was a hard man to work for. He expected the most out of you. He learned me to hitch a team when I was eleven, and he only showed me once. We had forty-four acres then, on Dickerson Road outside of Nashville. Now he's got 280 acres out in Goodlettsville, and he works it the old-time way. He plows right today with a horse and plow, and he can make you a roughhewn log house today just the way they used to. He knows every kind of tree there is, just by looking at it, and I guess he knows how to make just about anything you need."

Bill Monroe is a traditionalist in the strongest sense of that word. He is steeped in the rustic lore of his own forebears, of his father James and his mother Melissa, and of his kindly old uncle Pen, who used to squire Melissa down to the banks of the Green River in western Kentucky when they were young, to a spot that James Monroe would swim to from the other side to court her. Bill Monroe named his own two children Melissa and James to signify the depth of his love for the past. To a man like him, the new styles of life and music must have seemed almost heretical sometimes, and the departures of his bandsmen even worse.

It was particularly bad, for some reason, with Lester Flatt.

When Flatt and Scruggs joined the Opry in 1955, Flatt tried to pass a pleasantry with his old mentor a couple of times, but Monroe ignored each overture and that settled it. Lester Flatt's formative years in Overton County, Tennessee, had been about as stark as Monroe's own days in Rosine, and they had produced the same quiet fire of pride in Flatt's nature as Monroe's early days had in his own. Flatt tried only a couple of times. After that, for the next decade and a half, the two old masters worked the Opry the same nights and passed each other in the wings with never so much as a nod.

The fifties, good times for Flatt and Scruggs, were not so good for Bill Monroe.

His reputation as one of the Opry's biggest stars dimmed as the forces of television and rock and roll eroded some of the traditional country audience, coating many—especially among the young—with a thin veneer of sophistication and cynicism. A new teen-age generation of record buyers regarded country music, and especially bluegrass, as pretty old-fashioned and lacking in taste. Having no television show to popularize himself with, as Flatt and Scruggs had, Bill Monroe played his lonely music on the Opry broadcasts, worked the fields of his farms, and mostly just endured, awaiting a new time.

The salvation of bluegrass turned out to lie in what had seemed to be its nemesis: youth.

As the fifties wore on into the more serious sixties, a growing number of young people across America matured past primitive rock and roll but, remaining susceptible to powerful musical rhythms, began to become interested in the revved-up music of the past that they first heard played by Flatt and Scruggs. This music's strange combina-

OPPOSITE PAGE: James Monroe, right, says his father "pushed" him out onto some of the world's finest stages—Carnegie Hall, the Newport Folk Festival, and London's Albert Hall

313

Jim, right, and Jesse McReynolds

tion of driving, urgent speed, intricate instrumentation, and grave, traditional lyrics came to be regarded on the campuses as a sort of "source music," a residue of pioneer spirit with which young people oppressed by a national cold-war mentality could identify.

The Opry helped to nurture bluegrass in the sixties. In 1964, after the traumatic and reluctant hiring of Flatt and Scruggs had settled into dim memory, Opry manager Ott Devine doubled the bluegrass representation on the Opry, hiring both the traditional group of Jim and Jesse McReynolds and the electrified Osborne Brothers.

Devine's move reflected an increasing national interest in bluegrass, an interest partly due to the efforts of such urban partisans

as Ralph Rinzler of the Smithsonian Institution. Rinzler, a musician as well as historian, has played at various times with such differing groups as the New York-based Greenbriar Boys folk group and Monroe's own Blue Grass Boys. Rinzler and others like him helped see to it that Monroe, temporarily eclipsed by the dazzling successes of Flatt and Scruggs, was remembered in influential places.

Monroe's son James was just starting his career in the early sixties, working of course as a Blue Grass Boy. He got the same sort of initiation as a musician that he got hitching mules on his father's farm —quick and lasting.

"He shoved me out there," James recalled in 1972, with a grin.

"I didn't start playing until I was about twenty years old, and the first show I ever worked he put me on the stage with him with a bass when I didn't even know what a chord change was. I started out just trying to keep time. But I learned in some of the finest places you could learn: Carnegie Hall, the Newport Folk Festival, Albert Hall in London . . ."

In 1968, when Ott Devine was succeeded as manager of the Opry by an Akron, Ohio, native who had graduated from college with a major in economics, bluegrass acquired yet another—perhaps unexpected—friend. E. W. (Bud) Wendell had not grown up with any particular love for country music, but he had become quite familiar with the strength of its influence while working as a National Life salesman in the coalfields of West Virginia. When he was offered the chance to become manager of the Opry, he was properly impressed.

"I got to know some of the talent a little bit before I was given the job," Wendell recalls. "I liked them and was overwhelmed and awed by them, all at the same time. I was very conscious that I was getting an opportunity to work with a group of people that an awful lot of other people would have given their right arms just to have shaken hands with."

By the time Wendell took over the Opry, a bluegrass revolution was in full swing.

It took the form of the rural festival, an interesting contrast to the urban folk festival idea that had been in vogue for years. The bluegrass festival evolved using a pattern that has been widely imitated: it was staged on an extremely rural site where the land price was comparatively inexpensive, and it was usually located near some small town or community with a picturesque name.

Wendell remembers a typical one he attended on Memorial Day in 1972.

"It was at McClure, Virginia, about an hour north of Bristol," he says. "The last part of the way up there, the road was nothing but narrow curves. I didn't see a car coming or going, and I thought surely it had been called off. Then I rounded the last curve, and there were between fifteen and twenty thousand people sitting there on top of a mountain."

Bill Monroe says the first bluegrass festival he ever heard of was held in the early sixties at Fincastle, Virginia, in a sparsely populated area forty miles north of Roanoke. In 1966, Monroe founded his

OVERLEAF:
Bill Monroe and the Blue Grass Boys today

Opry executive E. W. (Bud) Wendell,
who became a devotee of bluegrass

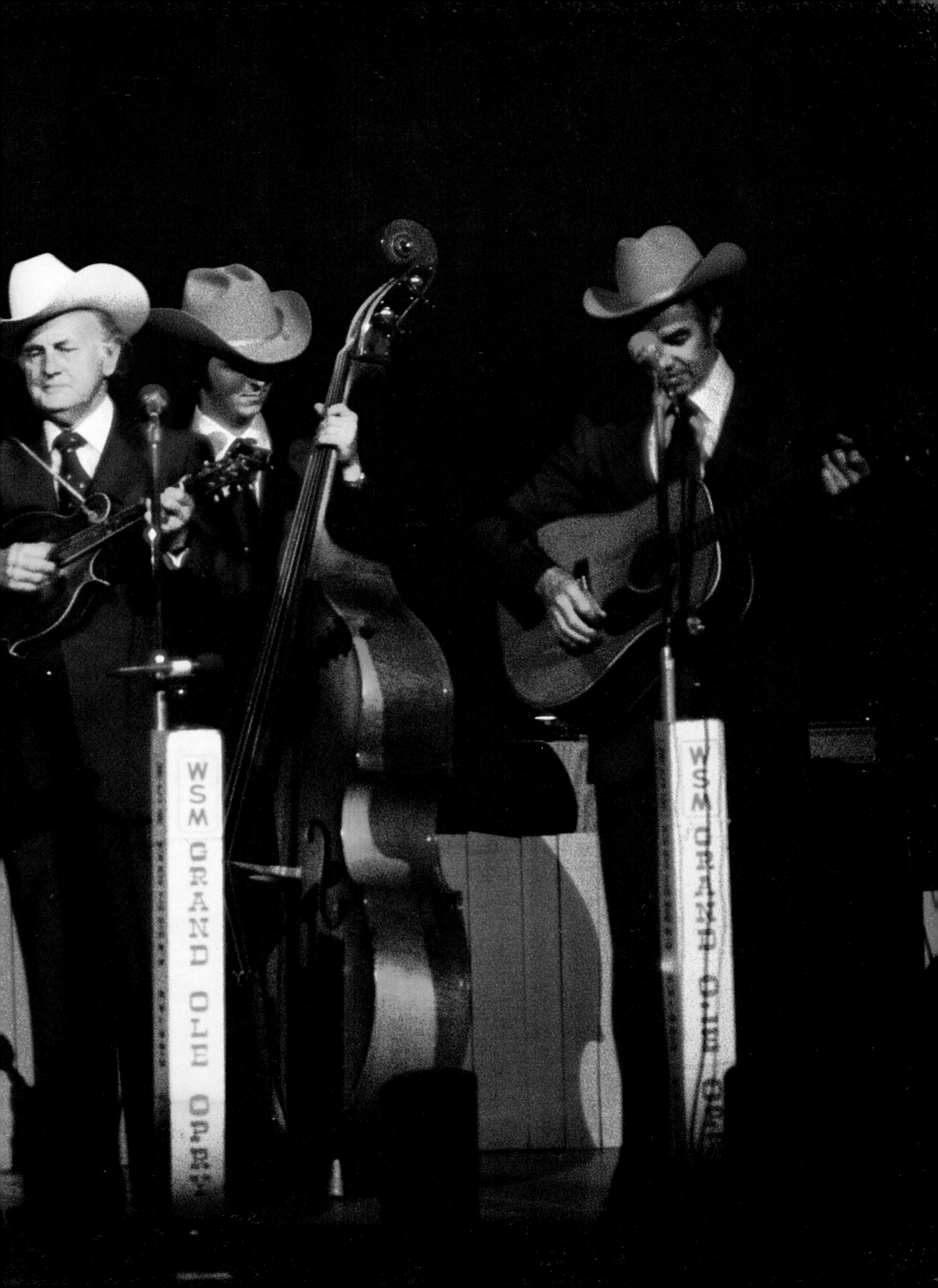
WSM
GRAND OLE OPRY
WSM
GRAND OLE

own annual festival at Beanblossom, Indiana, and others soon sprang up like weeds. They located in places like Damascus, Virginia, and Pinnacle, North Carolina. Almost from the beginning they seem to have drawn a strangely mixed crowd of country people and college-educated devotees.

From the beginning of their association at the Opry, Wendell became fascinated with Monroe, who was so old-fashioned that he would not have a telephone in his house and so secretive that for a long time not even the Opry management knew where his house was. Opry officials had to call the patriarch's ex-wife to get in touch with him at all. Wendell became even more intrigued by Monroe and his art when, in his first year as Opry manager, he attended Monroe's Beanblossom festival and saw the thousands of people gathered in a remote Indiana grove of trees on crude wooden benches to watch bluegrass being performed for days on end.

"Beanblossom kind of kindled a fire under me," Wendell recalls. "I liked the people who picked bluegrass, and I wanted to help them if I could. I didn't think they were getting the kind of recognition and attention they deserved, and I didn't think there was anybody else who could help them as much as the Opry could."

Wendell began to use his position toward that end, emphasizing bluegrass and its growing popularity in the frequent interviews he gave local and national reporters and magazine writers. Then, when WSM launched an annual week-long Nashville series of live performances called Fan Fair in 1971, Wendell gave bluegrass a definite boost by giving it its own special concert and making that concert the first of the entire week's events.

The 2,500 people who gathered in the Ryman Auditorium for the first annual Early Bird Bluegrass Concert heard James Monroe and the Midnight Ramblers, Ralph Stanley and the Clinch Mountain Boys, Carl Story and the Ramblin' Mountaineers, the Country Gentlemen, Jimmy Martin and the Sunny Mountain Boys, the Goins Brothers, Jim and Jesse and the Virginia Boys, Mac Wiseman, Don Reno and Red Smiley and the Tennessee Cut-Ups, and Lester Flatt and the Nashville Grass. Then Ralph Rinzler of the Smithsonian came out to introduce the finale.

"This man and his group comprise one of America's intangible national treasures," Rinzler told the audience.

"All this music is being played here tonight because one man, who joined the Grand Ole Opry thirty-two years ago, stood up for a kind of music he believed in when everything else was going electric.

"Bill Monroe."

In a conservative blue suit, the old man came out then and doffed his big white hat to the crowd. He spoke a few sentences in his quick, clipped brogue, more than normal for him. They sounded as abrupt to the ear as they look on paper. "This is the greatest bluegrass show ever put on in Nashville, Tennessee."

The entire audience of 2,500 immediately rose and cheered then, much the way the children of Israel must have cheered when they touched the other bank of the Jordan. The man on the stage of

Bill Monroe brings his stony dignity to a bluegrass son

the Ryman now, a sort of Moses of his kind, waited with seeming impatience for them to hush.

"I'm proud of the people playing on this program tonight," he went on rapidly. "A lot of them played for me and then went on to start their own groups and help hand this music down. I hope you all enjoyed your trip down here. Now here's the first number I ever did on the Grand Ole Opry. It's a kind of blues number. You'll find a lot of blues in bluegrass."

Then a fiddle started to whine in squalled submission, and Bill Monroe threw his head back and started the chillingly high, lonesome yell of joy and pain:

> Well, good moooornin' to you, captain.
> Well, good mornin' to you, suh-urrrrr!
> Do you need another muleskinnerrrrr
> Down on your new mud run?

Members of the audience screamed, shouted, and stomped as he went on through the rest of "Muleskinner Blues" and into "Uncle Pen," then to "McKinley's March" and "Footprints in the Snow." The music skimmed and lilted, the happy mandolin backing up the grave voice in a choppy rhythm within the verses and then bursting forth into furious melodies in between.

It probably went on for half an hour or more, but it seemed to pass in an instant. Suddenly, at an apparently prearranged moment, all the musicians who had been on the program that night came slowly and dramatically out onto the stage to surround Monroe. There were more than half a hundred of them, with their instruments, so many that the stage could hardly hold them and they had to stand in ranks. Following him, all of them together began to play the melody of an old standard, "Lonesome Road Blues," and Monroe, flushed with excitement now, explained this bluegrass symphony to the crowd.

"This is the only kind of music," he said, "where all of these musicians could walk out on a stage and play together and sound right. They like to compete with each other, but their final aim is just to put on as good a show as they possibly can and make the best music there is in the world: bluegrass music."

He began to sing the verses of "Lonesome Road Blues," and one at a time different members of the group on the stage came forward to one of the microphones and took a solo part. Don Reno came forward with the banjo, and then suddenly there was Lester Flatt, the long unwelcome prodigal son, now returned and singing along with his one-time employer.

That surprised a number of people that night.

With typical bluegrass reticence, Monroe and Flatt had neglected to announce the end of their long-standing feud, which had taken place some months before at Beanblossom, after Monroe's ex-wife hired Flatt as one of the groups to appear at Monroe's festival.

Flatt was standing in back of the primitive stage, tuning up

Bill Monroe, left, and his one-time
lead singer Lester Flatt in 1972

and getting ready to go on, when Monroe suddenly strode up and offered his hand. He said three words.

"Welcome to Beanblossom."

Almost as if the eighteen bitter years had never been, Lester Flatt perfunctorily shook the proffered hand.

"Thank you," he said. He did it routinely, in Monroe-style grand simplicity.

CHARLIE WALKER

STU PHILLIPS

AN ERA ENDS – THE RYMAN CLOSES

Jack DeWitt called Irving Waugh into his office one day in August 1967 and told him confidentially that he was going to retire. He suggested that Waugh, as heir apparent to the WSM presidency, might want to do some thinking about the state of things before the following March, when DeWitt would step down. Waugh was quite surprised. He and DeWitt had never been particularly close, Waugh moving in a wide circle that included many music business friends while DeWitt was generally preoccupied with his electronic experiments. Now, at sixty-two and in fine health, occupying a job that had never seemed to tax him particularly, DeWitt had decided to take early retirement, entrusting to Waugh all the policies with which Waugh had disagreed for twenty years.

"I went back over to my office," Waugh recalls, "and I thought, 'My God, there are problems here. What are going to be our priorities?' I had felt for a long time that because of some of the things that had been done, WSM was becoming a backwater instead of a leader. I felt that the Opry, in particular, was something that had to have immediate attention."

To understand the daring steps Waugh subsequently took, it is helpful to know a few things about him. A unique combination of businessman and thespian, he is a tough salesman with a pronounced flair for the romantic that seems to be left over from his youthful days when he "fooled," as he puts it, with the theater. His first job in radio was as one of the players on the CBS radio network's "March of Time" series, in which actors dramatized the news of the day.

When Jack Stapp hired him as an announcer, Waugh gained the same early contact with hillbilly music that everybody else at WSM got in those days. It was a kind of music he had known nothing about, despite his Virginia birth and raising. Waugh's Virginia was the cultivated Tidewater, not the rustic Blue Ridge.

"It was Jack Stapp's practice to have the newest announcer open up the station every morning," Waugh recalls, "and any Opry musician who happened to wander in at that hour was allowed to go on the air.

"None of the really big bands, like Acuff's, ever came in at that time of day, of course. The regulars I had for programming were Paul Howard and his band, Zeke Clements and his band, and a chap named Tommy Thompson who knew one song—'Cool Water,' I believe. I was also responsible for getting up three newscasts. Anyway, I'd put these people on the air, and I'd kid with them a little, and the listeners would send us cakes, boxes of fried chicken, bourbon. This surprised me. Because I was on the show, I was immediately accepted by the listeners. The only reason I say that is because they would send *me* bourbon and fried chicken, too.

"I went out with some of the bands on evening trips. We'd drive up to Clarksville, or down to Shelbyville, in a car with a bass fiddle on top. Zeke would pay me $5 to go with him, and I'd sing 'Come Sit under the Apple Tree with Me' or something—I had two or three things I knew. I could use the $5. But I was interested in the reaction.

The Ryman Auditorium

OVERLEAF: Colorful backdrops advertise sponsors' wares

Zeke, whom you couldn't call slender even then, was accepted as a star in those towns."

Waugh worked the Opry stage only a couple of times at most, on occasions when Judge Hay and Ford Rush were on the road with Acuff or Monroe or somebody and such normal replacements as Louie Buck were out with influenza or something. He was never considered a successful Opry announcer, probably because of his urbane speech and manner, but he became profoundly conscious of the Opry and its commercial possibilities.

When Waugh began considering measures to get the Opry moving again, he decided that he wanted to start fresh, with a new manager. Ott Devine, who had managed the show through the end of the difficult fifties and throughout most of the sixties, retired six weeks after DeWitt, and Waugh replaced him with Bud Wendell, who had been DeWitt's administrative assistant—a man who knew virtually nothing about country music and had had no prior experience in dealing with it.

"But Bud was a good administrator and a good businessman, and I wanted someone who didn't have any scar tissue, who hadn't been involved in any of the fights between the factions at WSM or in the music industry," Waugh says.

"I asked him to go down there and breathe some life into it, to get close to the managers and the talent."

What Waugh wanted, in other words, was for Wendell to begin trying to bridge the gulf between the Opry and the rest of the country music industry. Wendell made great strides in this direction. The new Opry manager began showing up at virtually every music-related function held in Nashville, and he got local and national publicity for the show—not so much by fancy press agentry as by simply exploiting the Opry's legitimate claims to public attention.

"I like to remind the Nashville Area Chamber of Commerce that the Opry crowd is Nashville's biggest convention gathering of the year—and it happens every weekend—an average gathering of 8,000 people every Friday and Saturday," Wendell told the *Tennessean* in 1972. He pointed out that in 1971, for the first time in its history, the Opry's attendance rose above 400,000.

When Wendell took over, the Opry had long since passed its low point. In the early sixties the attendance had recovered from its fifties dip to such a degree that Devine moved the free Friday night show, which had been held in WSM's studios since its inception in the late forties, and brought it to the Ryman. Changing its name to the Friday Night Opry, he had started charging admission. In the latter years of his tenure as manager Devine had also continued to add impressive new stars to the show, including Del Reeves, Jack Greene, Jeannie Seely, Charlie Walker, Stu Phillips, and Ray Pillow. When Wendell took over, he continued this policy of aggressive acquisition, hiring Dolly Parton, David Houston, Barbara Mandrell, George Jones, Tammy Wynette, Jeanne Pruett, Jerry Clower, Tom T. Hall, and the Four Guys. He also rehired Little Jimmy Dickens.

In 1972 Wendell was promoted to the new position of general

Fans line up in an alley behind the Ryman waiting to be admitted for the second show

Street scene
in front of the Ryman

BELOW:
A crowd milling outside
the Ryman in the forties

ABOVE: Members of a 23-member family who drove 3,000 miles from California to see the Opry proudly display their tickets for a photographer.
RIGHT: The wife holding an Ernest Tubb songbook and the husband holding their baby, a couple enjoys the Ryman Auditorium's Opry show in 1946

LEFT: This 72-year-old man from Apex, North Carolina, came to Nashville for one of the Grand Ole Opry's birthday celebrations. BELOW: Four Texans who drove to Nashville from Dallas to see the Opry in 1967

OPPOSITE PAGE:
ABOVE: Seen from the side and above, through the maze of ropes that controlled the backdrops and curtains, a Ryman Auditorium performance of the Opry somewhat resembled a marionette show. BELOW: Another view of the chaos that seemed to surround performers at the Ryman. At the front of the stage, Porter Wagoner waves in applause for Bill Monroe and the Blue Grass Boys

LEFT: Friends and relatives of stars and sidemen sat on benches just behind the Ryman's stage. BELOW: In one of the Ryman's most familiar scenes, members of the audience troop to the front of the stage to snap photographs of a star—in this case guest performer Johnny Cash

One of the few areas where smoking was allowed

manager of both Opryland and the Opry. Onetime Opry announcer Hal Durham, a former program director of WSM Radio, became manager of the Opry.

As Wendell set about implementing Waugh's policies at Ryman Auditorium in early 1968, Waugh began to look critically at the auditorium itself. The Ryman was a historic, expensive-to-maintain structure that National Life had rather considerably taken off the hands of the city of Nashville in 1964, even though the songlike price was only some $200,000. For a long time people had been asserting that the Ryman was a firetrap, and for a long time WSM had been denying it. Waugh himself thought that the building was unsafe, and he began studying what might be done about it.

"First we tried to see whether it could be made fire-resistant or fire-retardant and air-conditioned at a reasonable cost, and whether we could buy property around it so that the stage, the dressing rooms, and prop areas could be enlarged," Waugh says.

"We finally concluded that we couldn't do these things, that we would have to take the house down. When we decided that, we decided that instead of rebuilding down there we should go outside the city to a place where we could control our own environment. That led me to try to sell National Life on a feasibility study for what turned out to be Opryland.

"Opryland grew out of the need for an Opry House. When I first started working on the idea, I figured it would take at least $5 million to build an Opry House, and I felt you couldn't justify spending $5 million just to house a Friday night-Saturday night radio show. We then started studying whether we could generate other sources of revenue. In my mind the Opry House was always to be the centerpiece of the park, and I think it is. The house wound up costing $15 million instead of five. If we'd known that in the beginning, I guess we'd never have done it. I've got to say this about National Life, though: while waves of nausea swept over Bill Weaver at times, he backed us absolutely all the way."

William C. Weaver, Jr., is tall and vibrant and looks a dozen years younger than his present age of sixty-two. He is even charismatic in a folksy Southern way that humanizes but makes no attempt to hide his abilities as a maker of money. Weaver apparently has been an astute businessman all his life. At twenty-eight, when he married a daughter of Edwin Craig and entered the National Life pecking order, he was chairman of the board of the McWhorter-Weaver appliance company in Nashville.

Since 1973 he has been chairman of the board and chief executive officer of National Life and its holding company, the NLT Corporation, as well as WSM Incorporated. Weaver's office is as lofty as his title. Located in a corner of a top floor of the new twenty-eight-story National Life home office building in downtown Nashville, it allows Weaver to look out—and pleasurably down—on what *used* to be the highest building in Nashville, the Life and Casualty Tower, which belongs to National Life's local rival, the Life and Casualty Insurance Company.

Tom T. Hall, the singer whose prolific, distinctive songwriting has won him the nickname "The Storyteller," was a member of the Opry for a while during the seventies

Ray Pillow

OVERLEAF:
This kind of scene on the Ryman stage may have given birth to the term "Grand Ole Uproar," one of the Opry's many nicknames. Here, the Wilburn Brothers sing while a crowd of stars and music businessmen mills around

ABOVE: Charlie Walker, a big Texan who was one of country music's best-known disc jockeys before reaching stardom with the classic honky-tonk song "Pick Me up on Your Way Down," joined the Opry in the early sixties. RIGHT: Stu Phillips uses a soft singing style like that of the late Jim Reeves

ABOVE: The Four Guys—from left, Gary Buck, Brent Burkett, Sam Wellington, and Rich Garratt—joined the Opry in the seventies to work as both a background and a featured group. Garratt has since been replaced by Dave Rowland. RIGHT: Little Jimmy Dickens, a diminutive Opry star of more than two decades ago, recently returned to the cast

The new National Life building is a monument to many things, and one of them is the Grand Ole Opry. Ever since the days when Roy Acuff's name became known across the land, National Life agents have been getting themselves invited into modest homes all across the South and Midwest with a tip of the hat and a pleasant: "Good afternoon, I work for the company that owns the Grand Ole Opry, and Roy Acuff [or Minnie Pearl, Red Foley, Ernest Tubb, Jim Reeves] asked me to come by and give you a personal hello. May I come in?"

Weaver says he has no way of measuring the effect that the Opry has had on National Life's business, but he estimates that it has been considerable.

Perhaps a sense of euphoria brought on by the imposing new home office building contributed to the spirit with which National Life's officers accepted Waugh's brave new idea. Unquestionably this acceptance was aided by the fact that Weaver and some of the other officers shared a trait not even Waugh had had in the beginning: in his teens Bill Weaver had listened to WDAD, to such people as Dr. Humphrey Bate and DeFord Bailey, and he had *always* liked and understood hillbilly music.

The preliminary feasibility study Waugh asked for and got in 1968 cost $20,000. It was approved by both Dan Brooks, chairman of the board of National Life then, and Edwin Craig, who had retired in 1965 and become honorary chairman. The feasibility study set in motion a huge undertaking, much larger than even Waugh realized at the time. Waugh's idea was to illustrate country music's role as a musical melting pot by surrounding the Opry with live performances of the other kinds of music to which the American people have given rise—blues, jazz, Western, folk, and the rest. It would be a "theme park" somewhat resembling the ones at Disneyland and Six Flags over Georgia, but in keeping with the outdoor, natural image of country music it would be as genuine as possible, with real trees and flowers and the best and most authentic building materials.

It began as an expensive project and grew more and more so before it was finally finished.

"If the people up at National Life had taken the $43 million we spent out there and just invested it, there's no question that they could have gotten a better dollar return," Waugh says. "But this helps their people in the field. My argument was, if I'm a guy selling insurance for you in Kansas City, I'm selling against the giants—New York Life, Prudential, and so on—and I represent a company back in the little town of Nashville, Tennessee. Anything extra that can give me a little stature is going to help me if I'm worth a dime as a salesman."

But it was a risky undertaking, as the National Life executives —and especially Irving Waugh—fully realized. What if it was built and nobody came to see it? It was based on the theory that the Opry would draw country music fans to the park and that the park would draw non-country-music fans to the Opry out of curiosity. But who knew for sure? Opry tickets would probably have to be more expensive than the $3 that was being charged at the Ryman, and the price of a ticket to Opryland would certainly be even higher.

There were yet other problems, pressing ones.

A public outcry greeted the announcement that National Life and WSM planned to raze the historic Ryman and use parts of it to build a chapel at Opryland. Preservationists argued that the former tabernacle was one of the most important buildings in Nashville's history, not only because of its role as the thirty-year home of the Opry, but also because it dated from the Gay Nineties and had been Nashville's principal auditorium for half a century. WSM and National Life were reluctant to mar their good image by tearing down a piece of country music's heritage, so the Ryman's future was put on ice. Meanwhile, tourists still clog its aged doors to view the dusty stage Hank Williams walked and sang on.

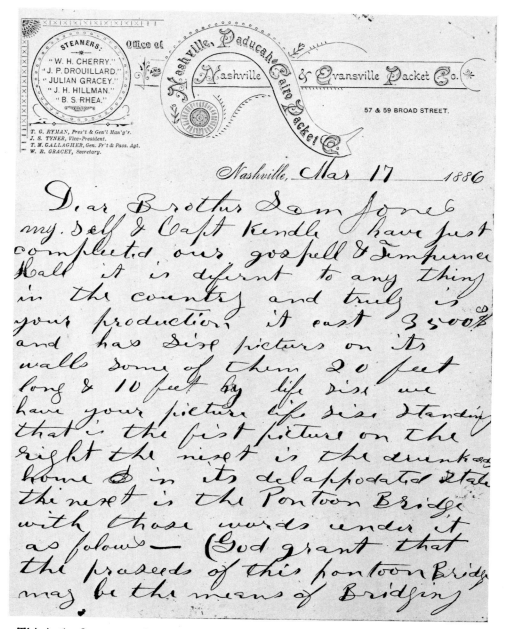

This is the first page of a letter from Captain Tom Ryman, the steamboat captain who built the Ryman Auditorium, to the Reverend Sam P. Jones, the evangelist whose fiery sermons inspired him to build it

The letter reads:

Nashville, Mar 17, 1886

Dear Brother Sam Jones,

Myself & Capt Kendle have just compleeted our gospell & Tempernce Hall, it is difernt to any thing in the country and truly is your production. It cost 3500.00$ and has six pictures on its walls some of them 20 feet long & 10 feet hy—life sise. We have your picture life sise, standing that is, the first picture on the right. The next is the drunkard's home in its delappodated state. The next is the Pontoon Bridge with those words under it as folows— "God grant that the proseeds of this pontoon Bridge may be the means of Bridging many soles over to a better world." The profits of the Bridge boght the hall. The next Picture is a long valey or road with too angels driving the devel before them and men with axes in the rier busting whisky barels, very impressive. The next is a moto in large letters as folows— "In the naim of God morality and honest goverment be truthfull honest & sober." The next is a bar room seen, one man has killed another. The next is a pile of whisky barells with snakes all among them and men around about with snakes around them, also bones skuls &cc, and the salvation army in the distance, women prevailing with the men, also an angel coming down with a drawn sword in the act of cuting of the heads of the snakes. The next and last is the Devel runing a large coper distilery, he is dooing his own firing up. It is all very atractive with appropriate motoes. This hall is finished, has a seating capacity of only 250 but is intended to run every night from 8 till 9 o clock. It has a nice alter, orgin &cc, fine shandoliers, carpeted about the alter with mating in the ile. This man Kindle who is paying one 4th of this hall is the man I had you to talk to. He then had a very fine saloon in our city but has sold it out and has a steamboat here and wont alow a man to run on her that drinks. He is talking of building a new boat and naiming her "Sam Jones." Now what we want and will doo is to run this hall non sectarian nightly the saim as Steave Halcorn does his in Louisville.

Now what we want is if posible as you are passing through going home after your meating in Chicago, I would never get dun apreciating it if you would stop and dedicate this hall of worshop. If you havent passed this rout don't let that stop you. I will make that all right and moer too. My ideer is to call all the prechers of the difernt denomonations at this dedication and show the world that we can have a place of worshop that is free of any colection being taken up whatever, and purialy an out post to ketch siners and alow them to go in any church they like. Now don't refuse as I beleave this thing will be the begining of a great move in that direction. Anser at once and let me no what day and hour you come, so I can anounse it in the paper, and I would like your advice as to the ider of caling on the prechers of all the denomonations. If it should be nice weather it might be well to erect a stand in front of the building and adress the people in the street as the hall is small. An erly reply will be looked for.

Your friend & Brother,
T. G. Ryman

One of the bigger Nashville businesses that have grown up around the Grand Ole Opry is that of conducting organized groups of weekend visitors on tours of Nashville and its environs. The tours sponsored by the Opry itself still depart from the Ryman Auditorium, home of the Opry for three decades. They vary in length of time spent and number of places visited, but a typical tour first visits the Country Music Hall of Fame, which houses a large collection of hats, boots, bandanas, guitars, and other memorabilia of the stars. One section includes a "Gallery of Stars" (right) and a theater in which a motion picture about country music's history is shown...

Leaving the Hall of Fame, the tour moves on into some of Nashville's more fashionable suburbs to visit the homes of stars. Often visited ones include those of George Jones (top) and Minnie Pearl (center). Others are the home of Webb Pierce, whose guitar-shaped swimming pool and musical mailbox advertise his success, and the home of the late, great Hank Williams —the Cadillac in which he died can be seen in the garage at left. A typical tour ends back at the Ryman, where visitors listen to a guide's concluding remarks in the middle of the historic stage

344

Roy Acuff clowns for Brother Oswald at the construction site of the new Opry House

At the dedication ceremonies of Opryland. From left are Irving Waugh, President of WSM; G. Daniel Brooks, chairman of the boards of the NLT Corporation, the National Life and Accident Insurance Company, and WSM; Mike Downs, Opryland's General Manager; William C. Weaver, Jr., President of National Life; and Sam Fleming, President of the NLT Corporation

At the Opryland site, labor problems sometimes stopped construction, thereby allowing inflation to do its dirty work as the cost of building materials soared. The Opry's own special labor force, its stars, watched the colossus rising on Nashville's suburban horizon and began to examine their own traditionally scanty remuneration very critically. "My friend Bill Graham at Show Biz [the television syndication empire] told me, 'Of all the dull things you've done in your life, this Opryland scheme is the stupidest one of all,'" Waugh recalls with a grin.

"Bill said, 'In your declining years, you should play your lousy game of golf and enjoy what little time you have left.' He was very serious about it. He said, 'You're going to get your—'" Waugh pauses— "'fired.'" Graham would probably have been right, Waugh guesses, if Opryland had failed. But National Life's executives stood behind him and his grandiose plan. The Opry had never been much of a profit-maker—it had not even charged admission until 1939, and after that most of the gate receipts were eaten up by talent fees and other overhead costs. But it had always been a priceless public relations tool, and they were gambling that Opryland would turn out to be the same. So when a million dollars was swallowed in a single bite by galloping inflation, Dan Brooks merely philosophized: "Well, Irving, you know, you never *can* build anything for what they tell you you can."

The construction estimates may have proved too modest, but Waugh's theories about the interplay between the different crowds to be attracted by the Opry and Opryland turned out to be correct. In the Opry's first year at Opryland, the show drew twice as many people as it had at the Ryman Auditorium the previous year. During the summer months, weekend matinees were required to satisfy the increased demand, even though the new Opry House contains 4,400 seats, some 1,300 more than the Ryman.

In short, Opryland has done what it was designed to do.

"It has gotten an awful lot of publicity in newspapers and magazines throughout the country," Waugh notes proudly, "and in a considerable number of the articles, National Life has been mentioned prominently."

Also, at increased admission prices it is finally in the black. "It's not a gold mine, but it's working for us," Waugh says.

The show that is working is, of course, an almost totally different phenomenon from the one that inspired the Opry's original designers.

The four old string bands that lasted into the sixties have shrunk now to just two, the Crook Brothers and the Fruit Jar Drinkers, as age overtakes the original cast members. George D. Hay is dead and Edwin Craig is gone also. Some of the rowdy old-time spirit of the show seems to have gone, too, and it is mourned both by performers like Bashful Brother Oswald Kirby and by skillful merchandisers like Irving Waugh.

"Roy Acuff was sitting here the other day giving me a hard time," Waugh said recently, with a rueful grin.

"I said, 'Roy, you know, *you* don't perform the way you did

OPPOSITE PAGE: Acuff, flanked by Charlie Collins and Oswald Kirby, fiddles as the new Opry House is constructed, watched from above by a workman

RIGHT: Fruit Jar Drinkers at the backstage entrance of the Ryman shortly before the move to the new Opry House. BELOW: Roy Acuff tosses his yoyo toward Oswald Kirby's feet

OPPOSITE PAGE: Herman Crook blows his harmonica as some of the Opry's other venerated oldsters supply accompaniment. Barely visible behind them at right, a square-dance troupe performs

when I first came here. Back then, your unit really had a ball. Now, I know you're a lot older than you used to be, and a little more dignified, but Oswald always used to fall off the stage into the lap of the fat lady, and somebody always got picked up and tossed in the RC cooler, and somebody always pulled somebody else's shirt off. Those were corn-ball things, but the audience just whooped it up. The people really enjoyed it, because the average American family doesn't get to see live entertainment. People enjoyed these things, but nobody does them anymore.' "

Waugh would like to see a return to some of the wild old crazi-ness. He would like to see, as he puts it, "some indication that the talent is having fun, instead of being just so many singers staring down a microphone." What he wants, in fact, would seem to be a return to the simple concept George D. Hay preached for most of his adult life: the principle that the Grand Ole Opry, to be truly grand, had to remain grandly simple, "close to the ground."

"The Grand Ole Opry is as simple as sunshine," Hay said in the most famous passage he ever wrote.

"It has a universal appeal because it is built upon good will, and with folk music expresses the heartbeat of a large percentage of Americans who labor for a living. There is no trick about it, and it requires no fancy key to open its front door.

"The latch-string is always out."

OVERLEAF:
The crowd lines up for the Ryman's last
Saturday-night Opry show, on March 9, 1974

The last song sung on the stage of the Ryman Auditorium
climaxed the weekly Friday-night "Grand Ole Gospel" show. An
old hymn called "Will the Circle Be Unbroken," its singers
included Carl Perkins, Gordon Terry, the Reverend Jimmy Snow,
Mother Maybelle Carter, Johnny Cash, Hank Snow, June
Carter Cash, and the LeFevres, a gospel group

Taking down the sign
after the Ryman's last
Grand Ole Opry show

The new Opry House

OSBORNE BROTHERS

CHARLIE LOUVIN

OPRYLAND U.S.A. – NEW HOME OF AMERICAN MUSIC

HANK LOCKLIN

opened in 1972 and attracted some 1,400,000 visitors, handsomely exceeding the most ambitious first-year attendance forecasts. When the Grand Ole Opry moved into the new Opry House at Opryland in 1974, the show quickly doubled the attendance it had drawn in its last year at the Ryman Auditorium. Now situated in a lavish "family entertainment park," performed on a splendid stage and flanked by the most modern television equipment in existence, the Grand Ole Opry is on the threshold of unprecedented new national popularity.

The future has been bright enough to prompt the Opry's stars to ask for and get a substantial raise in their Opry pay. In 1974 Vic Willis, head of the musicians' union negotiating team, succeeded in getting fees raised by 100 percent—from $30 to $60 per show for stars and $15 to $30 per show for sidemen. This means that an Opry star can make $120 on a Saturday night, when the Opry has an early show and a late one. The star can also get $60 for playing the Friday night show and yet another $60 for a weekend matinee show. Sidemen receive exactly half these fees.

"When I first came here in 1946, a sideman made $6 a show," reminisces Vic Willis. Tongue firmly in cheek he adds, "I told Irving and Bud during the negotiation meetings that I had seen the talent compensation on the Opry skyrocket from $6 to $15 in just twenty-eight short years."

The Opry park, in which the Opry House is located, calls itself the "Home of American Music," and it offers more entertainment than a family can avail itself of even in a very full day. Ten different live shows are put on in five separate music areas, each representing an era that gave birth to a form of American music: Opry Plaza features country music; the Hill Country area, folk music; New Orleans, jazz and blues; the West, cowboy and Spanish-American music; and the Music of Today, rock. The ten shows performed in these areas range from intricately choreographed and lighted productions to simple concerts by individual Opry stars on the Opry House stage.

Opryland's music is surrounded by scores of other attractions, including 14 rides, games of skill, 19 restaurants with individual menus, 24 curio and craft shops, scores of concession stands, and herds of wild and domestic animals. Buffalo, elk, and longhorn steers graze on an open range area of the park. A herd of white-tailed deer and a

OPPOSITE PAGE: A television camera sits beneath a maze of ceiling lights and stage controls in the new Opry House, graphically illustrating the technological capabilities behind the relaxed atmosphere of the Opry stage

OVERLEAF: A television studio located in the new building. INSET: An engineer studies monitors in the control room

wide variety of domestic farm animals are available for children to pet, and in a ravine which visitors may enter only in protected areas there are bobcats, wolves, mountain lions, a pair of African lions, and bears.

Opryland is certainly glamorous and exotic, especially when compared with George D. Hay's original conception of the old barn-dance that made it all possible. Yet Opryland is aimed at giving pleasure to the same people Hay wanted the Grand Ole Opry to entertain —families of "hard-working Americans."

These scenes show some of the things Opry-land's new television equipment was designed to capture. OPPOSITE PAGE, ABOVE: Tennessee Ernie Ford leads the cast of a recent network production in front of the park's American Music Theatre. BELOW: Minnie Pearl clowns on a similar show. ABOVE: Johnny Cash, his wife June Carter, and their daughters Rosie and Carleen make a guest appearance at the new Opry House. OVERLEAF: Cash sings on one of the many network appearances he has filmed in Nashville since 1969

LEFT: Children are greeted near the park entrance by some of Opryland's animated instruments—Frankie Fiddle, Delilah Dulcimer, Barney Bass, and so forth. BELOW: The Dixieland band makes one of several daily music marches through the park

PRECEDING PAGES:
A crowd of visitors streams across a wide courtyard near Opryland's entrance area. INSET: Members of the park's Dixieland band play in one of the bandstands

371

The Clown Show, below, and one of the contemporary music shows, at right, hint at the variety of performances in Opryland's entertainment pageant

OVERLEAF: The high-kicking square dancers of the "My Country" show celebrate the Grand Ole Opry's fifty years. INSET: A rock group sings in the park's contemporary music area

The cast of "Showboat '75" performs old and new riverboat music on a steamboat set in still another outdoor theater

"Indians" dance over "victims," above, in a performance in Opryland's Western section. OPPOSITE PAGE, ABOVE: The cast of a show in the Music of Today area strikes a pose of triumph. BELOW AND OVERLEAF: The cast of another contemporary show engages in a frenetic dance, the action dissolving into a swirl of color and motion

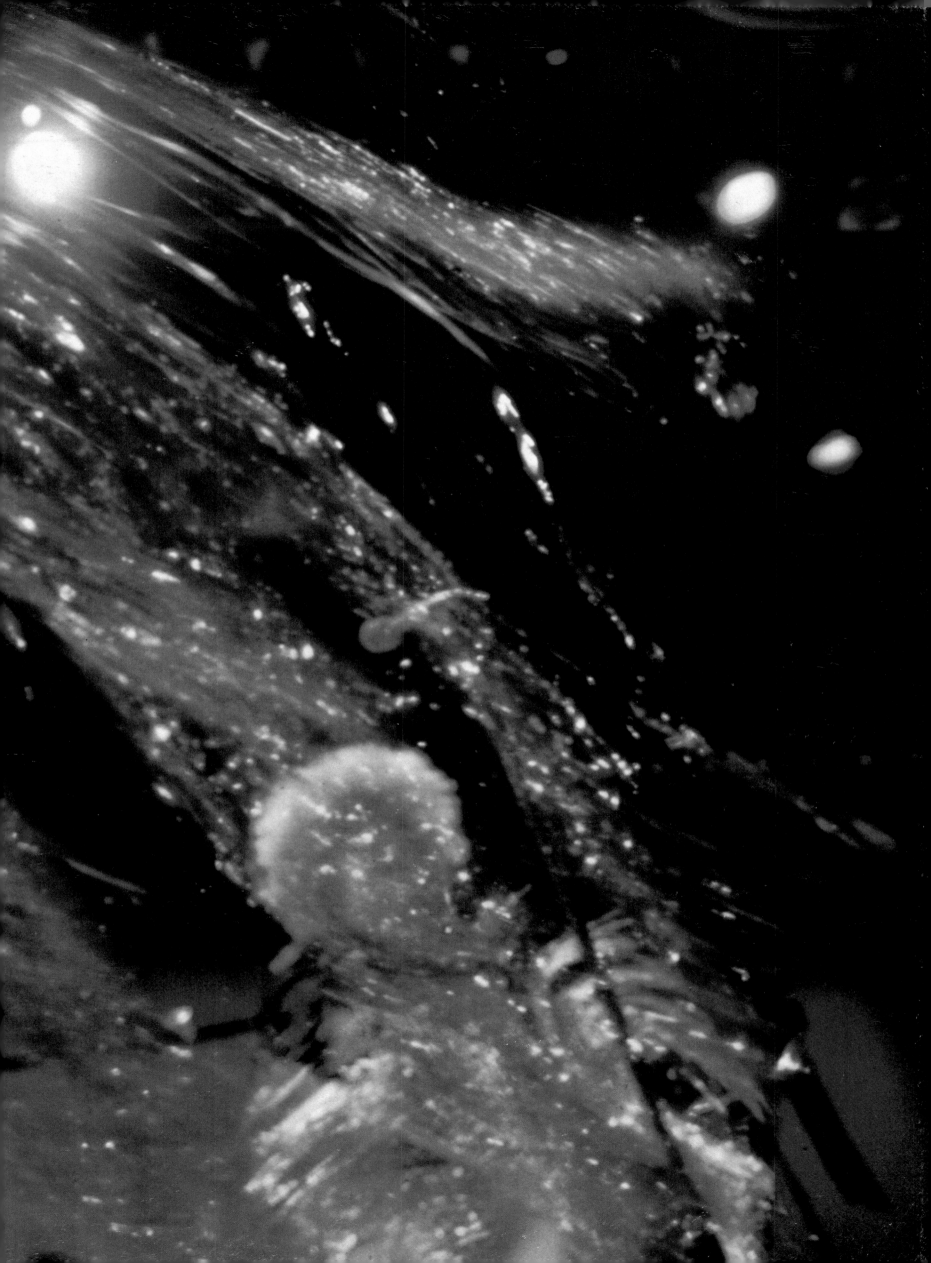

Opryland U.S.A. has its restful areas, too. ABOVE: Charlie Collins,
left, and Oswald Kirby do a little placid picking on a porch
near the Opry House. OPPOSITE PAGE: A father and daughter
receive a spontaneous welcome to the Roy Acuff Music Hall.
Inside, musicians Tut Taylor, left, Charlie Collins, center, and
Oswald Kirby get together for an impromptu jam session
against an appropriate background of instrument displays, and
visitors wander through the exhibits.

Opryland's Sky Ride Cable Cars overlook
insets of some of the many entertainment rides
that can be seen from above Opryland's crowded
forests. From left, these include the youngsters'
Red Baron Airplane Ride, the more grown-up
Timber Topper Roller Coaster, and the Flume
Zoom Log Ride. There are also Tin Lizzie
antique cars and locomotives like the ones below

ABOVE: The Raft, a motor-powered excursion cra
takes visitors across a three-acre lake. OPPOSITE PAG
Scenes from a variety of the park's live-anim
amusements. TOP LEFT: An attendant holds apart tv
of the playful performers in the Barnyard Circu
RIGHT: A cow participates in a barnyard band l
ringing a bell. CENTER LEFT: A young visitor hugs o
of the forty-six residents of the Deer Petting Farr
RIGHT: A Barnyard Circus performer industrious
beats a drum. BOTTOM LEFT: A recalcitrant go
frightens one of its young attendants. RIGHT: T
performing cow practices on the harmonic
OVERLEAF: The Opryland Carous

DISCOGRAPHY

ROY ACUFF	Greatest Hits, Columbia, CS1034
	Roy Acuff and His Smoky Mountain Boys, Capitol, DT-1870
	Back In The Country, Hickory, HR-4507
BILL ANDERSON	Greatest Hits, MCA Records, MCA-13
	Still, MCA Records, MCA-100
EDDY ARNOLD	Cattle Call, RCA, LSP-2578
	All Time Favorites, RCA, LSP-1223(e)
	Welcome To My World, RCA, LSP-4570
ERNIE ASHWORTH	The Best of Ernie Ashworth, Hickory, LPS 146
CHET ATKINS	Down Home, RCA, LSP-2450
	Guitar Country, RCA, LSP-2783
BOBBY BARE	The Best of Bobby Bare, RCA, LSP-3479
	Bobby Bare Sings Lullabyes, Legends and Lies, RCA, CPL 2-0290
JIM ED BROWN	Morning, RCA, LSP-4461
	Best of Jim Ed Brown, RCA, APL 1-0324
ARCHIE CAMPBELL	The Best of Archie Campbell, RCA, LSP-4280
BILL CARLISLE	The Best of Bill Carlisle, Hickory, LPS 129
THE CARTER FAMILY	The Best of The Carter Family, Columbia, CS9119
JOHNNY CASH	I Walk The Line, Columbia, CS8990
PATSY CLINE	Greatest Hits, MCA, MCA-12
	Sentimentally Yours, MCA, MCA-87
	A Portrait of Patsy Cline, MCA, MCA-224
JERRY CLOWER	Yazoo City, Mississippi Talkin', MCA, MCA-33
	Mouth of Mississippi, MCA, MCA-47
WILMA LEE & STONEY COOPER	The Great Speckled Bird: A Tribute to Roy Acuff, Skylite, SC730
SKEETER DAVIS	The Best of Skeeter Davis, RCA, LSP-3374
	Skeeter, RCA, LSP-4486
ROY DRUSKY	Peaceful, Easy Feeling, Capitol, ST-11339
LESTER FLATT	Country Boy, RCA, APL 1-0131
	Kentucky Ridgerunner, RCA, LSP-4633
LESTER FLATT & EARL SCRUGGS	Columbia, C32244
	At Carnegie Hall, Columbia, C58845
	At Vanderbilt University, Columbia, C58934
LESTER FLATT & MAC WISEMAN	Lester 'n' Mac, RCA, LSP-4547
RED FOLEY	Songs of Devotion, MCA, MCA-86
	Beyond The Sunset, MCA, MCA-147
	The Red Foley Story, MCA, MCA-2-4053
DON GIBSON	The Very Best of Don Gibson, Hickory, HR4502
THE GLASER BROTHERS	Vocal Group of the Decade, MGM, M3G4976
JACK GREENE	There Goes My Everything, MCA, MCA-251
	Greatest Hits, MCA, MCA-291
JACK GREENE & JEANNIE SEELY	MCA, MCA-288
	Two For The Show, MCA, MCA-77
TOM T. HALL	The Storyteller, Mercury, SR61368
GEORGE HAMILTON IV	Greatest Hits, RCA, APL 1-0455
DAVID HOUSTON	Greatest Hits, Columbia, BN26342
	The Day That Love Walked In, Epic, KE31385

DAVID HOUSTON & BARBARA MANDRELL	A Perfect Match, Epic, KE31705
JAN HOWARD & BILL ANDERSON	For Loving You, MCA, MCA-365 Singing His Praise, MCA, MCA-143
FERLIN HUSKY	The Best of Ferlin Husky, Capitol, SKAO-143
STONEWALL JACKSON	Recorded Live At The Grand Ole Opry, Columbia, C30469 Greatest Hits, Columbia, CS9177
SONNY JAMES	Young Love, Capitol, ST-11196
NORMA JEAN	The Best of Norma Jean, RCA, LSP-4227
JIM & JESSE	Diesel On My Tail, Epic, BN26314
GEORGE JONES	Take me, TCA, LSP-4787 A Picture of Me Without You, Epic, KE31718 The Best of George Jones, RCA, APL 1-0316
GEORGE JONES & TAMMY WYNETTE	Me And The First Lady, Epic, KE31554 We Go Together, Epic, KE30802
GRANDPA JONES	Everybody's Grandpa, Columbia, SLP 18083 Hits From Hee Haw, Columbia, SLP 18131
DOUG KERSHAW	Cajun Way, Warner Bros., 5-1820
HANK LOCKLIN	Bless Her Heart . . . I Love Her, KCA, LSP-4392 The Best of Hank Locklin, RCA, LSP-3559(e)
CHARLIE LOUVIN	It Almost Felt Like Love, United Artists, UA-LA 248G
BOB LUMAN	Greatest Hits, Epic, KE32759 Lonely Women Make Good Lovers, Epic, KE31746 When You Say Love, Epic, KE31375
LORETTA LYNN	Coalminer's Daughter, MCA, MCA-10 Blue Kentucky Girl, MCA, MCA-80 You Ain't Woman Enough, MCA, MCA-6 Don't Come Home A-Drinkin, MCA, MCA-113 You're Lookin' At Country, MCA, DL 7-5310
THE ERNEST TUBB/LORETTA LYNN STORY	MCA, MCA 2-4000
BARBARA MANDRELL	The Midnight Oil, Columbia, KC32743
JIMMY MARTIN	Good 'n' Country, MCA, MCA-81
BILL MONROE	Beanblossom, MCA, MCA 2-8002 Greatest Hits, MCA, MCA-17 The High Lonesome Sound, MCA, MCA-110 Bluegrass Instrumentals, MCA, MCA-104 Bill and Charlie Monroe, MCA, MCA-124 I'll Meet You in Church Sunday Morning, MCA, MCA-226
GEORGE MORGAN	Red Rose From The Blue Side Of Town, MCA 4222
THE OSBORNE BROTHERS	Pickin Grass and Singin' Country, MCA, MCA-468 Bobby and Sonny, MCA, MCA-502 Ru-beeee, MCA, MCA-135 Modern Sounds Of Bluegrass, MCA, MCA-108
DOLLY PARTON	Coat of Many Colors, RCA, LSP-4603 Joshua, RCA, LSP-4507 The Best of Dolly Parton, RCA, LSP-4449 Golden Streets of Glory, RCA, LSP-4398 Jolene, RCA, APL 1-0473n My Tennessee Mountain Home, RCA, APL 1-0033
DOLLY PARTON & PORTER WAGONER	Burning The Midnight Oil, RCA, LSP-4628
THE BEST OF PORTER WAGONER & DOLLY PARTON	RCA, LSP-4556
WEBB PIERCE	Greatest Hits, MCA, MCA-120
RAY PILLOW	Countryfied, ABC-Dot, DOSD 2013
RAY PRICE	All-Time Greatest Hits, Columbia, KE31364 Danny Boy, Columbia, CS9477
JEANNE PRUETT	Satin Sheets, MCA, MCA-338 MCA, MCA-388

JIM REEVES	He'll Have To Go, RCA, LSP-2223(c)
	Distant Drums, RCA, LSP-3542
	Songs To Warm The Heart, RCA, LSP-2001
	A Touch Of Velvet, RCA, LSP-2487
	Am I That Easy To Forget, RCA, APL 1-0039
	Blue Side of Lonesome, RCA, LSP-3793
	Moonlight and Roses, RCA, LSP-2854
TEX RITTER	Hillbilly Heaven, Capitol, ST-1623
	Fall Away, Capitol, ST-11351
	The Best of Tex Ritter, Capitol, DT-2595
MARTY ROBBINS	Gunfighter Ballads and Trail Songs, Columbia, CS8158
	Devil Woman, Columbia, CS8708
	All-Time Greatest Hits, Columbia, KG31361
	Bound For Old Mexico, Columbia, KC31341
	Tonight Carmen, Columbia, CS9525
JIMMIE RODGERS	The Best of The Legendary Jimmie Rodgers, RCA, LSP-3315(e)
	Train Whistle Blues, RCA, LPM-1640
	Never No Mo' Blues, RCA, LPM-1232
	This Is Jimmie Rodgers, RCA, VPS-6091(e)
EARL SCRUGGS	Earl Scruggs Revue, Columbia, KC32426
	Dueling Banjos, Columbia, C32268
	His Family and Friends, Columbia, C30584
	I Saw The Light, Columbia, KC31354
	Nashville's Rock, Columbia, CS1007
JEANNIE SEELY	Can I Sleep In Your Arms/Lucky Ladies, MCA, MCA-385
	Greatest Hits, Monument, KZ31911
	Little Things, Monument, SLP 18104
JEAN SHEPARD	Slippin' Away, United Artists, UA-LA144F
	I'll Do Anything It Takes, United Artists, UA-LA307
	Sings Poor Sweet Baby And 10 Other Bill Anderson Songs, United Artists, UA-LA363
CARL SMITH	The Way I Lose My Mind, Hickory, H3G4518
CONNIE SMITH	The Best of Connie Smith, RCA, LSP-3848
	If It Ain't Love, RCA, LSP-4748
	Just One Time, RCA, LSP-4534
	God Is Abundant, Columbia, KC32492
HANK SNOW	Hello Love, RCA, APL 1-0441
	The Best of Hank Snow, RCA, LSP-3478(e)
	Sings in Memory of Jimmie Rodgers, RCA, LSP-4306
	This Is My Story, RCA, LSP-6014(e)
HANK SNOW & CHET ATKINS	Reminiscing, RCA, LSP-2952
HANK THOMPSON	Twenty-Fifth Anniversary Album, Dot, DOS 2-2000
MEL TILLIS	I Ain't Never/Neon Rose, MGM, 4870
TOMPALL & THE GLASER BROTHERS	Now Country, MGM, 4620
ERNEST TUBB	Greatest Hits, MCA, MCA-16
	Just Call Me Lonesome, MCA, MCA-209
	The Ernest Tubb Story, MCA, MCA 2-4040
	I've Got All The Heartaches I Can Handle, MCA, MCA-341
	One Sweet Hello, MCA, MCA-294
JUSTIN TUBB	Justin Tubb, Hilltop 209
PORTER WAGONER	Confessions Of a Broken Man, RCA, LSP-3593
	The Carroll County Accident, RCA, LSP-4116
	Skid Row Joe/Down In The Alley, RCA, LSP-4386
	The Farmer, RCA, APL 1-0346
PORTER WAGONER & THE BLACKWOOD BROTHERS	The Grand Ole Gospel, RCA, LSP-3488
BILLY WALKER	The Billy Walker Show With The Mike Curb Congregation, MGM, 4863
	Billy Walker's All-Time Greatest Hits, MGM, 4887
	When A Man Loves A Woman, MGM, 4682
CHARLIE WALKER	I Don't Mind Going Under, RCA, LSP-4737
	Break Out The Bottle, RCA, APL 1-0181

KITTY WELLS	Dust On The Bible, MCA, MCA-149
	Greatest Hits, MCA, MCA-121
	Sincerely, MCA, MCA-501
	Kitty Wells Story, MCA, MCA 2-4031
DOTTIE WEST	Country Sunshine, RCA, APL 1-0344
	I'm Only A Woman, RCA, LSP-4704
	The Best of Dottie West, RCA, LSP-4811
THE WILBURN BROTHERS	A Portrait, MCA, MCA 2-4011
	Take Up Thy Cross, MCA, MCA-217
HANK WILLIAMS	In The Beginning, MGM, 4576
	Twenty-Four Of Hank Williams' Greatest Hits, MGM, 4755-2
	I Saw The Light, MGM, 3331
	Hank Williams On Stage, MGM, 3999
	Luke The Drifter, MGM, 4380
	Lost Highway And Other Folk Ballads, MGM, 4254
	I Won't Be Home No More, MGM, 4481
	The Essential Hank Williams, MGM, 4657
WILLIS BROTHERS	In The Beginning (with Hank Williams), MGM, 4576
DEL WOOD	Ragtime Glory Special, Lamb & Lion, LL 1009
JOHNNY WRIGHT & KITTY WELLS	Heartwarming Gospel Songs, MCA, MCA-142
TAMMY WYNETTE	Stand By Your Man, Columbia, BN26451
	Your Good Girl's Gonna Go Bad, Columbia, BN26305
	Take Me To Your World, Columbia, BN26353
	The Ways To Love A Man, Columbia, BN26519
	D-I-V-O-R-C-E, Columbia, BN26392
	Bedtime Story, Epic, KE31285
	Greatest Hits, Columbia, BN26486
FARON YOUNG	Step Aside, Mercury, SR61337
	The Best of Faron Young, Mercury, SR61267

INDEX

All numbers refer to pages. Numbers in *italic type* refer to illustrations.

ACKNOWLEDGMENTS

There are so many people who have been of the utmost help to me in my association with country music over the years that it would be futile to attempt to remember them all at the same time. The role of some in the research for this book, however, has been so large that it would be almost an unkindness not to mention them.

Roy Acuff, Minnie Pearl, and Vic Willis gave selflessly of their time again and again, as did Alcyone Beasley, who was particularly helpful in illuminating the shadowy period of the Opry's birth. The files of the Country Music Hall of Fame Library and Media Center were also very helpful, and much information in George D. Hay's *A Story of the Grand Ole Opry* could not have been acquired anywhere else. Bill C. Malone's *Country Music U.S.A.* and Robert Shelton's *The Country Music Story* were very helpful references.

Several present and former employees of WSM Inc. were of immeasurable assistance in establishing the sequence of events and the atmosphere surrounding them. They include John H. (Jack) DeWitt, Jr., Robert Cooper, Ott Devine, Aaron Shelton, Bill Williams, and Dee Kilpatrick. Hal Durham and Jerry Strobel supplied valuable advice. Without Irving Waugh and E. W. (Bud) Wendell I could not have begun — much less completed — this project.

But there have been many others outside the music business who have been unselfishly helpful also. My wife Donna was indispensable to the task of producing the manuscript for deadline, transcribing many of the taped interviews, and then final-typing the entire manuscript. Gene Roberts and Jon Katz of the *Philadelphia Inquirer* were generous and encouraging in allowing me a three-month leave of absence. *Inquirer* Book Editor Larry Swindell was of great assistance with advice at various times, and Bill and Candy Preston of the *Nashville Tennessean* went far beyond the call of friendship in allowing my wife and me the run of their home while we were in Nashville.

Finally, there are of course the people at Harry N. Abrams, Inc. — Harry Abrams himself, Executive Editor John Hochmann, Managing Editor Margaret Kaplan (who first thought of doing this book), Barbara Lyons, Director of the Photo Department, and designer Arnold Skolnick. Each of them put up with the ignorance and naivete of a first-time author who was a complete stranger to New York book publishing, and they dealt carefully and sensitively with the project. I think they have done the Grand Ole Opry proud.

PHOTO CREDITS

Courtesy Alcyone Bate Beasley: 96; Courtesy Capricorn Records: 257; Courtesy Country Music Foundation: 26, 67, 73 above, 105, 140 above, 180, 240 below; Courtesy Country Music Hall of Fame: 54; Courtesy Epic/Columbia Records: 58; Marshall Fallwell, Jr.: 278; Grand Ole Opry Archives: 23 center, 64 above, 68 below, 70, 71, 75, 100 top and bottom, 102, 103 above, 108, 109, 110 below, 115, 119, 120, 121, 123, 126, 131, 132, 134, 135, 137, 138 above, 139 below, 140 below, 147 below, 154, 156, 158 below, 161, 172, 174 below, 176, 177, 219, 224-25, 230 above, 233 below left, 236 below, 239 below, 249, 260, 261, 287 above, 297 left column, 315, 329 below, 330 below, 333 below, 341; Grand Ole Opry Archives, Les Leverett photographer: 53, 64 below; Gerald Holly: 298, 346 above, 347, 362 inset, 364, 366-67, 368 inset, 370, 374 inset, 379 below, 380-81, 382, 383 above right and below, 389 left bottom and three on right, 390-91, 392; Les Leverett: 22 above right, 25, 30, 32 inset left, 33 inset right, 34-35, 37 below, 41 above left, 43, 44, 45, 46, 51, 52, 55, 56, 59, 62 above, 65 below, 153, 164, 237, 245, 246, 251, 253, 266, 273, 276, 283, 285 below, 289 below, 294 above, 295 below, 296, 301 above, 313, 325, 335, 342, 343, 344 left, top, center on right, 345, 346 below, 348 above, 350-51, 351-52, 379 above; Les Leverett Archives: 68 above, 73 below, 80, 85 below, 86 above, 87, 92, 94, 95, 99, 100 second from bottom, 101, 103 below, 104, 110 above, 122, 127, 128, 133, 157, 158 above, 159, 173, 216, 226 below, 234 below right, 236 above, 241 above; Kit Luce: 18-19, 23 top, 24, 31 above, 34 inset, 40-41, 40 above right, 41 above right, 57, 62 below, 65 above, 259, 263, 264, 270, 271 above, 277, 289 above, 292 above, 338, 339, 365; Jim McGuire (Grease Brothers): 16-17, 20, 21, 22 above left and below, 31 below, 32-33 and 32 right inset, 35 inset, 37 above left and right, 40 above left, 42, 48, 69 above, 165, 167, 170, 181, 182, 262, 269, 284, 285 above, 288 below, 299, 300 above, 301 below, 303, 309 above, 311, 314, 317, 318-19, 328, 329 above, 332 above, 333 above, 334, 344 bottom right, 354-55, 356-57, 378, 383 above left; Courtesy *Nashville Tennessean*: 81, 304-5, 309 below, 321, 330 above, 331, 332 below; Opryland Public Relations: 358, 360, 361, 362-63, 368-69; Opryland Public Relations, Bill Lafevor photographer: 371, 372, 373, 374-75, 376-77, 384-87, 388, 389 left top and center; Courtesy RCA Records: 288 above, 294 below; Bob Schanz Studio: 271 below; Courtesy Top Billing, Inc.: 272 below; Sam Trent: 33 left inset, 47, 49, 50, 60, 61, 161, 267, 272 above, 336-37, 348 below; Courtesy Ernest Tubb: 66; WSM Archives: 23 bottom, 69 below, 72, 79, 84, 85 above, 86 below, 88-89, 90-91, 100 second from top, 111, 113, 114, 117, 118, 129, 130, 138 below, 139 above, 141, 142, 143, 144, 145, 146, 147 above, 151, 155, 160, 163, 168-69, 174 above, 218, 220, 222, 226 above, 227, 228, 229, 230 below, 232, 233 above left and right, below right, 234 above, below left, 235, 238, 239 above, 240 above, 241 below, 242, 247, 250, 256, 258, 274, 275, 287 below, 292, 293, 295, 297 right column, 300 below, 310, 326-27, 349; WSM Archives, Les Leverett photographer: 27, 223, 290, 291.

The text of this book was set in Bookman, a handsome type that was originally cut as a bold face for Miller & Richard's Old Style. The type was set by Lexicraft Typographers, New York.

The book was printed in five-color offset by the Veritone Company, Melrose Park, Illinois. The four-color separations were supplied by D C & S Incorporated, New York. The text paper is 80-pound Flokote, manufactured by S. D. Warren Co., Westbrook, Maine. The music section paper is 80-pound Hammermill Offset, Laurentine finish. Both were supplied by the Lindenmeyr Paper Corporation, New York. The book was bound by Rand McNally and Company, Hammond, Indiana.